FAITH STRENGTHENED.

חזוק אמונה

OR

FAITH STRENGTHENED.

---◆---

"Know, therefore, this day, and reflect in thy heart, that the Lord he is God, in heaven above, and on the earth beneath, there is none else."—DEUTERONOMY, *Chap.* iv. *ver.* 39.

---◆---

TRANSLATED BY

MOSES MOCATTA

---◆---

HERMON PRESS
NEW YORK

First edition: London, 1850
Reprinted: HERMON PRESS, New York, 1970
LC 74-136768
ISBN 0-87203-062-8

THE TRANSLATOR'S

ADDRESS TO HIS CO-RELIGIONISTS.

As we Israelites do not seek to impose our faith on others—a practice altogether repugnant to Judaism—it is necessary to premise that the following work is intended exclusively for distribution among our Hebrew community.

Having made this declaration, the Translator informs his Readers, that the ensuing work will be found to be a faithful version of a valuable theological treatise, entitled חזוק אמונה; or, FAITH STRENGTHENED. It was originally composed in Hebrew by Isaac ben Abraham, an Israelite, a native of Lithuania. The work was published A.M. 5393; and in De Rossi's " Dizionario

Istorico," the author is designated as the most powerful opponent and refutant of the doctrines and dogmas
of Christianity, that had ever appeared among the
Jews.   Indeed, an attentive perusal of the little volume
cannot fail to convince us, that he was not only. an able
and a skilful controversialist, but an eminent biblical
scholar, a man of deep and extensive research; and
earnest in his investigation of truth.   The grand design
of his polemics, as he himself tells us, is to establish and
make manifest the sublime truths of Israel's Faith,
and expose and refute the erroneous views on which
Christianity is founded.   For this purpose his arguments are essentially based on Scripture authority,
inasmuch as he derives his entire chain of proofs from
apposite biblical texts, with which authorities every
page of his work abounds.   Arguments and opinions
founded on sanctions so high and authoritative, demand
our highest respect and most serious meditation.   The
sound and critical knowledge of the sacred language of
our forefathers, for which our author was distinguished,
and his perfect familiarity with Bible phraseology,
obviously and emphatically enabled him to produce a
more exact and accurate version of the *original* text,
than it is possible to find in any authorised English
version of the Bible.   The result of this superior and
decisive advantage was, that he was enabled to obtain

a clearer and more definite conception of the real
meaning and purport of those obscure and difficult
passages which we find dispersed throughout the Law
and the Prophets, and which are so arrogantly and so
constantly cited by Christian theologians in support of
their creed and doctrine. Of those intricate texts, our
Author has given most ample and lucid explanations,
and by a train of the most logical, and conclusive
reasoning, he ably and forcibly refutes the erroneous
and fallacious interpretations put upon them by the
opponents of Judaism. And, more forcibly to disprove
the arguments of his adversaries, and demonstrate the
false and untenable foundation upon which they stand,
he has, in a cursory view of each book of the so-called
New Testament, shown the glaring inconsistences apparent in them, and detected and exposed the manifold
discrepancies subsisting among their several authors,
and the endless and contradictory misquotations from
the Hebrew Scriptures which appear in those writings.
Thus has our Author presented his people with a well-
selected compendium of religious instruction, containing
those grand fundamental principles of Judaism, —
namely, the belief in ONE INDIVISIBLE GOD, and THE
ADVENT OF A FUTURE MESSIAH. To this mass of
Scriptural knowledge let the biblical student resort,
and therein he will find a most valuable aid, with an

immense economy of time and labour. To this store-house of Scriptural information let the youth of our community also repair, and it cannot fail to afford them ample materials for their perfect conviction of the truth and purity of our holy faith, and weapons of defence against the obtrusive efforts of the over-zealous proselyte-seeker, and the insidious attacks of the hireling missionary.

Such are the claims and merits, the purport and intent, of FAITH STRENGTHENED; but great and invaluable as those claims and merits are in the maintenance and elucidation of our Holy Faith, its worth and usefulness are but little known and imperfectly understood beyond the pale of the theological scholar, the work having been written in the Hebrew language. Actuated, therefore, with a wish to make its invaluable knowledge universally accessible to his Jewish brethren, the Translator has used his best endeavours to render it into the vernacular language of the country, in order that it may no longer be a sealed book, but may freely circulate among all grades and classes of the Jewish community, both in the mother country and in the colonies, and become, in the domestic circle and the private closet, a handbook, and a text authority of the principles and doctrines of our Holy Religion.

It may here be desirable to remark, that as the style of the Author was rather diffuse, and his language quaint and inharmonious, the Translator has adopted a more condensed and a more congenial phraseology. He has also omitted the superfluous repetition of the same arguments and quotations with which the original work was needlessly overlaid; as also certain epithets and harsh expressions, in which the Author, in despite of the moderation he professed, occasionally indulged ; but which doubtless are referrible to the persecuting spirit of the times in which he lived. To those who are acquainted with the metaphorical style of the East, and the unadorned simplicity of European phraseology, it is unnecessary to state the difficulties attending the translation of a work like this, so as to adapt it to the taste of educated Englishmen. The difficulty of the task was further enhanced by the daily impediments to which the infirmities incident to old age cast in the way of an Octogenarian. That task, however, has been sweetened by the comfort and serenity of mind which accompany purely spiritual and religious undertakings, and has cheered on its aspirant, with the hope that his toilsome, but gratifying, undertaking, will not only tend to raise and excite a spirit of religious inquiry among all classes of the Jewish community, particularly the young and the inexperienced, but will impart new vigour, and bring new honour on the name and profession of the Israelite.

That FAITH STRENGTHENED may realize the exalted aim of its author, must be the ardent wish of every sincere admirer of, and faithful adherent to, the sound and pure principles of that Revelation the Almighty vouchsafed to bestow on his chosen people.

ABSTRACT FROM THE AUTHOR'S PREFACE.

My religious zeal was aroused, on finding that the name of the Supreme Being was dishonoured, and our Holy Law profaned, by the very people who had been appointed to be the guardians of faith and the witnesses of those grand truths which make the simple man wise, the sorrowing heart glad, and the dim eyes bright. To my grief, I found that the inquisitive and indefatigable study of religion, which yields due reward to its zealous followers, was not cultivated among us as in former days, and am persuaded that ignorance and growing misapprehensions have added mental to physical burdens. Persecutions arising from religious hatred were heaped upon the children of my faith in all quarters of the globe, and were ever increasing in acrimony, not less in consequence of the low state of knowledge possessed by the Jews in matters of theological controversy than by the confused and mistaken notions which Christians had formed of Judaism. But it is absolutely imperative on man to be at all times prepared to repel any attack made on his belief. In conformity with this observation, our sages have recorded their opinion in the following axiom:—" Man ought assiduously to study his own faith, and be competent to give a proper reply to his antagonists," more particularly when we consider that, in the majority of cases, the opposition to our doctrines rests on the misinterpretation of those Scriptures of which we alone are the legitimate heirs and expounders.

Influenced by the foregoing reflections, I have undertaken this humble work, which, in its narrow compass, embraces a subject of the utmost importance. It is intended to afford a stronghold to the sincere believer in the Sinaic revelations who may be incapable of defending himself, and whose opinions may be exposed to the persevering attacks of his assailant. I refer my co-religionist so situated, to an attentive perusal of the " FAITH STRENGTHENED," wherein he will find an ample supply of arguments and proofs in favour and support of our venerable creed. In former years, when I investigated the works of several Christian divines, and had frequent disputations with other literary Christians, I made a point to reason in a mild and dispassionate manner. Indeed, I placed my reliance on the soundness of my position, by preserving a constant evenness of temper. Thus I rendered the discussions advantageous to myself and more acceptable to my opponents. Seeing that our Holy Scriptures contain immutable truths, revealed to us for the benefit of the whole human race, I have presented in this work such biblical passages as serve to illustrate the genuineness of Judaism, and also such as require elucidation, in order that the reader may fully perceive that, whatever seems obscure or tending to support Christianity, is, indeed, merely so in form, and relates wholly and exclusively to the sacred cause of Judaism—a cause which no argument whatever can depreciate, for the leading object of our faith is to make erring men look up to the unerring Deity, and inspire the belief that one indivisible God rules over the destinies of all, requiring no mediator or intercessor to obtain remission for our sins.

I have endeavoured not merely to explain such passages of our Scriptures as are obnoxious to misconstruction, but also to arraign before the tribunal of common sense the assertions made by Christians which tend to throw discredit on the truths of the Jewish Faith. For this purpose, I found it advisable to subdivide this work into two parts. The first portion is devoted to an examination of the objections raised by Christians against our religion, and to the proofs cited by them for the corroboration of their own doctrines. The refutation I have given it, is in many cases, based on the contradictory nature of their own statements. The second portion comprises a careful review and refutation of the glaring inconsistencies that are discoverable in the New Testament. With the view to render the argument introduced into this work more cogent and conspicuous, I have allotted in the first part a separate chapter to each particular subject of discussion. In the second part, it has appeared preferable to adopt distinct chapters for those passages of the New Testament which call for a special animadversion and refutation. May the God of all Spirits, who has rendered wisdom unfathomable, and who scrutinizes all hidden thoughts, bestow a blessing on my humble efforts, forgive all my unconscious errors, uphold me in my pure faith, and grant his Divine protction to me and all Israel. Amen.

FAITH STRENGTHENED.

CHAPTER I.

I was once asked by a Christian scholar, "Why do you Jews refuse to believe that Jesus Christ was the Messiah, evidence concerning him having been given by the true prophets, in whose words you also believe?"

And this is the answer which I gave him: How is it possible for us to believe that he was the Messiah, as we do not see any actual proof of his Messiahship throughout the prophetic writings. As for the passages which the authors of the Gospel adduce from the words of the prophets, to demonstrate that Jesus the Nazarene was the Messiah, they advance nothing relating to *him*, as will be shown in the second part of this work, in which we shall, in regular succession, point out the fallacies set forth in the Gospel. On the other hand, we shall see many incontrovertible proofs in support of our conviction that Jesus was by no means the Messiah. A few of these arguments may be here introduced,

He was not the Messiah is evident:—

1st, from his pedigree;

2ndly, from his acts;

3rdly, from the period in which he lived; and

4thly, from the fact that, during his existence, the promises were not fulfilled which are to be realised on the advent of the *expected* Messiah, whereas the fulfilment of the conditions alone can warrant a belief in the identity of the Messiah.

1st. As to the pedigree of Jesus, he was not a descendant of David, being merely affiliated to him through Joseph, as is testified in the Gospel. For in Matthew, chap. i., it is written, that Jesus was born of Mary during her virginity, and that Joseph knew her not until she had given birth to Jesus. According to this statement, the pedigree of Joseph can be of no avail to Jesus, and at the same time it is quite evident that the ancestry of Mary was unknown to the authors of the Gospel. But even the relationship of Joseph to David is wanting in proof, there being a discrepancy between Matthew and Luke in their account of his pedigree, which appears clearly when we compare the Gospel of Matthew, chapter i., with that of Luke, at the end of chapter iii. Here we see conflicting testimonies; and where that is the case no belief can be attached to either statement. The prophets, on the contrary, predicted to us that the expected Messiah should be no other than a descendant of David.

2ndly. As to the works of Jesus, we find that He says of himself, Matthew x. 34. " Think not that I am come to make peace on earth; I came not to send peace but the sword, and to set a man at variance against his father, and the daughter against her mother, and the daughter-in-law against her mother-in-law." On the other hand, we find Holy Writ attributing to the true and expected Messiah actions contrary to those of Jesus. We see here that Jesus says of himself, he is not come to make peace on earth, whereas Scripture says of the true and expected Messiah, in Zechariah ix. 10., "And he shall speak peace unto the heathen," etc. Jesus says he came in order " to send the sword on earth," but Scripture says, Isaiah ii. 4., "And they shall beat their swords into ploughshares, and their spears into pruning-hooks; nation shall not lift up sword against nation, neither shall they learn war any more." Jesus says he came "to put father and son at variance," etc, but Malachi says (at the end of his book) that "before the coming of the true Messiah the prophet Elijah shall appear, and turn the heart of the fathers to their children, and the heart of the children to their fathers." Jesus says, concerning himself, Matthew xx. 28, that he is not come to be served by the son of man, but to serve others. Concerning the true Messiah, however, Scripture says, Psalms lxxii. 11, " Yea, all kings shall prostrate themselves before him; all nations shall serve him." And Zech ix. 10, " His dominion shall be from sea even to sea, and from the river even to the end of the earth." Thus states also Daniel, vii. 27, " And all rulers shall serve him and obey him."

3rdly. As to the period of his existence, it is evident that he did not come at the time foretold by the prophets; for they predicted the advent of the Messiah to happen at the latter days, see Isaiah ii. 2, "And it shall come to pass in the latter days, that the mountain of the Lord's house shall be established on the top of the mountains," etc. Further we read there, verse 4, concerning the king Messiah, " And he shall judge among the nations and arbitrate among many people, and they shall beat their swords into ploughshares, and their spears into pruninghooks," etc. Thus is also recorded in Scripture concerning the wars of Gog and Magog, which are to take place in the time of the king Messiah. *Vide* Ezekiel xxviii. 8, "After many days thou shalt be visited; in the latter years thou shalt come into the land that is brought back from the sword," as will be explained in the proper place. The same is evident from Hosea, iii. 5, "Afterward shall the children of Israel return, and seek the Lord their God, and David their king, and shall revere the Lord and His goodness in the latter days."

So we read also in Daniel ii. 28, "And (God) maketh known to the king Nebuchadnezzar what shall be in the latter days." Which passage refers to the subsequent prophecy, *ib.* ver. 44, "And in the days of these kings shall the God of heaven set up a kingdom which shall never be destroyed; and the sovereignty shall not be left to other people," etc. Hence we see clearly that the prophets predicted that the coming of the true Messiah would happen at the "latter days," and not before.

4thly. We have to consider the promises contained in the words of the prophets, which were not fulfilled in the time of Jesus, but are to be realised in future at the time of the true Messiah, who is still expected. They may be classed under the following heads:—

(*a.*) At the time of the king Messiah there is to be only one kingdom and one king, namely, the true king Messiah. But the other empires and their rulers shall cease at that period, as we read in Daniel ii. 44, " And in the days of these kings shall the God of heaven set up a kingdom which shall never be destroyed; and the kingdom shall not be left to other people, but it shall break in pieces and consume all these kingdoms, and it shall stand for ever." Whereas, we now actually see that many empires, different in their laws and habits, are still in existence; and that in each empire a different king is ruling; consequently the Messiah is not yet come.

(*b*). At the time of the king Messiah, there is to be in the world but one creed and one religion, and that is the religion of Israel, as is proved by Isaiah (lii. 1), " Awake, awake, put on thy strength, O Zion; put on thy beautiful garments, O Jerusalem, the holy city: for henceforth there shall no more come into thee the uncircumcised and the unclean." And further (chap. lxvi. 17),

" Who sanctify themselves and purify themselves [we prefer the literal translation of this obscure passage to the unwarranted and still more obscure translation of the Authorised Version] in the gardens, behind *one* in the midst of them who eat the flesh of the swine, and the abomination, and the mouse, shall be consumed together saith the Lord." " And (ver. 23) it shall come to pass, that from one new moon to another, and from one sabbath to another, shall all flesh come and worship before me, saith the Lord." Moreover, it is written in Zechariah (xiv. 16), " And it shall come to pass, that every one that is left of all the nations which came against Jerusalem shall even go up from year to year to worship the King, the Lord of hosts, and to keep the feast of tabernacles." In the same book (chap. viii. 23) we read, " Thus saith the Lord of hosts, In those days it shall come to pass, that ten men of nations of diverse languages shall take hold, even shall take hold of the skirt of a Jew [Authorised Version renders it " of him that is a Jew"], saying, We will go with you ; for we have heard that God is with you." There are many other passages in that book to the same effect.

(c.) At the time of the Messiah, the idolatrous images and their memorial, as also the false prophets and the spirit of profanity are to vanish from the earth, as may be seen in Zechariah xiii. 2. " And it shall come to pass in that day, saith the Lord of hosts, that I will cut off the names of the idols from the earth, and they shall no more be remembered, also I will cause the prophets and the unclean spirit [literally ' the spirit of uncleanliness'] to pass away from the earth." So also it is written in Isaiah ii. 18. " And the idols he shall utterly abolish." So it is also said in Zephaniah ii. 11. " The Lord will be terrible unto them, for he will cause all the gods of the earth to waste away, and men shall worship Him, every one from his place, even all the isles of the heathen."

(d.) At the time of the Messiah, there will be no sins and iniquities in the world, particularly not among the Israelitish nation. Thus we find in the law (Deuteronomy xxx. 6.), " And the Lord thy God will circumcise thine heart and the heart of thy seed to love the Lord thy God with all thine heart and with all thy soul, that thou mayest live." Again, in Zephaniah iii. 13. " The remnant of Israel shall not do iniquity, nor speak lies, neither shall a deceitful tongue be found in their mouth." Again, in Jeremiah iii. 13. " At that time they shall call Jerusalem the throne of the Lord, and all the nations shall be gathered unto it, to the name of the Lord, to Jerusalem, neither shall they walk any more after the imagination of their evil heart." Again, in Ezekiel xxxvi. 25. " And I will sprinkle clean water upon you: from all your impurity, and from all your idols, will I cleanse you. And I will give unto you a new heart, and a new spirit will I put within you, and I will take away the stony heart out of your flesh, and I will give you a heart of flesh. And I will put my spirit within you, and cause you to walk in my statutes, and ye shall keep my judgments and do them." Moreover, see Ezekiel xxxvii. 23. " Neither shall they defile themselves any more with the idols nor with their abominations, nor with their transgressions, and I will save them out of all their dwelling-places wherein they have sinned, and I will cleanse them, and they shall be my people, and I will be their God, and David my servant shall be king over them, and they shall have one shepherd, and they shall walk in my judgments and observe my statutes and do them."

(e.) At the time of the king Messiah and after the

war with Gog and Magog there will be peace and tranquillity throughout the world, and men will no longer require any weapons of war. So it is written in Isaiah ii. 4. " And they shall beat their swords into ploughshares, and their spears into pruning-hooks; nation shall not lift up sword against nation, neither shall they learn war any more." See also Ezekiel xxxix. 9. " And they that dwell in the cities of Israel shall go forth and shall set on fire and burn the weapons, both the shields and the bucklers, the bows and the arrows, and the handstaves and the spears, and they shall burn them with fire seven years (ib. ver. 10.) so that they shall take no wood out of the field, neither cut down *any* out of the forests, for with the weapons shall they kindle the fire." With these words agrees the prophecy of Hosea ii. 20. according to the division of chapters in the Hebrew Bibles, (in the English version it is chap. ii. ver. 18.) " and I will break the bow and the sword and the battle out of the earth, and I will make them to lie down safely." So says also Zechariah ix. 10, " And the battlebow shall be cut off, and he shall speak peace unto the heathen," etc.

(*f.*) At the time of the king Messiah there will be peace in the Holy Land between the ferocious and domestic animals, so that they will not injure each other, and much less injure a human being, as is evident from the following prophecies of Isaiah xi. 6. " The wolf also shall dwell with the lamb, and the leopard shall lie down with the kid, and the calf and the young lion, and the fatling together, and a little child shall lead them." (Ver. 7) " And the cow and the bear shall feed together; their young ones shall lie down together, and the lion shall eat straw like the ox." (Ver. 8) " And the sucking child shall play on the hole of the asp, and the weaned child shall put his hand on the cockatrice's den." (Ver. 9) " They shall not hurt nor destroy in all my holy mountain, for the earth shall be full of the knowledge of the Lord," etc. and (ib. lxv. 25) "And the wolf and the lamb shall feed together, and the lion shall eat straw like the bullock, and dust shall be the serpent's meat. They shall not hurt nor destroy in all my holy mountain, saith the Lord." (See also Ezekiel xxxiv. 25) " And I will make with them a covenant of peace, and will cause the evil beasts to cease out of the land, and they shall dwell safely in the wilderness, and sleep in the woods." (Ver. 28.) "And they shall no more be a prey to the heathen, neither shall the beast of the land devour them," etc. (See also Hosea ii. 20, or in the English version, 18) "And in that day will I make a covenant for them with the beasts of the field, and with the fowls of heaven, and with the creeping things of the ground," etc.

(g.) At the time of the Messiah there will be no troubles, cares, and anxieties, among the restored Israelites, who will then be blessed with a prolonged and more happy life, as is foretold in the following passages of Isaiah (lxv. 16). " He who blesseth himself in the earth shall bless himself in the God of truth, and he that sweareth in the earth shall swear by the God of truth, because the former troubles are forgotten, and because they are hid from mine eyes. (Ver. 19) " And I will rejoice in Jerusalem, and joy in my people, and the voice of weeping shall no more be heard in her, nor the voice of crying." (Ver. 20) " There shall be no more thence an infant of days, nor an old man that hath not filled his days, for the child shall die a hundred years old, but the sinner being a hundred years old shall be accursed." (Ver. 21) "And they shall build houses and inhabit them, and they shall plant vineyards and eat the fruit of them." (Ver. 22) " They shall not build and another inhabit, they shall not plant and another eat, for as the days of a tree shall be the days of my people, and mine elect shall long enjoy the work of their hands."

(*h*). At the time of the Messiah the *Shechinah* (effulgency of divine presence) shall return to Israel as in former days, and the people of Israel increase in prophecy, wisdom, and knowledge, as may be seen by the following quotations from the prophets. (Ezek. xxxvii.26) " Moreover I will make a covenant of peace with them; it shall be an everlasting covenant with them: and I will establish and multiply them, and set my sanctuary in the midst of them for evermore." .(Ver. 27) " My residence also shall be among them. Yea, I will be their God, and they shall be my people." (Ver. 28) " And the heathen shall know that I the Lord do sanctify Israel when my sanctuary shall be in the midst of them for evermore." (Ib. xxxix. 29) " Neither will I hide my face any more from them, for I have poured out my Spirit upon the house of Israel, saith the Lord God." (Ib. xliii. 7) " And he said unto me, Son of man, the place of my throne, and the place of the soles of my feet where I will dwell in the midst of the children of Israel *for ever*," etc. (Ib. xlviii. 35) " And the name of the city from that day shall be, ' The Lord is there' " (Joel ii. 27) " And ye shall know that I am in the midst of Israel, and that I am the Lord your God, and there is none else; and my people shall never be ashamed." (Ib. iii. 1; in the English Version ii. 28) " And it shall come to pass afterwards, that I will pour out my spirit upon all flesh, and your sons and your daughters shall prophesy, your old men shall dream dreams, your young men shall see visions." (Ib. iii. 17) " So ye shall know that I am the Lord your God dwelling in Zion my holy mountain: then shall Jerusalem be holy, and there shall no strangers pass through it any more." (Ib. iii. 21) "For I will avenge their blood that I had not avenged, for the Lord dwelleth in Zion." (Zec. ii. 14; in the English Version, ii. 10) "Sing and rejoice, O daughter of Zion, for, lo! I come and dwell in the midst of thee, saith the Lord." (Isa. xi. 9) "For the earth shall be full of the knowledge of the Lord as the waters cover the sea." (Jer. xxxi. 34) " And they shall teach no more every man his neighbour, and every man his brother, saying, Know the Lord: for they shall know me, from the lowest of them to the highest, saith the Lord: for I will forgive their iniquity, and remember their sin no more."

The above indications pointed out by the prophets as indispensable attributes of the true Messiah, have not been fulfilled in Jesus the Nazarene. Nor have we hitherto seen realised the prophetic assurances already named, or others that we have omitted, to avoid prolixity. And we therefore arrive at the just conclusion, that the true and expected Messiah has not yet come. In him alone all the predicted attributes undoubtedly will be manifested, and through him alone and in no other way, the scriptural promises will be accomplished.

CHAPTER II.

AN argument has been adduced by Christians, to the effect, that the Almighty has rejected the Israelitish nation, because they would not listen to the teachings of the Messiah, his messenger, and because they executed judgment on him. The Lord has, therefore, say they, chosen the Christian nation, and he permitted Christ to suffer martyrdom for their sake and for the salvation of their souls, because they had acknowledged him and put faith in him.

REFUTATION.

This argument is unfounded; for the Christians themselves confess, that before the coming of Jesus, they (as Gentiles) denied the Almighty, and were idolaters. Even after the coming of Jesus, he was not received as a God, nor believed to be such until some hundred years subsequent to his existence. Yea, they (the Gentiles) themselves carried on exterminating persecution against him, his disciples, apostles, and followers. Nero, the emperor of Rome, for instance, caused Peter and Paul to die an unnatural death, on account of their endeavours to persuade and urge the people to believe in Jesus. Decius, the Roman emperor, caused, in a like spirit, Laurentius to be roasted alive in the year 254 of the vulgar era, because he persuaded people to embrace Christianity. So acted all the emperors that followed him; they persecuted the Christians, and killed the popes, and those who followed the religion of Jesus, as may be gathered from their ecclesiastical histories. The first Byzantine emperor who adopted the Christian faith, was Constantine, who established laws for his co-religionists 300 years after the death of Jesus. In his days lived Arius who composed a controversial work against the Christian dogmas, but Constantine lent no ear to his opinions. After the death of this monarch, Constantine the Second attached himself to the sect of Arius, and slighted the established doctrines; and his succeeding relative Julian, likewise adhered to the Arian views, and rejected the general principles of the Christian Faith. His example was imitated by several of his successors. There are, even in our times, people who acknowledge the authority of Arius, and who constitute the sect called by his name. This (the original repudiation of Christianity by the Gentiles) is also to be noticed among the [ancient] inhabitants of Prussia; when bishop Adelbert of Prague came to them to instruct them in his religion in the year 990, of the Christian era, they cut him in pieces. The Prussians and Poles were not converted to the Christian religion before the eleventh century, and the Scandinavians not until after the 1400th year of the vulgar era, as is stated in the Ecclesiastical histories. The majority of the followers of Christianity continue even at the present day to adore in their places of worship images of gold and silver, wood, and stone, and many of them shew divine reverence to the wafer, or sacramental bread by prostrating themselves before it.

These practices they keep up in contradiction to the teachings of Jesus: who rigorously impressed upon his disciples and apostles to abstain from them, as well as from the eating of the sacrifices offered up to idols. We also find in the Gospel, they are forbidden to eat blood, or the flesh of strangled animals; which interdictions are disregarded even by the most scrupulous Christians. They likewise desecrate the true Sabbath-day, the stringent commandment of which, was kept by Jesus, and subsequently by his disciples and his followers, during the period of 500 years. From that period, the ancient law was superseded by the Pope enjoining to celebrate the first day of the week, Sunday, as the sacred day. Hence arises the question: How can they boast to be the preferred nation, selected in reward of their homage to Jesus; or how can they assume the name of Christians, since there exists among them, no longer any observer of the Mosaical precepts, which Jesus himself declared inviolable? Besides, they deviate from his statutes by adding to, and diminishing from the dictates of the Gospel, while he pronounced severe maledictions against those who should venture to add or to diminish from his words, as may be learned from the passages above referred to, and will be set forth more fully in chapter xlix. of this work.

CHAPTER III.

A MEMBER of the Greek Church, once addressed me in the following words:—"Do you know wherefore you have no longer a king of your own people? It is because you have rejected the faith of Jesus Christ and His kingdom, for He was the king of Israel. On this account the empire of Israel has been destroyed."

I replied to him: " It is known, and evident from the words of the prophets, that in consequence of our manifold iniquities, our kingdom was destroyed in the time of Nebuchadnezzar, when this king led Zedekiah, king of Judah, captive to Babylon.

" This event took place more than four hundred years before the existence of Jesus. The Jews were then successively subjects of the Babylonians, Medes, and Greeks. Long before the birth of Jesus we had been kept in servitude by the Romans. You may see that proved in your Gospel of Luke, iii. 1, 'In the fifteenth year of Tiberius Cæsar, Pontius Pilate being governor of Judea,' etc. See also John xix. 15, 'Pilate saith unto them, Shall I crucify your king? The chief priests answered, We have no king but Cæsar.' Now, as to your ascribing to Jesus the government of Israel, we are at a loss to know who made him king, and where he ruled over Israel. You, members of the Greek Church, were the parties who first acknowledged Christianity in the kingdom of your Messiah, and you still continue in your faith in Him; and, nevertheless, your

C

government has been destroyed, and you have no longer
a king of your own people : for a Mohammedan ruler, the
Turkish sultan, who is now in possession of the Holy
Land, extends his sway over Greece.

There are many other Christian states which formerly
elected their own kings, and now are subjected to the
Ottoman power.   On the other hand, you see the
Mahommedans not only disbelieving the doctrines of
Jesus, but even mercilessly persecuting the followers of
his faith, and notwithstanding this, the empire of
the Turks enjoys undisturbed prosperity.

CHAPTER IV.

An eminent disciple of Martin Luther one day, thus
argued with me :—"You know that in our gospel, Acts,
v. 34, it is mentioned that Rabbi Gamaliel, a learned
and distinguished man, addressed the by-standing Jews
in the following terms: (Ver. 38) ' Refrain from these
men, and let them alone, for if this counsel, or this work
be of men, it will come to nought; (ver. 39) but if it
be of God ye cannot overthrow it, but it will continue
firm, and ye must rebel against the intentions and the
counsel of God.'   To this he brings forward an example
in Theudas and Judas of Galilee, who came forward as
Messiahs of their own accord, without approbation and
decree of the Almighty, and were in a short time utterly
destroyed, with all their followers.

"You see then with your own eyes (said the Lutheran)
that this faith, that is to say, the faith of Jesus and his
apostles, has not been destroyed these 1500 years and
more; consequently the before-mentioned trial (of the
veracity of the Christian faith proposed by the Jewish
doctor) is a convincing and perfect proof, that the words

and acts of the founders of Christianity met with the full approbation of God."

Upon this, I gave him the following reply:—The words reported in the gospel as having been used by Rabbi Gamaliel are not accredited among us; but were it even acknowledged that Rabbi Gamaliel did thus express himself, we know that he did not speak in a prophetic spirit, for he was no prophet, but that he expressed merely his views from what he had experienced in his own time of Theudas and Judas of Galilee. Hence it is possible he might have uttered his views, as Scripture says (Psalm xix. 12), "Who can be aware of errors," etc. On the other hand, you may perceive incontrovertible testimony of the contrary from the idolatrous service which preceded Jesus, and which was renewed after his time, and did not cease for so many centuries. You well know that the worship of idols was introduced previously to the existence of our ancestor Abraham; for Terah the father of Abraham was an idolater, as is recorded in scripture, Joshua xxiv. 2. concerning the father of Abraham and Nahor, "and they served other Gods."

Since that period to the present time, 3000 years and more have elapsed; and the worship of images still continues. For we see your Evangelists, who follow in the steps of Martin Luther, accuse those who walk in the faith of the pope of Rome of rendering homage to images in their houses of worship; yet it is manifest, that image-worship proceeds from the will of God.

Thus has also the infidel Mohammed instituted the spurious religion of the Islams. A religion the falsity of which you yourself acknowledge, and nevertheless this delusion lasted for above 1000 years, and is to this day not put down.

Would you say then that these two creeds, viz.,

Popery and Mohammedanism because they are not yet abolished, were established by the approbation or command of God? I have not the slightest idea, that a reasonable being can entertain such a supposition: but the fact is, that the Almighty says "leave the foolish-minded to themselves, for in futurity they will have to render account of their action" (vide treatise *Abodah Zarah*, on occasion of a question asked of Rabbi Gamaliel). Moreover it is known, from the words of the prophets, that idolatry will continue till the time of the Messiah, whose advent we expect; for concerning that period see Isaiah ii. 18., " And the idols he shall utterly abolish." Again Zephaniah ii. 11., "The Lord will be terrible unto them, for he will bring low all the gods of the earth," "and men shall worship Him every one from his place, even all the isles of the heathen." Again Zechariah xiii. 2., " And it shall come to pass in that day, saith the Lord of hosts, that I will cut off the name of the idols out of the land, and they shall no more be remembered" etc. Then will be fulfilled the passage contained in the same prophet, xiv. 9. "And the Lord shall be King over all the earth, in that day the *Lord shall be One and His name One.*"

CHAPTER V.

THE same personage argued with me another time, and said, "You ought to know that, as long as you fulfilled the behests of God and his commandments, you were prosperous in this world; for the kings of Israel were great and mighty, so that our forefathers, and many other Gentile nations, were held under subjection by you; but now, since you have sinned against God, the case is reversed; for the rule has departed from you and passed over to us, so has our subjection departed from us and passed over to you. For, at present, you have no king or prince among you, and you are held under subjection by all nations. At the same time, our prosperity is a great proof of the goodness of our faith, as your former prosperity was a proof of the goodness of your faith, hence this your degraded state must be considered a convincing illustration of your evil doings in rejecting our creed." To this I replied:—

" Your argument is fallacious in all its bearings, for in this world there are many wicked men, whose lot is as prosperous as if they were truly righteous men, while we frequently see the pious labouring under severe afflictions; an instance of this we find in the success of Nebuchadnezzar the *wicked*, and Alexander the Great, who extended their rule over a great part of the world, and especially over the land of the Israelites, nor had there ever been seen kings more prosperous in their government than they were. Yet they, with all their success, cannot be brought forward as an argument in favour of the superiority of the faith of the Gentiles over that of the subjugated Israelites, it being a well-known fact that they (the great kings) were worshippers of idols and the planets. Now in our day even you, Christians, agree that Islamism is nothing but a false system introduced by their pretended prophet Mohammed ; nevertheless, they are prosperous in this world, and their religion and power spread over a large portion of Asia and Africa: consequently, how can you say that their prosperity is a proof of the goodness of their creed, seeing also that Scripture shews the reverse. Thus Jeremiah says, xii. 1, " For the Lord chastiseth him whom He loveth," etc. The argument, therefore, which you derived from your prosperity in favor of your religion, is groundless, and must appear so to every man of good sense.

CHAPTER VI.

A CHRISTIAN scholar argued once with me, saying, " We have examined the words of the prophets, and have not found that even a single allusion was made or a prophecy revealed, concerning the captivity in which you at present are—namely, the captivity into which you were brought by the Romans. All the prophets speak only about the captivity and the conquest of Babylon by the Medes and Persians, yet not a word is contained in Holy Writ concerning your present captivity nor your deliverance from it, nor of the downfall of the Roman dominion. How can it then be known, that the appointed Messiah has not arrived, or that he is to arrive at some future period—since all the promises recorded in the works of the prophets were fulfilled at the time of the second temple—and it is this to which Matthew alludes, xi. 13, ' For all the prophets and the law prophesied until John [the Baptist].' "

Upon this I made the following reply:

It is not to be wondered at, that you do not find any statement in the writings of the prophets, concerning the present captivity and the redemption therefrom, etc., for it is written Psalm xiv. 70, " He declareth His word unto Jacob, His statutes and His judgments unto Israel. He has not dealt so with any nation, nor has He made known His judgments unto them."

But I will shew, first, distinct prophecies concerning our dispersion and our scattered state in this exile—a dispersion which is wonderful—a scattered state, which is unprecedented, for where have we seen a*ny other* nation spread throughout all parts of the earth?

Secondly. I will bring forward prophecies fixing our continuance in this captivity for a protracted period extending to the latter days; and also promises of the prophets regarding our redemption from this captivity; and likewise many predictions from the sacred writers respecting the overthrow of the Roman and other powers who must be deemed unworthy to be allied with the nation of Israel at the time of its restoration. There are several other prophecies yet unaccomplished, which will come to pass at the appointed season.

Now referring to the prophecy concerning the captivity: viz., the captivity effected by the Romans, we read in the law (Deut. xxviii. 64), " And the Lord shall scatter thee among all people, from the one end of the earth even unto the other;" for, in the Roman captivity, the Jews belonging to the second temple were dispersed and scattered in divers countries then possessed by the Romans. They brought with them people of various nations to besiege Jerusalem for they could not make an easy conquest on account of the great valour of the Jews. Such was not the case at the destruction of the first temple, the Jews being then too few and weak, so that the unaided Babylonians were sufficient to reduce them and to lead them into captivity; they were, therefore, only banished to Babel, as we read at the end of the Second Chronicles (xxxvi. 20), " And them that had escaped from the sword carried he away to Babylon, where they were servants to him and his sons, until the reign of the kingdom of Persia." Thus we find also in Ezra (ii. 1), " Now these are the children of the province that went up out of the captivity of those who had been carried away, whom Nebuchadnezzar, the king of Babylon, had carried away to Babylon,

and came again unto Jerusalem and Judah, every one
into his city." See also in the same prophet (i. 2), " All
the vessels of gold and of silver were 5400; all these did
Sheshbazzar bring with them of the captivity that were
brought up from Babylon into Jerusalem." You see
here, from the testimony of Scripture, that the Israelites
were only exiled to Babel, and returned only from
thence. When we therefore read in Deut. (xxx. 3),
" That then the Lord thy God will turn thy captivity, etc.,
and gather thee from all the nations whither the Lord
thy God has scattered thee," we cannot possibly ascribe
it to the captivity of Babel, but only to that of Rome.

When, further, the prophet Ezekiel says (xxii. 15),
" And I will scatter thee among the heathen and disperse
thee in the countries and cause thy impurity to cease,"
we cannot possibly refer it to any other than this last
captivity, viz., the Roman captivity. For in the captivity of Babylon their impurity was not removed from
them. When they had left Babylon and arrived in the
Holy Land, there were still among them men who had
taken heathen wives, who profaned the sabbath and
committed many more iniquities; hence they became
again subject to captivity for their many sins. To this
must be referred the remark of the prophet, that by
reason of the length of this sad captivity, our sins and
our impurities will be removed from us, so that we shall
not be exiled again. See Lamentations (iv. 22), " The
punishment of thy iniquity is accomplished, O daughter
of Zion; he will no more carry thee away into captivity,
etc." See also Amos (i. 6), " Thus saith the Lord, For
three transgressions of Gaza, and for four, I will not
turn away the punishment thereof, because they carried
away captive the whole captivity, to deliver them up to
Edom"; and in the same chapter (ver. ix.), " Thus saith
the Lord, For three transgressions of Tyre, and for four, I

will not turn away the punishment thereof, because they delivered up the whole captivity to Edom, and remembered not the brotherly covenant."

These prophecies referred to the future: viz., to the destruction of the second temple, for those who had escaped from the captivity of Titus and fled to the countries of the Philistines and to Tyre, both adjacent to the Holy Land, were seized and delivered up to the hand of Edom; that is, Titus and his army; for the Nazarene Nations, and the Romans at their head, are alluded to in Scripture under the title of Edom, or daughter of Edom, in like manner as those nations which were converted to the creed of Islam, are called by the Hebrews, Ismaelites, on account of their supposed ancestor Ismael.

Now, what the prophet says (Amos i. 9) concerning the *whole* captivity, means, that there remained no fugitive or runaway who was not subject to the yoke of the Romans, while there had remained many remnants during the Babylonian captivity who did not yield to the supremacy of the Chaldeans; and, therefore, went to Egypt, as Scripture testifies (see Jeremiah xliii. 7), "So they came into the land of Egypt, for they obeyed not the voice of the Lord." As to the expression of Amos (i. 9), "And they remembered not the brotherly covenant," it alludes to the covenant that existed between Hiram, king of Tyre, and King Solomon; for Scripture says, "That they made a covenant together and addressed each other as brothers (see 1 Kings ix. 13).

We shall now proceed to consult scripture respecting our continuance in this protracted captivity; and we shall perceive that after having surmounted many days of trouble and affliction, the Lord will have mercy again on us in the latter days ; and we shall be convinced that, though our deliverance is so long deferred, the

Lord will not forget His covenant and His oath which He swore unto our fathers. See Deut. iv. 30, 31, " When thou art in tribulation, and all these things are come upon thee, even in the latter days, thou shalt turn to the Lord thy God, and be obedient unto His voice. For the Lord thy God is a merciful God, and He will not forsake thee, neither destroy thee, nor forget the covenant of thy fathers which He sware unto them." Hosea iii. 4, " For the children of Israel shall abide many days without a king, and without a prince, and without a sacrifice, and without an image, and without Ephod, and without Teraphim—afterwards shall the children of Israel return and seek the Lord, their God, and David their king, and shall reverence the Lord in the latter days." This prophecy evidently refers to our present exile; for we have no king, and no prince in Israel, but are under the dominion of Gentiles and their monarchs. We cannot offer sacrifice to God, or seek information by means of the Urim and Thummim, neither is there a false *oracle* of the Teraphim, which, according to the representation of idolaters, revealed coming events—besides all Israelites are now in captivity, and what the prophet says, " Afterwards Israel shall return," refers to the latter days, close to the time of salvation when the children of Israel shall come back penitently and seek the Lord their God, and David their king, for then they will regret their ejaculation (1 Kings xii. 16), " What portion have we in David? neither have we inheritance in the son of Jesse;" for he who denies the kingdom of David is as sinful as if he had rebelled against the Lord himself, who has given an everlasting dominion unto David and his seed. At the time of salvation shall be fulfilled the saying of Jeremiah xxx. 9, " They shall serve the Lord their God, and David their king, whom I will raise up unto them." We find besides an allusion to the redemption from the captivity by the Romans in the law, as well as in many passages of the Prophets (see Deut. xxx. 3) " Then the Lord thy God will turn thy captivity and have compassion on thee, and will return and gather thee from all the nations;" and (ver. 4.) " If any of them be driven out to the uttermost of heaven, from thence will I the Lord thy God gather thee and from thence will He fetch them.' (Ver. 5.) " And the Lord thy God will bring thee into the land which thy fathers possessed, and thou shalt possess it, and He will do thee good and multiply thee above thy fathers (ver. 6). And the Lord thy God will circumcise thy heart, and the heart of thy seed, to love the Lord thy God with all thine heart and with all thy soul, that thou mayst live." We see that these passages were not fulfilled on the return of Judah and Benjamin from Babylon; for the number of those who returned amounted to only 42,360, as recorded in Ezra ii. The majority remained in Babylon because they were unwilling to go back to Jerusalem. How then can it be maintained that the promise has been fulfilled, which declares " if any of them be driven out to the uttermost part of heaven, from thence the Lord thy God will gather thee, and from thence will He fetch thee."

If even at the time of the second temple, during an abode in the Holy Land, the Lord has not done us more good, nor multiplied us more than our fathers—how can it be asserted that the promises have been fulfilled ? viz. " And He will do thee good and multiply thee above thy fathers." For during all the days of the second temple we were in distress and trouble. See Daniel ix. 25 " And after three score and two weeks the streets shall be built again and the wall even in troublesome times." See also the prophecy of Isaiah xliii. 5 " Fear not, for I am with thee; I will bring thy seed from the East, and

gather thee from the West." (Ver. 6). "I will say
to the North give up, and to the South keep not back.
Bring my sons from far and my daughters from the end
of the earth." Again (xi. 12), "And he shall set up
an ensign for the nations, and shall assemble the outcasts of Israel, and gather together the dispersed of
Judah from the four corners of the earth." See also
the prophecy of Ezekiel xxxix. 28, "But I shall gather
them into their own land, and leave none of them any
more there" (namely in the land of the enemy).

Assurances of this description, were not realised at
the exit of the Israelites from Babylon to Jerusalem, for
they not having been dispersed, after the captivity of
Babylon, in the four quarters of the globe, how can the
promise have been fulfilled that says, "And He shall
assemble the outcasts of Israel, and gather together
the dispersed of Judah from the four corners of the
earth?"

There having remained many in the captivity of
Babylon, as we have mentioned above, how was the
prophecy brought to pass which states "And I will
leave none of them there any more?" We have further
to shew that during the time of the construction of the
second temple, the prediction was not fulfilled which
is contained in Isaiah lx. 10, "And the son of the
strangers shall build up the walls; and kings shall
minister unto thee." For at that time the heathens
derided the Jews, saying (Nehem. iv. 2) "What are
these feeble Jews doing"? etc. And they prevented
and interrupted them in building up the walls; moreover the passage, "And kings shall serve thee" was not
fulfilled at that period; for we read in Ezra ix. 9 "We
are bondsmen; yet our God has not forsaken us in our
bondage, but hath extended mercy unto us in the sight
of the kings of Persia." This is also written in

Nehemiah ix. 36. " Behold we are servants this day, and for the land that Thou gavest unto our Fathers to eat the fruit thereof, and the good thereof, behold we are servants in it." (Ver. 37) " And it yieldeth much increase unto the kings whom thou hast set over us, because of our sins: also they have dominion over our bodies and over our cattle at their pleasure, and we are in the greatest distress." Further, we find in Isaiah lx. 11, " Therefore thy gates shall be open continually, they shall not be shut day or night." This prediction did not come to pass during the second temple. For we observe in Nehemiah vii. 3, " And I said unto them, let not the gates of Jerusalem be opened until the sun be hot," etc. Hence you may conclude, that not only these promises, as well as the above-mentioned assurances, were not fulfilled during the time of the second temple, but that just the contrary took place in respect to them as we have already related. We must therefore arrive at the conviction, that these prophecies and promises, and many others not mentioned here, referred to our redemption from the captivity in which we *now* are.

We shall now proceed to consider the predicted downfall of the Gentile nations, which is to take place in the days of the expected Messiah. Concerning that period, we read in Numbers xxiv. 17. " I see it, though it will not *happen* now; I behold it, though not nigh, there shall come a star out of Jacob, and a sceptre shall rise out of Israel, it breaketh down the corners of Moab and crusheth all the children of Seth." The king Messiah, whose grandeur and lustre make him comparable with the stars of heaven, will, according to this prophecy, subject to his power all the children of Seth, and He will perform such heroic deeds as were never accomplished before Him.

To the exploits of this king, are referable the con-
quests predicted in the above chapter of Numbers, "And
Edom shall become an inheritance, and Seir shall be a
possessor of its enemies, and Israel shall do valiant
deeds; and he who is descended from Jacob shall rule,
and he that escapeth from the city [of the enemy] shall
perish."

The many predictions regarding Edom recorded in
Isaiah, Obadiah, and other prophets, have, by our laws,
been explained as alluding to Rome, which, since the
time of the destruction of the second temple, has exhibited the fiercest persecutors, and most implacable
enemies of the Jews and their faith.

To this effect, Isaiah says, xxxiv. 8, " For the Lord
hath a day of vengeance, a year of retributions for the
controversy of Zion." Every iniquitous act committed
by the adversary of Zion will meet with condign visitation, and human liberty shall triumph on the ruins of
tyranny. Hence he says, " And the redeemed of the
Lord shall return and enter Zion with joy, and everlasting gladness shall be upon their head. Exultation
and rejoicing shall reach them, and sorrow and affliction shall flee from them far away." The comfort promised in the Lamentation of Jeremiah will then be
realised, for in iv. 22, it is said: " The punishment of
thine iniquity, O daughter of Zion, has been fulfilled;
he will no more lead thee into captivity. He has visited
thine iniquity, O daughter of Edom, he hath laid bare
thy sins." Love will then be shewn by the Gentiles to
the Jews, and according to Isaiah, lxvi. 20, " They will
bring your brethren from among all the Gentiles as a
gift unto the Lord . . . . to Jerusalem, my holy
mountain." An objection has been raised against a
complete restoration of the Jews, grounded on some
partial texts of Scripture; but let us refer those who

make the allegation, to the following scriptural passages which afford a complete refutation of such a supposition: For Joel says, " Egypt shall be a desolation, and Edom a howling wilderness, on account of the violence done to the *children* of *Judah,* and on account of the innocent blood which they shed in their land. But Judah shall dwell for ever, and Jerusalem from generation to generation."

We should not take these words in the narrow limits in which they may present themselves to readers, who fix upon a single scriptural passage without comparing it with the more extensive detailed passages of a similar character. In fact, we have already stated, that by Edom we understand Rome; and we must, with justice to truth, submit that Egypt means the heavy yoke of the Mahommedan power.

The Ishmaelites (or Mahommedans) have traced their origin back to Hagar, " the Mitzrith," or Egyptian bondwoman, and were, therefore, called by the prophet, Mitzrayim (Egyptians).

It appears also perfectly accountable that the prophet speaks of the children of Judah rather than of the whole house of Israel. For, on the overthrow of the Ten Tribes, the name of the prevailing and distinguished tribe of Judah was adopted to designate the whole nation of Israel. Hence he says, " And Judah shall remain there and for ever, and Jerusalem from generation to generation." Obadiah actually predicts that all Israel (not only Judah) shall obtain the ultimate victory. He says, " And the house of Jacob shall be as a fire, and the house of Joseph as a flame, and the house of Esau as stubble," etc. And he concludes by saying, " And the saviours shall go up to the mount Zion, to judge the mount of Esau, and the kingdom shall belong unto the Lord."

We will now, for the sake of clearness, review in

regular order the prophecies which are unfulfilled, and are yet to come to pass in the days of the expected Messiah.

1. The ingathering of the Ten Tribes, and their union with Judah and Benjamin under the dominion of one king of the house of Judah (see Ezek. xxxvii. 16), " And now, O son of man, take unto thee one staff, and write thereon, for Judah and Israel," etc.

2. The rise of Gog and Magog, and their incursions into the territory of Israel (see Ezek. xxxviii. and xxxix. See also Zech. xiv. 12), " And this shall be the plague which shall strike all the nations who have carried their hosts against Jerusalem," etc.

3. The Mount of Olives shall be rent asunder (see Zech. xiv. 4), " And his feet shall stand on that day on the mount of Olives, which is before Jerusalem, and the mount of Olives shall be rent asunder in the midst of the east and the west, so as to become a very extended valley," etc.

4. The river of Egypt shall be divided, and dry up prior to the gathering of the exiles of Judah (see Isaiah xi. 15, 16).

" And the Lord shall cause the tongue of the sea of Egypt to be dried up, and He will wave His hand against the river in the strength of His spirit, and He will smite it into seven rivers. And men shall walk through it dry shod, and it shall be a path for the remnant of his people which shall remain from Assyria as it was unto Israel on the day when they went out of Egypt."

5. Ezekiel xlvii. "The waters issued out from under the threshold of the house eastward. And by the river shall grow all trees for meat, whose leaf shall not fade, nor the fruit thereof be consumed. It shall bring forth new fruit according to his month. Because their waters

they issued out of the sanctuary, and the fruit thereof shall be for meat, and the leaf thereof for medicine." See ver. 1 and 12, Zechariah, xiv. 8, " And it shall be in that day that living waters shall go out from Jerusalem, half of them toward the former sea, and half of them toward the hinder sea, in summer and in winter shall it be." Joel iii. 18, " It shall come to pass in that day, that the mountains shall drop down new wine, and the hills shall flow with milk, and all the rivers of Judah shall flow with waters; and a fountain shall come forth of the house of the Lord, and shall water the valley of Sheetim."

6. The conversion of the Gentiles to Judaism, see Zech. viii. 23, " They will say (to the Jews), We will go with you, for we have heard that God is with you."

7. The annual pilgrimage of the remnant of all nations to Jerusalem " to bow down to the King the Lord of Hosts," etc. see Zech. xiv. 17.

8. The celebration of the Sabbath, and the new moons by all the Gentiles (see the end of the Book of Isaiah ver. 23.)

9. The total extinction of idolatry. See Isaiah ii. 13, " And the idols he will consume completely;" and xlvii. 17, " They shall turn backward, and be filled with shame who trust in images, and say unto the molten statues, Ye are our gods!" See also Psalm xcvii. 7.

10. Unity of faith shall prevail throughout the world. See Isaiah xlviii., " By myself have I sworn, saith the Lord, righteousness hath come forth from my mouth, and a word which shall not emptily return, namely, that *unto me every knee shall bend, and by me every tongue shall swear.*" Zech. xiv. 9, " And the Lord shall be a King over the whole earth; on that day shall the Lord be *one and his name One.*

11. The kingdom of Israel shall be the principal one in existence. See Isaiah lx. 10, " And the children of

strangers shall build thy walls, and their kings *shall serve thee.*" Also ibid, " For the nation and the kingdom which shall not be willing to serve thee shall perish, and the people shall be utterly destroyed." Daniel vii. 27, " And the kingdom and the dominion and the multitude of kingdoms under the whole heaven shall be given to the people of saints of the most high, whose kingdom shall be an everlasting kingdom, and all rulers shall serve and obey Him."

12. Peace shall be restored after the subjugation of the resisting powers. See Isaiah ii. 4, " And they shall strike their swords into ploughshares and their spears into pruning hooks; nation shall no more lift up sword against nation, and they shall no more learn warfare." Hosea iv., "And the bow and the sword and the warfare I will break down and remove from the land, and ye shall rest in security."

13. That there should be peace and harmony even among the animals, in the land of Israel; nor should they harm man. See Isaiah xi. 6, " The wolf shall also dwell with the lamb, and the leopard shall lie down with the kid, and the calf, and the young lion, and the fatling together; and a little child shall lead them." (Ver. 7) "And the cow and the bear shall feed; their young ones shall lie down together, and the lion shall eat straw like the ox. (Ver. 8) And the sucking child shall play on the hole of the asp, and the weaned child shall put his hand on the cockatrice' den. (Ver. 9) They shall not hurt nor destroy in all my holy mountain, for the earth shall be full of the knowledge of the Lord as the waters cover the sea."

The like auspicious promises are repeated and amplified Isaiah lxv. 6, and Ezekiel xxxiv. 25. Also in Hosea ii. 28, we read, "And in that day, I will make a covenant for them with the beasts of the field, and with the fowls of heaven, and with the creeping things of the ground," etc.

14. Sin shall no longer prevail. See Deut. xxx. 6, "And the Lord shall circumcise thy heart and the heart of thy seed to love the Lord thy God," etc. Isaiah lx. 21, "And thy people, being righteous altogether, shall possess the land for ever. They are scions of my planting, the work of my hands, my glory." Jerem. iii. 17, "At that time they shall call Jerusalem the throne of the Lord, and all nations shall straightway flock into it, and shall no more go after the perversion of their evil heart." Ibid, chap. l. 20, " In those days and at that time, saith the Lord, the iniquity of Israel shall be sought and not be, and the sin of Judah, and it shall not be found, for I shall forgive those I shall leave behind." Ezekiel xxxvi. 25, 26, " And I shall sprinkle upon you pure water, and ye shall be clean; from all your impurities will I cleanse you," etc. " And I will give unto you a new heart, and a new spirit will I put into you, and I will remove the heart of stone out of your flesh; and I will give unto you a heart of flesh, and my spirit will I put into you, and I will do it so that you shall walk in my statutes, and observe my judgments and do them." Again, ib. xxxvii. 23 and 24, " Neither shall they defile themselves any more with their idols, nor with their detestable things, nor with any of their transgressions; but I will save them out of all their dwelling-places, wherein they have sinned, and will cleanse them, so that they shall be my people, and I will be their God. And David my servant shall be king over them; and they all shall have one shepherd; they shall also walk in my judgments and observe my statutes and do them."

15. Ancient troubles and sorrows shall cease for ever. See Isaiah lxv. 16, "He that blesseth himself in the land shall bless himself with the God of Truth, and he that sweareth in the land shall swear by the God of Truth; for the former troubles shall be forgotten, and

be withdrawn from mine eyes." Again (ver. 19), "And
I shall exult in Jerusalem, and rejoice in my people.
The voice of crying shall not be heard," etc.

16. The Divine presence (Shechinah) shall be restored, as is promised in the prophecy of Ezekiel xxxvii.
26, 27, and 28, " And I shall make unto them an everlasting covenant, yea, an everlasting covenant it shall
be unto them.   And I shall favour them and multiply
them, and I shall put my sanctuary in the midst of
them, my divine presence shall for ever be among them,
and I shall be unto them as a God, and they shall be
unto me as a people, and all the nations shall know that
I the Lord am sanctifying Israel, since my sanctuary
shall for ever be amongst them."   Again, ib. "And I
shall not hide any more my countenance from them,
since I have poured my spirit over the house of Israel,
saith the Lord God."   Joel ii. 27, "And ye shall know
that I am in the midst of Israel, and I am the Lord your
God residing in Zion my holy mountain; and Jerusalem
shall be holy, and strangers shall no more pass through
it."   See also Isaiah xi., "And the earth shall be full of
knowledge of the Lord as the waters cover the sea."

17. The prophet Isaiah will appear before the coming
of that "great and awful day" (see the end of Malachi).

18. The future temple will be rebuilt according to
the design predetermined by the Almighty (see Ezekiel
xl. to xlv).

19. The ancient division of the Holy Land will be
resumed. See Ezekiel xlvii. 13, commencing "Thus
saith the Lord your God, This is the border whereby
ye shall inherit the land according to the twelve tribes
of Israel," etc.

20. The resurrection will take place in those latter
days. See Deut. xxxii., "Behold I, even I, am ever
the same, and there is no other god with me.   I bring

to death, and I bring to life again; I crush and I heal again," etc. Isaiah xxvi. 19, "Thy dead shall live again, together with my dead body shall rise again. Awake and sing, ye that live in the dust,"etc. See also Daniel xii. 2, "And many of those that sleep in the dust shall awake; these for eternal life and those for disgrace and everlasting horror."

These points are subjects of ardent expectation, and will surely be fulfilled at the appointed time of the King Messiah. Nothing that is promised will be withheld, "for God is not a man who lieth."

A strong corroboration of our belief in the triumphs of the Messiah is afforded us by the description of the fifth kingdom in Daniel ii. The fifth kingdom, not represented by any part of the image seen in Nebuchadnezzar's vision, will subsist for ever; that is to say, the state and the faith of Israel will supersede all other kingdoms and creeds. This is predicted in the following words of Daniel ii. 44:—"And in the days of those kings, the God of heaven will set up a kingdom which will never be destroyed, and his kingdom will not be left to another people, but it will crush and demolish all those kingdoms, and it shall last for ever." Israel is called "The people of saints (or holy people) of the most High," a designation of which we find many instances in our Holy Scriptures.

The epithet "holy people" is given us, for example, in Deut. vii. 6, "For thou art a *holy people* unto the Lord thy God, and He has chosen thee to be unto Him a people select from all the nations," etc. Isaiah lxii., "And they shall call them, The holy people, The redeemed of the Lord." Jeremiah ii. 3, "Israel is holiness unto the Lord, the firstling of his produce," etc.

The important passage in Daniel vii. 18, "And the saints of the most high shall receive and possess the

kingdom to eternity and to the eternity of eternities,"
etc., relates, therefore, as every unbiassed reader must
perceive, to the people of Israel, and to no other nation,
for surely the same Providence which has established us,
and has blessed us with a holy revelation, will also watch
over us and render our future condition great, glorious,
and free from the recurrence of past dangers.

CHAPTER VII.

CHRISTIANS have raised the following argument against
our restoration:—They say, in the captivity of Egypt
you [Jews] have been kept four hundred years;
in that of Babylon, seventy years; but in subjugation
by the Romans your captivity has been prolonged more
than 1500 years. Moreover, you had received predictions which determined with exactness the duration
of your two former exiles, while that of the present time
was not even revealed to the prophets, so that now it
may be said, You are suffering under the curse written
in Leviticus xxvi. 38, "And ye shall be lost among the
gentiles, and the land of your enemies shall consume
you." The very length of your exile is a proof that
God does not desire to lead you back to the land of
your fathers.

Reply:—The communication made to Abraham of the
period fixed for Israel's captivity in Egypt was merely
incidental, it being explanatory of the delay in the
appropriation of the territory promised to that patriarch.
When the Lord said to him, "Thou must know, thy
seed shall be strangers in a land which shall not be
theirs, and they shall make them serve, and shall afflict
them four hundred years," it intimated that the land
would only be allotted to the posterity of Abraham after

the iniquity of the first inhabitants of Palestine would be full, and when, according to the unerring Divine prescience, the fit time for releasing the Jews from their taskmasters, and for punishing the Canaanites, would arrive. The long period for Israel's humiliation in Egypt allowed, therefore, ample time for the nations of Palestine to repent and to abandon their evil doings. The length of the Babylonian captivity was, according to our humble view, limited to seventy years, because seventy sabbatical years had been neglected. The duration of the exile of the Jews was thus appointed to be equal to the number of years during which the divine ordinance of abstaining from husbandry and of giving rest to the soil, had been broken. Thus we read in Leviticus xxvi. 34 and 35, " Then shall the land enjoy her sabbaths, as long as it lieth desolate, and ye shall be in your enemies' land, even then shall the land rest and enjoy her sabbaths. As long as it lieth desolate it shall rest, because it did not rest in your sabbaths, when ye dwelt upon it." With this passage we compare the following of 2 Chronicles xxxvi. 21 :—" To fulfil the word of the Lord by the mouth of Jeremiah until the land had enjoyed her sabbaths, for as long as she lay desolate she kept sabbath, to fulfil three score and ten years."

The special object of the captivity of Babylon had been attained by the short exile, the wider object of their present exile, however, requires a more prolonged period. We have now to expiate the sins committed from the time of Israel's first entrance into the Holy Land,—sins which have created a division between us and the Lord; therefore, Divine Wisdom has ordained that we shall abide our time in dispersion until the approach of the latter days. Thus says Ezekiel xxii. 15, " And I will scatter thee among the gentiles and disperse thee in the countries, and will consume thy filthiness out of thee. To this captivity also alludes the promise in Lamentations iv. 22, " Thine iniquity, O daughter of Zion, is ended; He will no more cause thee to go into captivity." We have already, in a former quotation from 2 Chronicles, shown the real cause of the second captivity, and are now enabled satisfactorily to infer from the above extract from Lamentations that troubles endured in our present exile have been decreed with the view of purifying us from our sins, and of bringing to pass the prediction in Deut. xxx. 6, "And the Lord will circumcise thy heart and the heart of thy seed, to love the Lord thy God with all thy heart and with all thy soul for the sake of thy own life." In regard to this present captivity, it is also said in Ezekiel xxxvi. 26 and 27, "And I will give unto you a new heart, and a new spirit I will place in the midst of you." Again (ib.), "And I will make that you shall walk in my statutes and observe my judgments and do them." There are many other promises which have not as yet been realized, because the ancient sins are not completely eradicated. We have moreover to state that the time of the ultimate redemption is unrevealed, because the knowledge of it would not encourage the timorous if they were to perceive it to be at too remote a distance, to persevere in godliness, nor would it avail the refractory, who would be the more presumptuous if they were to notice that the approaching restoration is not delayed by their own evil ways. The founder of the Christian faith was himself of opinion that the period of the restoration was to remain unknown to his disciples, and he gave, in the book of Acts i. 6 and 7, a striking proof that he was neither a messiah nor a divine being. We find there, " When they [viz., the apostles], therefore, were come together, they asked of him, saying, Lord,

wilt thou at this time restore again the kingdom to
Israel?   And he said unto them, It is not for you to
know the times or the seasons, which the Father hath
put in his own power."   The term of this captivity has
indeed not been confided to any man, and is solely known
to God, whose knowledge is unsearchable.

Our opinion, that our restoration depends on repentance, is founded on the following passage from
Deut. xxx. 1 to 6:—"And it shall come to pass when
all these things are come upon thee, the blessing and
the curse, which I have set before thee, and shall call to
mind among all the nations whither the Lord thy God
hath driven thee; and thou shalt turn unto the Lord
thy God and shalt obey His voice according to all that
I command thee this day, thou and thy children with
all thine heart and with all thy soul: that then the Lord
thy God will turn thy captivity and have compassion on
thee, and will return and gather thee from all the
nations whither the Lord thy God hath scattered thee.
If any of thine be driven out unto the uttermost parts
of heaven, from thence will the Lord thy God gather
thee, and from thence will He fetch thee; and the Lord
thy God will bring thee into the land which thy fathers
possessed; and thou shalt possess it, and He will do thee
good and multiply thee above thy fathers, and the Lord
thy God will circumcise thy heart and the heart of thy
seed," etc.

On our own will, then, depends our repentance, and
consequently also the abbreviation of the period of our
captivity.

From the verse in Leviticus xxvi. 38, " And ye shall
be lost among the gentiles, and the land of your enemies
shall consume you," it must not be inferred that an
irrevocable loss or a total perdition is meant.   The
Hebrew word expressive of loss, " Abad," alludes to the

temporary state of despair,—a state in which a man is unable to escape the impending danger, though relief and deliverance may be his portion at some future day. Hence Isaiah xxvii. 13, "And the *lost ones* in Assyria and those exiled in the land of Egypt shall come," etc.

If "Abad" (to lose or be lost) were to be taken in the sense of complete perdition or cessation of existence, it could not have been said in Leviticus xxvi. 44, "And even this, when they shall be in the land of their enemies, I shall not reject them nor abhor them so as to consume them and to break my covenant with them, for I am the Lord their God." See also Isaiah lxvi. 22, "For as the new heavens and the new earth which I am making remain before me, saith the Lord, so shall your seed and your name remain." Jeremiah xxx. 11, "For I am with thee, saith the Lord, to save thee; though I make a full end of all nations whither I have scattered thee, I will not make a full end of thee; but I will correct thee in measure and will not leave thee altogether unpunished."

The warning pronounced in Leviticus xxvi. 38, "And the land of your enemies shall consume you," has, unfortunately been fulfilled in a grievous measure; many of our brethren have sealed with their blood their fidelity to the faith of their fathers, undergoing the penalties described in Psalm xliv. 22, "For thy sake we are slain all the day long, we are considered like sheep for the slaughter."

The argument, that the length of our present captivity is a proof of our total rejection from the special favour of the Almighty has no reasonable foundation whatever. The designs of the Almighty take their regular and unerring course through hundreds and thousands of years. They are most wisely conceived, although their working and ultimate completion escape our perception, or extend beyond our terrestrial existence. Besides this, their own history elucidates the truth of the saying uttered by the psalmist (Psalm cx), "A thousand years are in Thine eyes, only like yesterday which is past." The world had existed more than two thousand years before the Almighty revealed Himself, and chose "a nation from the midst of a nation, with trials, and signs, and miracles, and warfare, and a strong hand and an out-stretched arm, and awfully great doings."

Finally, we would remind those who taunt us with an everlasting abandonment, because of the restoration not having as yet been granted to us, that the salvation through Jesus, which forms their religious boasting, and which, according to their doctrines, saved the souls of the pious patriarchs from the dominion of Satan, did not come to pass till about four thousand years after the creation of man, why should they then object to our waiting for the time of favour when the appointed period of our restoration shall arrive?

CHAPTER VIII.

WE were once questioned by a Christian, how we could expect to be reinstated in the inheritance of our several tribes, seeing that we are totally unaware of which tribe we are descended, and being so completely mixed up with each other as not to possess any means of tracing our pedigree?

To this we replied:—

The tribes led into captivity by Salmonassar, king of Assyria, were not destroyed, but merely transported from one country to another. Judah, the principal tribe, and Benjamin, remained alone in Palestine. Many of the exiles of the ten tribes who returned settled among the tribe of Judah, who, continuing in the land of their fathers, gave the name of Judah (in Latin *Judæus*---hence the curtailed name *Jew*, formerly spelt *Jue*) to the whole remnant of Israel.

Thus we find in the book of Esther, that Mordecai, though descended from Benjamin, was called, like all the other exiles of Persia, a Jehudi (*i. e.*, a Judæan, or Jew). The descendants of the priests and the Levites have to this day retained the knowledge of their origin. Those who are ignorant of their origin will, at the time of our restoration, be endowed by Divine aid, with the necessary knowledge of their descent. For the prophet Elijah will come before " the great and awful day," and he will turn the heart of the children to their fathers'!

WE SHALL NOW PROCEED TO THE EXPLANATION OF SUCH BIBLICAL PASSAGES AS ARE ASSUMED BY CHRISTIANS TO BEAR REFERENCE TO CERTAIN POINTS OF THEIR FAITH.

CHAPTER IX.

GENESIS i. 1, " In the beginning Elohim [God] created the heaven and the earth." *Elohim*, ending in a plural form as though it meant *Gods*, has been interpreted by Christians as an evidence of the plurality in the Deity, consisting of the Father, the Son, and the Holy Ghost, who are denominated *Trinity*. Our view of the term *Elohim* is as follows:—

Those who are conversant with the Hebrew language are aware that *Elohim* relates not merely to the Supreme Being, but also to angels and human authorities. Manoah, the father of Samson (mentioned in Judges xiii. 22), after he found that he had perceived " an angel of the Lord," said, " We shall surely die, for

we have seen *Elohim*." In reference to human authorities, we read in Exodus xii. 9, " Before the Elohim
[judges] the cause of the two men shall be brought,
and he, whom the *Elohim* [judges] shall declare guilty,
shall pay twofold unto his neighbour." Having thus
shewn that the word *Elohim* bears various interpretations, it is perfectly out of question to refer it in the
first verse of Genesis, to a plurality of persons in the
Deity, of which assumption no corroboration whatever
is given in our Revelation.

We should like to understand how the name of Elohim, given by God to Moses, Exodus vii. 1, in the
words, " Behold I have made thee an *Elohim* to
Pharaoh," can be allowed by Christian expounders to
allude to a plurality of persons, and represent in a
mortal creature a visible Trinity?

Suppose, for argument's sake, Elohim does allude to
a plurality of persons, how could the occurrence of
Eloha (the singular form of Elohim) be justified? Thus
we find in Deut. xxxii. 15, " And he forsook the Eloha
[God] who made him," and Psalm l. 22, " Ye who forget
Eloha [God]." Again, how can the advocates of the
existence of a Trinity account for the alternate employment of Elohim and Eloha? See Isaiah xliv. 6, "And
besides me there is no Elohim"; and, in ver. 8, we read,
" Is there an Eloha besides me?" If the truth of the
doctrine of the Trinity depend on the term " Elohim,"
the word " *Eloha* " most decidedly disproves it, since it
renders the allusion to a plurality perfectly unnecessary.

The real object in the plural form in *Elohim* is to
represent authority and power. The genius of the
Hebrew language admits this particularity not merely
in *Elohim*, but in words of profane signification. Thus
is used *Adonim* (lords) instead of *Adon* (lord). For
instance, Isaiah xix. 4, " In the hand of a hard *Adonim*

[lord, literally lords];" Genesis xxxix. 20, "And the *Adonai* [lords instead of *Adon*, Lord] took him, viz., Joseph," etc.; Exodus xxi., "If בְּעָלָיו [*Baiolov*, his master] is with him," etc.

The plural form is used instead of the singular in many modern languages (for instance *you* instead of *thou*).

CHAPTER X.

GENESIS i. 26, "And God said, We will make man in our image according to our likeness, and they shall rule over the fish of the sea," etc.

From the words, "We will make man," the Christian expounders of this verse infer, that an allusion to a plurality of divine persons is made.

Refutation :— If the verb נַעֲשֶׂה *Naasseh*, we will make, related to a divine plurality, why do we find immediately afterwards the singular form, "And God created man in *His* image?" or why not, "And *they created man?*" The same explanation which we have given in the preceding chapter on the employment of the plural form, holds also good in regard to the present passage.

To bring to mind the manifold powers of the Almighty employed in the creation of the noblest of His creatures, the plural is employed by way of high distinction. We will point out some other passages which contain the verb in the plural for the sake of emphasis, although they indicate a strict unity of person. Genesis xi. 7, " Go to, let us go down and let *us* confound their speech," instead of "let *me*," etc. Job xviii. 2, " Ye shall understand, and then *we* will speak" (instead of *I will* speak).

The words of the Almighty, " We will make man in our image," may have been addressed to the Angels,

for " He maketh known his will to his servants." Thus
we find in Genesis xviii. 17, " Should I conceal from
Abraham what I am doing?" In the same chapter
occurs a parallel expression to the above-mentioned
passage in Genesis xi. 7; but there the singular number
is used, " I will go down and see." If a doctrine of
plurality of personages were to be enforced by the gram-
matical form of words, the very alterations which occur
between the singular and the plural would frustrate
such a doctrine, and suggest doubt and uncertainty
instead of confidence and conviction. Our Holy Scriptures contradict in the most direct terms every opinion
which departs from the belief in an immutable unity,
or ascribes corporeity to him in whose spiritual likeness
the soul of man is created with the object of acknowledging, obeying, and adoring the eternal *one God*.

It is remarkable, that Christians are desirous to make
us believe in the doctrine of the trinity, which is so
totally unauthorised by our Holy Bible, and even by
their own New Testament.

Our Divine Law tells us expressly in Deut. vi. 4,
" Hear, O Israel, the Lord our God is one Lord."

Ibid. iv. 35, " Thou hast been shewn these things, in
order to know that the Lord is God, and there is none
besides Him."

And again, ib. (ver. 39) " Thou shalt know to-day and
take it to heart, that the Lord he is God in heaven above,
and on the earth beneath, and there is none besides."

Isaiah xliii. 2, says, " I, even I, am the Lord, and
there is no saviour besides me."

Ibid. xliv. 6, " Thus saith the Lord the King of Israel
and his Redeemer, I am the first and I am the last, and
besides me there is no God."

Ibid. lv. 5, " I am the Lord, and there is none else
besides me."

Again (ver. 6), " In order that they shall know, from
the rising of the sun [east] unto the west, that there is
no one besides me; I am the Lord, and there is none
else."

Ibid, xl. 18, "And to whom will you liken God, and
what likeness have you to compare with him."

Jeremiah x. 6, " There is none like Thee, O Lord.
Thou art great, and thy name is great in power."

Hosea xiii. 4, " I am the Lord thy God from the land
of Egypt, and thou shalt know no God but me; and
there is no Saviour besides me."

Psalms lxxxvi. 10, " For thou art great and doing
miracles; Thou alone art the Lord."

Nehemiah ix. 6, " Thou alone art the Lord, Thou
hast made the heavens, the heavens of the heavens, and
all their hosts," etc.

1 Chronicles xvii. 20, " There is none like unto thee,
and there is no God like unto thee, and there is no God
besides thee, according to all we have heard with our
ears."

We might adduce numerous other similar corroborative
passages, were it needful. In order to counteract the
dangerous effect of the belief in a good and evil principle (a belief prevailing in Persia, etc.), our Divine
Instructor tells us, " Behold now that I even I am ever
the same, and there is no God with me; I kill and I
bring to life; I crush and heal again." Isaiah xlv. 7,
" He formeth light and createth darkness, maketh peace
and createth evil; I the Lord am doing all these things."
The Deity, who calls into being conditions and events of
totally opposite natures, and who, by mere power of
will brings things into being, or reduces them into
annihilation, is, according to all scriptural testimony,
the most absolute Unity, and, as such, without the
slightest shade of mysticism. This Unity can alone be

comprehended by our finite understanding. He who alone possesses absolute power, and is the first cause, is the Creator of Beings who depend on His will, remain ever, and in every respect, subjected to His Supreme Mandate, and are liable to change and decay. Hence, also, human reason subscribes to the doctrine that God is an absolute and a perfect Unity.

This absolute Unity cannot, under any logical view, be divided into a Duality or a Trinity. If such division is to be forced upon the faith of man, reason remonstrates against it; the faculty of thought given to us by the Almighty protests against a false representation of the Divine Being, and proves that God has constituted the mind in such a manner as to worship Him in accordance with His true attributes. From the moment that a divisibility of essence is attributed to God, we should be compelled to maintain, with the Polytheists, that He is deficient of omnipresence, and that He is comparable with created matter. How can we, then, repudiate such clear testimonies of God's unity, as are contained in passages like the following, Isaiah xl. 18 : "And unto whom will ye liken God, and what likeness have ye to compare unto Him"? We cannot even grant that God from His own resolve would reproduce, and double or treble Himself. Such an assumption could only spring from the narrowest views of a sophistical or a perverted mind; but it could not emanate from a faith which commands veneration and rational obedience.

Even the authors of the New Testament have given opinions which disprove the untenable position of the Christians who make belief in the Trinity an indispensable portion of their creed. Matthew xii. 32, says, "And whosoever speaketh a word *against the Son of Man*, it shall be forgiven him; but whosoever speaketh against the Holy Ghost, it shall not be forgiven him,

neither in this world, neither in the world to come."
The same is repeated in Mark iii. 28, 29, and Luke
xii. 10. These authorities of the Christians have their
data here clearly averred that there is no identity
between the true Deity and the personages subsequently
added to the name of the Divine Being. In Mark
xiii. 32, we have also a proof of the want of identity
between the Son and the Father: " But of that day and
that hour knoweth no man, no, not the angels which are
in heaven, neither the *Son*, but the Father."

Nor do we find throughout the New Testament any
evidence to show that the belief in a Trinity constitutes
a part of the code of Christianity, or that Jesus and
God are to be held as One and the same Being. On
the contrary, Jesus himself is made to profess, in
Matthew x. 40, " He that receiveth you receives me,
and He that receiveth me receiveth Him that sent me."
Here Jesus puts himself merely as a messenger of God.
Paul, in his epistle to the Romans v. 15, also says,
" The gift by grace, which is by *one man* Jesus Christ,"
etc. Matthew xx. 18, again says, " Behold, we go to
Jerusalem, and the *Son of Man* shall be betrayed,"
etc.; and in verse 28 he states, " Even as the Son of
Man *came not to be ministered unto*, but to minister,"
etc.

In the very prayer instituted by Jesus, and denominated after him " The Lord's Prayer," his disciples are
taught to invoke the Father who is in heaven, but are
not told to use the combination subsequently made of
Father, Son, and Holy Ghost. We see clearly that the
New Testament affords not a single evidence to authorise a change from the pure belief in the Divine Unity
to the complex aud unintelligible dogma of that of the
Trinity.

CHAPTER XI.

GENESIS ii. 17, "And from the tree of knowledge of good and evil thou shalt not eat. For on the day thou shalt eat thereof thou shalt surely die." The religious authorities of the Christians deduce from this passage the belief that Adam, by transgressing the Divine prohibition, forfeited individually, and through him all his posterity, the enjoyment of the everlasting beatitude of the soul, and that he and his seed, including our patriarchs, prophets, and pious ancestors, fell a prey to hell, from which they were only saved through the death and intercession of Jesus. The reduplication of the Hebrew phrase מות תמות (dying thou shalt die, or, thou shalt surely die), is taken to be a proper *testimony* of this singular tenet. As a further proof that the ancient personages mentioned in the Hebrew Scriptures were aware of the doom awaiting them after their quitting this life on earth, Christian authors have cited the lament of Jacob in Genesis xxxvii. 35, "I shall go down into *hell* (Sheol) to my son in mourning." Also the words of Hezekiah, in Isaiah xxxviii. 10, have been pointed out as corroborative evidence, for he says there, "I shall enter the gates of hell (Sheol)."

Refutation.—When Adam was told by the Almighty, "On the day thou shalt eat thereof thou shalt surely die," it was implied that Adam should actually be punished with the loss of life, on the very same day he should counteract the command of God; but we evidently see by his continued existence that he only ensured the penalty of death. A passage similar to the one we have just quoted occurs in 1 Kings ii. 37, where Shimei, once the insolent enemy of the fugitive king, David, was prohibited by the son of that monarch from quitting the capital; and he was told, "On the day thou shalt go forth from Jerusalem and pass the brook of Kidron, thou must know that thou shalt surely die." Yet Shimei was not punished with death on the same day he left Jerusalem. In like sense, we take the Divine injunction ending with the term, "Thou shalt surely die." It meant that on the day Adam would, by his disobedience, incur the displeasure of the Almighty, he would be afflicted by various punishments, such as reaping thorns and thistles, and living by his hard labour on the scanty produce of an unblessed soil, and until his severe trials should terminate in the fatal dispensation of death. This sentence being the most prominent and inevitable destiny of the transgressor, it was announced in the first instance, but not with the intent of its being *immediately* fulfilled.

As to the idea of the reduplication of the verb " to die," shewing that the punishment attending the transgression of Adam was of an hereditary nature, we have found in Scripture a complete refutation of such an interpretation; for we read in Deuteronomy xxiv. 16, "Fathers shall not die for children, nor children for fathers." The principle here laid down cannot solely be referred to the sentence of death, but relates also to every minor punishment, so that neither parents nor children are to be amenable to punishment for each other's misdeeds.

The reader, on referring to the whole matter of Genesis iii., will perceive that it had not been the object of the Almighty to remove Adam from the earth on the day he committed the transgression of the Divine command. The punishments Adam had to endure, received their completion only at his death. In the passage above cited, it is stated that the mission of the first patriarch was the propagation of his species. His mode of subsistence is there pointed out to consist in long and wearying toil, and only after a period predetermined "by the Almighty" the doom was to be accomplished, which was pronounced in the words, "Thou art dust, and unto dust shalt thou return." These last words evidently shew that the retribution of Adam's sin related to the body, and not to the soul, for nothing but the inanimate corpse is the prey of the earth its native element. Of that portion alone it is appositely remarked in Ecclesiastes xii. 7, " The dust returneth to the earth as it was, but the spirit shall return to God who gave it."

We see thus that the formula מות תמות ("dying thou shalt die," or " thou shalt surely die"), alludes to the perishable state of the body, and not to the state of the soul. But we have further evidence that the souls of the posterity of Adam were not consigned to perdition, in consequence of the sin of the first father; for we find in the Levitical laws that abscission of the soul from her people is to be the punishment for various sins. See, for instance, Leviticus vii. 27 : So that each man who dies in his own guilt must suffer for his own iniquity, and is severed from his people, that is to say, his soul is excluded from a reunion with the souls of those who have gone before him into the realms of bliss. On the other hand, we find numerous instances, that, in describing the death of the righteous, the text used runs thus : " And they were gathered unto their people," see, for instance, Genesis xxv. 17; Deut. xxxii. 50. A sentence in direct opposition to the annihilation of the soul, illustrating our argument, may be found in Leviticus xxii. 3, " That the soul shall be cut off from my presence, I am the Lord."

In these early records of humanity we have a clear lesson of the immortality of the soul. The pious and worthy are received into undisturbed beatitude, while those who defile themselves by sins are removed from the enjoyment of the glorious contemplation of the Deity.

Far be it, therefore, from us to put faith in the doctrine propounded by Christian divines, that the predecessors of Jesus were, without regard to their innocence or piety, totally and collectively abandoned, and consigned to the abode of hell. Far be it from us to believe that, that God causes " His pious servants to see perdition"; that He hated those who loved Him, or that He regarded them favourably while they lived on earth, yet disowned them after they had quitted the scenes of their pious aspirations.

It is utterly revolting to the mind to attribute to the Almighty the slightest degree of injustice, or of indifference to man, whether he be righteous or iniquitous. How could such a prophet as Jonah have prayed, Jonah iv. 3, " And now, O Lord, do Thou take my soul from me, for my death is better than my life." Would he, cognisant of the future punishment of the soul, have desired to be taken away from this earth, in order to undergo inevitable torments in after life? Again, when Enoch and Elijah were " taken away by God," as Scripture expresses it, and which removal could happen to the soul only, should we imagine that God designed to manifest His special love to them, by giving them over to constant torments in hell?

We have to combat another unfounded opinion set forth by our antagonists. They maintain that their " God Messiah," through his own death, saved the souls of those who had gone before him from their doom in hell. How can it be asserted that the first sin of the first man should meet with retrospective and prospective atonement, through the perpetration of a far more

heinous crime in laying a violent hand on the body of
a presumed Deity? The difficulty of the position of
those who maintain these views is increased by the very
words of Paul, in his epistle to the Romans v. 14:
" Nevertheless, death reigned from Adam to Moses, even
over them that had not sinned after the similitude of
Adam's transgression," etc.

In Leviticus xviii. 5, we find a still stronger proof of
the inconsistency of believing that a divine displeasure
was felt against all predecessors of Jesus. We read
there, " And ye shall observe my statutes and my commandments which man shall perform, and through
which he shall live." Scripture here points out to us in
the clearest and most incontestable manner, that immortal
bliss is conceded to the individual who faithfully adheres
to the Divine will, so that man is not in any respect
dependant on the acts which may have been performed
by his ancestors. We may now apply this reasoning
to the sin of Adam, since we see that man receives rewards
and punishments according to his performance of the
Divine commandments, and that he is individually responsible for his actions, also Adam could only be per-
sonally accountable for the sin he had committed.

The commandments, being denominated " a tree of
life, for those who take firm hold of them," do not
suggest that our terrestrial existence is to be prolonged
by their observance; but they are calculated to place us
on an equality of excellency with the patriarchs, the
chosen servants of God. Without closing our ears
against truth and reason, we cannot admit that a responsibility is imposed upon man for the sins of his first
progenitor. Man's own. immortal life is imperilled by
his own doings, and therefore God, in His Divine mercy,
has enjoined on us His commandments, " which man
performeth and lives thereby." Passages to the same

effect are repeatedly found even in the book of Ezekiel,
see xviii. 19, 20, where he speaks concerning the life of
the soul, " He who does judgment and righteousness
shall surely live and not die." And again, it is written
there, " And who does judgment and righteousness, his
soul shall live"; for except the life of the soul, there is
no life but what is succeeded by death.   From all that
has been adduced hitherto, it is clear, that the holy and
righteous men were not condemned to hell, nor afflicted
with the spiritual torments of the first man, they not
having rebelled against the Lord; but, on the contrary,
they found favour in His sight, and secured everlasting
salvation through their own merits, without requiring
extraneous interference to save their souls.   In support
of our conviction Ezekiel says, chap. xviii., " The soul
that sinneth shall die.   The son shall not be visited
through the iniquity of the father, nor the father
through the iniquity of the son," etc.   The object of the
prophet is to declare that there shall be no condemnation to the soul, except through its *own* crime, not
through the crime of another.   It is here in place to
settle an apparent contradiction of Scripture—namely,
We find stated in the ten commandments, " He visiteth
the iniquities of the fathers on their children," etc.;
from this an hereditary punishment seems obvious: but
on a close examination, this phrase is satisfactorily
explained.   The punishment of fathers on their children
takes place where the iniquity is continued to be exercised by the children; and therefore Holy Writ holds
out the threat of successive visitation, saying, *On those
who hate me*, which explanation is applicable to all
similar passages in Scripture.   Conformably to this interpretation, the author of the Lamentations says,
chap. v. "Our fathers sinned and are no more, and we
have borne their iniquities," which means, " Our fathers,

through their guilty conduct, brought on the troubles of the captivity, and they died in consequence of their misdeeds. We also, who succeeded them in this captivity, have added to our own transgressions those of our ancestors, by imitating their evil deeds, and thus fulfilling the prediction, Lev. xxvi. 9, " And they who are left among you shall pine away in *their* iniquity in your enemy's land, and also through the iniquities of their fathers retained among them they shall pine away." The pious contemporaries of the captivity, however, as for instance, Jeremiah, Baruch the son of Nerejah, Ezekiel, Daniel with his companions, and others, were benefited through the very trials which they shared with their sinful brethren; for among the Gentile governments they were raised to far greater distinction than they had attained under the kings of Israel. These advantages they enjoyed solely through the care with which they avoided the deeds of their wicked ancestors; and therefore they laboured not under the infliction of curses which the Almighty ordains to the race of sinners. The opinion of the Christians, that no salvation was granted prior to the death of Jesus, meets with another refutation in Luke xvi. 19: the history of the beggar Lazarus represents that he was after death to repose in beatitude on the bosom of the patriarch Abraham. This shews that Abraham and Lazarus were not in hell, and leads to the conclusion that the pious were not deprived of a felicitous eternity, even before Jesus was said to have redeemed them, but that the wicked only meet with merited retribution.

We return once more to the reduplication of the term *thou shalt surely die*, which, as we have before stated, has been misapplied to the death of the soul. The argument is totally wrong, and rests on the misapprehension of the Hebrew idiom, according to which the infinitive is frequently placed before the ordinary tense;

see, for instance, 2 Kings viii. 5, " Go and say, Thou shalt
surely not live; and the Lord revealed unto me that he
shall surely die" (the infinitive מות, die, and חיה, to live,
here accompanies the respective future tenses). The
sentence quoted here serves as a reply to the question
asked by the king, " Shall I recover from my illness ?"
(literally *live through*). The answer can only suit the
question. The enquirer asks merely whether he is to
live on or die (in a bodily sense), and the answer refers
to the death with regard to the body only, and is given
with the double verbs. Such a reduplication occurs also
in 1 Samuel xiv. 4, where Saul says, מות ימות יונתן,
"Surely Jonathan shall die," and in the same book (xxii.
16), מות תמות אחימלך, " Surely, Ahimelech, thou shalt
die. Though the threat of death is expressed with the
repetition of the verb מות (to die) it has no other signification than bodily death. Other verbs are repeated
in a like manner, for instance, Ex. xxi. 20, נקם ינקם, he
shall surely be revenged: Ibid (xix. 13, או יסקל סקול
ירה יירה, " He shall surely be stoned or shot through."
Genesis xv. 13, ידע תדע (knowing thou shalt know)
" thou shalt surely know." On the other hand, we find
in Scripture that the use of the simple unrepeated verb,
מות, to die, is sufficient to indicate perdition of the soul,
as, for instance, Eze. xviii. 20, " The soul that sinneth
it shall die," היא תמות. From the preceding proofs and
argument it is established that there is not the remotest
allusion to hell in the lament of Jacob. Genesis xxxvii.
35, " I shall go down into the grave (Sheol) unto my
son mourning." Neither in the thanksgiving or
Hezekiah (chap. xxxviii. 10), where he says, " I shall
go to the gates of the grave שאול (Sheol). Thus we
find also in the Psalms (xlix. 15), " Like sheep they
are laid into the grave (Sheol)." Again, " Sheol cannot
thank thee." In these passages, the word מות (maveth)

death might be used appropriately for Sheol (the grave). In other parts likewise Sheol is used as the resting place of the inanimate body; for instance, Job xiv. 13, "O that Thou wouldst hide me in the (Sheol);" Eccles. ix. 10, "In the (Sheol) whither thou art going;" Gen. xxxvii. 35, "I will go down into the grave (Sheol) unto my son;" and instances where Sheol means the depth of the earth are to be met with in the Psalms (cxxxix. 8), "If I make my bed in the grave (or depth of the earth), Thou art there;" and Job xi. 8, "And deeper than the grave what canst thou know?"

CHAPTER XII.

Genesis iii. 15, "And I will put an enmity between thee and the woman, and between thy seed and her seed. It shall bruise thy head, and thou shall bruise his heel." The Christians attempt to strengthen their faith by maintaining that the words, "it shall bruise thy head," is a type of Jesus, who is to kill Satan, styled in holy writ "the serpent."

Refutation.—The interpretation is fallacious, for if the passage under consideration meant that Jesus was to kill Satan, that is to say, destroy the cause of sin, there ought not to be any sinners among his believers, but since they still continue committing sins, that opinion is overthrown both by their practical life and by the same verse on which they found this doctrine. The end of the passage (thou shalt bruise its heel) shows the unsoundness of such assertions. How could the serpent (sin) do injury after its being destroyed? Moreover, how could Satan induce the Jews and the heathen to kill Jesus and his disciples, he (Jesus) already

having destroyed Satan. Paul himself affords a refutation by promising (Romans xvi. 20), "And the God of
peace shall bruise Satan under your feet *shortly*." The
same writer, in his first Epistle to the Thessalonians,
states (chap. ii. 18), "Wherefore we would have come
unto you, even I, Paul, once and again, but Satan
hindered us." This tends to show that, even after the
death of Jesus, in the times of Paul, Satan had still
preserved his existence and exercised his dominion
over those who had been saved through Jesus, and that
the Gospel is at variance with this symbolical interpretation.

CHAPTER XIII.

GENESIS xxii. 18, " And in thy seed shall the nations
of the earth be blessed, because thou (Abraham) hast
obeyed my voice." On this verse the Christians found
the assertion, that the promise given to Abraham as to
the blessing of all nations through his seed, had no
reference to the whole race of Abraham's descendants,
but specially and exclusively to Jesus as the pre-eminent
posterity of the patriarch; that, therefore, this promise
was never realized on other individuals.

Refutation.—Here, again, we have to treat with a
palpable fallacy, because the Christians generally argue
in favour of their religion from detached portions of the
prophecies, without going deeply into the sacred subject
and studying the context. The slightest attention to
the verse which precedes the one cited, will enable us to
judge that no *single* individual is meant by the Divine
bounty. For there we see plainly predicted, " For I
will surely bless thee, and multiply thy seed like the
stars of heaven, and like the sand on the shore of the
sea, and thy seed shall inherit the gates of his enemies;

and with thy seed shall be blessed all the nations of the earth," refers to the whole posterity, which is to be abundant as the stars of heaven, and the sand on the shore of the sea. Through the *entire* seed, through the whole people of Israel the other nations of the earth are to be blessed. Moses gives his testimony to this in addressing the people of Israel, Deut. i. 10, " The Lord your God hath multiplied you; and behold ye are this day as the stars of heaven for multitude." To this effect, also, the Almighty gave His assurances to Israel and Jacob, see Genesis xxvi. 4, " In thy seed shall all the nations of the earth be blessed"; and Ib. xxviii. 14, the Lord says to Jacob, " And thy seed shall be as the dust of the earth, and thou shall spread abroad to the west, to the east, to the north, and to the south, and through thee and thy seed shall all the families of the earth be blessed." The Divine promises of love agree with the one given to Abraham in Genesis xii. 3, " And I will bless them that bless thee, and curse them that curse thee; and in thee shall all the families of the earth be blessed"; and Ib. xviii. 18, " And Abraham shall surely become a great and mighty nation, and all the nations of the earth shall be blessed in him."

The patriarchs had become a blessing to all the nations of the earth by fearlessly acknowledging the existence, unity, and omnipotence of the Lord, and by proclaiming His name in all their migrations; and they had raised themselves above all other people by their communion with the Divine Being, who awards true blessing and spiritual beatitude.

An equal reward of bliss was appointed unto their children following their paths and observing the virtuous acts of their forefathers. Agreeably to this, Scripture declares, Genesis xviii. 19, " For I know him, that he will command his children and his household after him, that they shall keep the way of the Lord, to do justice and judgment, that the Lord may bring upon Abraham that which He hath spoken of him." See also Isaiah li. " Look unto Abraham your father, and unto Sarah that bare you: for I called him alone, and blessed him and increased him." It is well known no spiritual blessing has ever fallen to the lot of the Gentiles, unless conveyed to them through the medium of Israel's religion. This will be borne out by the following quotations:—Numbers x. 32, " And it shall be, if thou go with us, yea it shall be, that what goodness the Lord shall do unto us [Israelites] the same we do unto thee [Gentiles]". Isaiah xiv. 1, " For the Lord will have mercy on Jacob, and will yet choose Israel, and set them in their own land, and the strangers shall be joined with them, and they shall cleave to the house of Jacob." Ib. lvi. 6, " Also the sons of the strangers that join themselves to the Lord to serve him and to love the name of the Lord to be his servants, every one that keepeth the Sabbath from polluting it, and taketh hold of my covenant." (Ver. 7) " Even them will I bring to my holy mountain, and make them joyful in my house of prayer," etc. Ib. lx. iii., " And the Gentiles shall come to thy light, and kings to the brightness of thy rising." Zechariah ii. 15 (English version, ver. 11), " And many nations shall be joined to the Lord in that day, and shall be my people, and I will dwell in the midst of thee, and thou shalt know that the Lord of Hosts hath sent me unto thee." Ib. viii. 23, " Thus saith the Lord of Hosts, in those days it shall come to pass that ten men out of all languages of the nations, shall take hold, even shall take hold of the skirt of him that is a Jew, saying, We will go with you, for we have heard that God is with you." And Psalms lxvii. 1, " God will be gracious unto and

will bless us, and cause His face to shine upon us."—
Selah. "That thy ways may be known upon earth,"
etc. Passages analogous to the preceding will be amply
discussed in the course of this work.

CHAPTER XIV.

Genesis xlix. 10, " The sceptre shall not depart from
Judah, nor a law-giver from between his feet, until
Shiloh come, and unto him shall belong the gathering
of the people."

The Christians argue from this verse, that the patriarch Jacob did hereby prophesy the coming of Jesus,
whom he (Jacob) called *Shiloh*, and through him (Jesus)
the prophecy was fulfilled; for the sceptre did not depart from the Jews until Jesus appeared: with Him
only departed royalty from the Jews.

The Refutation.— The Christians labour under the
misconception, that Jesus was a member of the tribe of
Judah, and king of the Jews. Now, were this inter-
pretion the true one, how can they reconcile it with the
fact, that the sceptre did *not* depart from Judah at the
advent of the so-called *Shiloh?* Moreover, we find that
Judah lost the sovereignty at the destruction of the
first temple, when Nebuchadnezzar led Zedekiah, king
of Judah, into captivity; an event which happened
430 years anterior to the birth of Jesus. During the
existence of the second temple, however, we find no
indication that a descendant of Judah governed Israel.
Herod and his descendant, who occupied the throne
until the fall of the second temple, were of low birth,
and belonged to the tribe of Judah. How can they,
therefore, maintain that the sceptre had not departed
from Judah, nor royalty from Israel, until the coming
of Jesus?

In investigating the true sense of the words, "The sceptre shall not depart from Judah (meaning the tribe of Judah), we perceive that the patriarch Jacob, by his blessing, bequeathed to Judah the supremacy over his brethren. Accordingly, he says, Genesis xlix. 8, "The children of thy father shall bow down to thee;" and on this account he compares him with the lion as the king among the animals. Hence we find the tribe of Judah taking the precedence in the encampments (see Numbers x. 13, et seq.), "And Nashon, the prince of that tribe, was admitted on the *first* day [of the dedication of the tabernacle] to offer up his sacrifice" (see Numbers vii. 12). Subsequently, when Joshua was dead, and the Israelites inquired of the Lord, Judges i. 1, " Who shall go up for us against the Canaanites *first* to fight against them? The Lord said, Judah shall go up," etc. From these passages it appears, that, after the leader had left the tribes without a successor, they inquired which of them should assume the rule and precedency, and the Almighty awarded it to the tribe of Judah who, 1 Chron. v. 2, was the most powerful among his brethren. This superiority may be ascribed to David, who said of himself, 1 Chron. xxviii. 4, " The Lord chose me before the house of my fathers to be king over Israel for ever; for he hath chosen Judah to be the ruler; and of the house of Judah the house of my father, among the sons of my father he willed to make me king over all Israel." From David the royalty descended to Zedekiah, king of Judah, who was of the seed of David. With this king the sovereignty departed from the tribe of Judah. There remained during the whole series of the two captivities only a few dignitaries as princes and chiefs of the captivities who had been denominated by the patriarch Jacob מחוקקים (law-givers).

During the existence of the second temple, and also at the time when the priests and their subordinates ruled, there were found princes, descended from David and from the lineage of Zerubbabel, as is stated in the work "*Seder Ngolam Zuta.*"

It is true, we find that originally King Saul was elected ruler, though not descending from the tribe of Judah, but from that of Benjamin; but, at that period, it was against the desire of the Almighty to admit a king. On that account he would not have a king chosen from the tribe to which the promise of a permanent dynasty had been given; and He appointed for them a king who should occupy the throne only for a short time. To this fact Scripture alludes, Hosea xiii. 11, " I gave thee a king in mine anger, and removed him in my wrath," for he and his children were slain, and the sway departed from him. All this misfortune came to pass, because the Israelites had desired a king in the time of Samuel, the prophet of the Lord, who was their judge and leader: hence we find in 1 Samuel viii. 7, " for they have not rejected thee, but me they have rejected from ruling over them." Yet, even in the times of Samuel, the dignity of the leadership was not totally removed from the tribe of Judah, for David was the man who conducted Israel to battle. Hence we must interpret the words " The sceptre shall not depart from Judah," according to their literal sense, viz., that the sceptre of royalty shall not be taken from Judah as long as the kingdom shall last. And the words "*nor a lawgiver from between his feet,*" viz., that the lawgivers shall not depart, must have reference to the sages and scribes who, being from the seed of Judah, were rulers and leaders during the captivity; for the chiefs of the captivity were descendants of David, and the majority of our exiled were from the tribe of Judah,

and many of them were of the lineage of David. They
distinguished themselves as scholars and theologians,
i.e. sages and scribes, and therefore they were called
lawgivers, in the same manner as Moses, the " chief of
the prophets," is called in the Hebrew מחוקק, " lawgiver," (see Deut. xxxiii. 21). For there is the portion
of the *lawgiver* concealed, " and he led the heads of the
people, and executed the justice of the Lord, and His
judgments with Israel." We see, also, in Judges,
" From Nachir descended lawgivers, and from Zebulon
those who handle the pen of the scribe," which refers
again to the sages and the learned who were the rulers
of their people. The words from " *his feet*" are synonymous with *his seed*. The word שׁילה (Shiloh) signifies
the youngest child, or *the last child*, and is derived from
the same root as וכשליתה (and towards her young one,
Deut. xxviii. 57), which the Chaldee version renders
" and towards the youngest of her children." The term
Shiloh refers to our expected king, Messiah, and who
will appear in the latter days and be one of the seed of
Judah. The words *until Shiloh shall come*, do not mean
that at the coming of Shiloh, the sceptre shall immediately depart; but, on the contrary, that it shall not
depart thereafter. The word עד (until) is used in the
same sense in the following instances, (Gen. xxviii. 15),
" For I will not leave thee *until* I shall have done
what I have promised unto thee;" and (Deut. vii. 24),
" No man shall be able to stand before thee *until* thou
shalt have destroyed them." The word יקהת meaning
" authority," in the verse of Genesis under consideration
recurs in the Proverbs, xxx. 17. The supreme power
and authority of the Messiah alluded to in Jacob's
prophecy is predicted, also, in Daniel, who says " And
all rulers shall serve and obey him."

CHAPTER XV.

DEUT. xiv. 13, " Thou shalt not eat any abomination."
The Christians adduce against this passage one from
Matthew xv. 11, " Not that which goeth into the mouth
defileth man; but that which cometh out of the mouth,
this defileth;" they consider us, therefore, in the wrong
for not eating of unclean animals.

Refutation. — Independent of motives of economy,
persons may refuse certain articles of food on different
grounds. The food may be too expensive, and, therefore, unsuitable to persons of a low condition; or it may
be of too inferior a quality, and, therefore, unfit for a man
in a high station of life. It is obvious that Christians
will not argue, that the food of unclean animals is denied us on account of the luxuriousness of such nourishment, or the unworthiness of the Israelites, for Scripture
inculcates the reverse, viz., that certain creatures are
unclean, and that the Israelites are to be a holy nation.
Hence, if Christians partake of food denominated unclean, they must consider themselves unholy. Our
conclusion is borne out by Scripture, for we read in
Lev. xi. 8, " they [certain animals] shall be unclean unto
you." This implies, that they shall be forbidden to you
Israelites, who are a holy nation, but not to you, the
Gentiles, who have not been equally distinguished by
the Almighty.

Of the same tenor is the admonition in Leviticus, xi. 43
and 44, " Ye shall not make yourselves abominable
with any creeping thing that creepeth, neither shall you
make yourselves unclean with them that ye should be
defiled thereby. For I am the Lord your God, ye shall
therefore sanctify yourselves and ye shall be holy: for I
am holy. Neither shall ye defile yourselves with any

manner of creeping thing that creepeth upon the earth."
See also Lev. xx. 25 and 26, "Ye shall therefore put
difference between clean beasts and unclean, and between
unclean fowls and clean; and ye shall not make your
souls abominable by beast or by fowl, or by any manner of living thing that creepeth on the ground, which
I have separated from you as unclean.   And ye shall
be holy unto me; for I the Lord am holy, and have
severed you from other people, that ye should be mine."
Also, Deut. xiv. 1, 2, & 3, " Ye are children of the Lord
your God: ye shall not cut yourselves, nor make any
baldness between your eyes for the dead, for thou art a
holy nation unto the Lord thy God.   And the Lord has
chosen thee to be a peculiar people unto himself above
all the nations that are upon the earth.   Thou shalt not
eat any abominable thing."   This portion concludes
with the words, " Ye shall not eat of anything that
dieth of itself, thou shalt give it unto the stranger that
is in thy gates that he may eat it, or thou mayest sell it
unto an alien: for thou art a holy people unto the Lord
thy God; thou shalt not seethe a kid in its mother's milk"
(ver. 21).   These verses afford sufficient evidence, that
such creatures, on account of their being unclean, were
prohibited food to the Israelites, who are a holy people,
designated the " children of the Lord."   For unclean
food defiles the body of him who eats of it; and a defiled
body infects the soul.   Now, a soul that is defiled will
not be admitted into the sanctuary, that is to say, before
the Divine presence, but will be deprived of a glorious
future.   The declaration of the revealed law, that unclean food defiles the body of the eater, at once over-
throws the argument of the Christians, " that things
entering the mouth do not defile a man, but only those
proceeding from the mouth.''

In what way can the opinion of the Gentiles, based on

their Gospel, be reconciled with the various precepts regarding certain animals expressed in many parts of our Holy Writ? for instance, " Do not defile yourselves by them." " Ye shall be defiled through them." " Do not defile your souls by the creeping things," etc. All this must bring conviction, that unclean food doth defile both body and soul. Who then will venture to render lawful what God has forbidden, and annul His statutes? Moreover, if the founders of Christianity had considered it lawful for the Gentiles to partake of unclean food, why did they prescribe to them (in Acts xv. 20), " to abstain from things strangled and from blood"? It ought also to be kept in mind, that Adam incurred punishment for transgressing a command which had been imparted to him *only once*. How much greater must the transgression be of those who venture to eat of unclean food which had been so repeatedly prohibited to them? Besides, we find great inconsistencies in this principle contained in the Books of Matthew and Mark (" That not what goeth into the mouth defiles," etc.), for many intoxicating drinks will doubtlessly defile when allowed to go down into the mouth of man in excess, while from the mouth of man come out the words of the living God, praises and thanksgivings to His glorious name, wise and moral maxims, and social converse for the interchange of ideas. All such utterance does not defile man; and he may through his words even deserve to be called a holy man.

As to our Sacred Scripture, it gives the assurance, that, in times to come, even the Gentiles will abstain from eating blood and unclean and abominable food. See Zech. ix. v. 7, " And I shall remove his blood from his mouth, and his abominations from between his teeth."

CHAPTER XVI.

DEUT. xxvii. 26. " Cursed is he who will not keep the words of this law to fulfil them; and all the people shall say Amen." The Christians infer from this verse, that the law of Moses curses all who neglect any commandment of the law, and there being so many commandments, no man can properly practise them: hence, all Jews must be cursed.

Refutation.—The tenor of this verse does not go to pronounce a curse against every one who will not keep the obligations and prohibitory laws set forth in the Books of Moses. A strict fulfilment of all the commandments is utterly impossible. Even our legislator Moses, the chief of prophets, observed only those which he found practicable *out* of Palestine; since many of the divine precepts had been especially adapted to and were solely practicable *in* the Holy Land. How much greater is the claim of other Israelites to be forgiven if they abandon certain precepts, the performance of which is rendered impracticable in consequence of existing circumstances? nor will they be included in the curse if they transgress a commandment when led astray by the impulse of passion, provided it be followed by sincere repentance, " for there is no righteous man on earth who will do good and not sin;" and repentance is the balm and remedy for the pain and the mortification of sin. An instance is afforded in King David, though he sinned in the case of Uriah, the Hittite, he was not cursed (by reason of his repentance); on the contrary, he was blessed by the Almighty with an everlasting benediction, since a covenant was made with him that his throne should never be destroyed. See Jer. xxxiii. 20, " Thus speaketh the Lord, if ye can break my covenant with the day and my covenant with the night, and there should not be day and night in their season, then may also my covenant be broken with David my servant, that he should not have a son to reign upon his throne." The merit of his general piety availed during a long period to him and his seed after him, and to all his nation. See Isaiah xxxvii. 35, " And I shall protect the city and save it for mine own sake and for the sake of my servant David." This is a clear evidence, that a man failing to observe a portion of the divine law will not be accursed, so long as no opportunity of evincing his obedience has been afforded him. In like manner will he be spared who, sinning under the influence of passion, resolutely abandons his error, and shews sincere contrition. Only such a man is cursed who refuses to believe in the revealed will of the Almighty, or who rejects and contemns the divine commands.

In corroboration of the argument, we may refer to the identical words of the passage under consideration, viz., " Cursed is he who will not keep the words of the law to fulfil them." If no exception whatever were admissible in the rigid observance of the divine precepts, the inspired penman necessarily would have said, " Cursed be he who will not keep *every word* of the law." The latter words, " to fulfil them," shews that the malediction concerns only those who evade the opportunity of manifesting their obedience. We further find in Deut. xxviii. 15, " And it shall come to pass, if thou shalt not obey the voice of the Lord thy God to keep and fulfil all the commands and statutes which I command you this day, all these curses shall come upon thee and reach thee." This warning does not refer to a person who neglects the keeping and fulfilment of *all* the commandments without *any* exception, but to him who does not listen to the voice of God, but impiously rebels against it, and shakes off the yoke of divine government. The curses will come upon him if he does not finally return to God with perfect repentance. It is acknowledged that God gave the law to His people from pure love, not for His own sake, but for their benefit; nor did He multiply His commandments to weigh His creatures down with their burden, and bring perdition upon man's soul, but to increase the claim of reward, and prepare the spirit for a glorious futurity. Not a single commandment is to be despised, for each contains the seed of heavenly bliss. The more strictly and diligently man conforms to the number of divine precepts, the greater becomes his worth and merit in the eyes of the Lord.

We find that Moses yearned to enter into the Holy Land in order to obtain an opportunity to fulfil all those commandments that had been ordained to be practised in Palestine. Here we must remind the reader that the curses proclaimed in Deut. xxvii., obviously relate to the commission of secret and revolting sins, for the maledictions contain the expression וְשָׂם בַּסָּתֶר "And who put it (viz., the idol) into a *secret place*," while overt transgressions meet punishment from the human tribunal. In a like manner we find, in the same chapter, that he will be cursed " who smites his neighbour *secretly*;" this alludes, also, to the slanderer who secretly injures his fellow-man. A parallel expression occurs in the 101st Psalm, in the words " Whoso privily slandereth his neighbour, him will I cut off." To avoid the error of its being understood with regard to corporal punishment, the law adds the words *secretly* or *privately*. A similar curse recoils upon him who refuses to observe certain laws, because he considers the word of God unimportant, a presumption which certainly ranks among the secret sins. To sum up our review of these twelve verses of Deut. xxvii., we remark, that in the same mode as the public transgressor is punished by public justice here below, so the secret transgressor will be punished by the invisible and supreme justice of our Heavenly Father. Only that man will be condemned who obstinately *persists* in vice and scornfully disdains mercy which the Lord offers to repentant sinners. This again may be illustrated by the words in (Deut. xxix. 29), " The secret things belong to the Lord our God, but matters revealed, belong to us and to our children for ever." The Christians have argued against us from this verse without fully comprehending its purport, and we can oppose them on their own grounds, by referring them to the concluding verses of their Gospel, viz., " For I testify unto every man that heareth the words of the prophecies of these books, if any man shall add unto these things, God shall add unto him the plagues that are written in these books; and if any man shall take away from the words of the book of these prophecies, God shall take away his part out of the Book of Life and out of the Holy City, and from the promises written in these books." Now the Christians must be well aware that they have acted in contradiction to these emphatic warnings, in having both added and diminished from their own doctrines. Thus, for instance, they have made an innovation by keeping the Sabbath on the first day of the week instead of the seventh, for which no sanction whatever can be found in the Gospel. On the other hand, they have totally disregarded commands enforced on them. See Acts xv. 20, where the eating of blood and of strangled creatures is forbidden. To these commands they actually do not conform, for they unscrupulously eat of both these forbidden articles.

CHAPTER XVII.

SOME Christian divines have asserted that the curses pronounced in Leviticus xxvi. 42, relate to the destruction of the first temple, and are therefore accompanied by the consoling words, " And I shall remember the covenant with Jacob, and also my covenant with Isaac, and also my covenant with Abraham I shall remember, and I shall remember the land." In the same light they view the passage, " And I shall remember unto them the first covenant that I brought them out of Egypt before the eyes of the Gentiles to be their God, I am the Lord." The Christians refer these topics to the remembrance of the second temple, and the redemption is said to allude to the captivity of Babel; but the subsequent curses contained in Deut. xxviii. are referred to the demolition of the second temple, and hence are unaccompanied by consolatory words as Israel is to have no restoration from this exile.

Refutation.—Scripture does not authorise the supposition that the first-mentioned curses refer to the destruction of the first temple only; the warnings contained in Leviticus with regard to the first covenant, though materially and principally referring to the first temple in which the captivity commenced, include, also, the destruction of the second temple and the afflictions suffered by Israel in the present captivity. At the same time we perceive that the curses contained in Deuteronomy mention facts relating exclusively to the first destruction. Among the maledictions mentioned in Leviticus xxvi. 31, we read, " And I shall destroy your *sanctuaries*," the latter word being in the plural must evidently be understood to include both the first and the second temple; nor can the word *sanctuaries*

refer to *palaces*; since the passage in Leviticus goes on to
say " And I shall not smell your sweet savours," therefore it naturally points to the sacrifices offered up in the
sanctuaries. Thus also the curses contained in Deut.
xxviii. 29, " The Lord shall cause thee to be smitten
before thine enemies; thou shalt go out against them one
way, and in seven ways thou shalt flee before them."
This undoubtedly did not take place during the time of
the second temple, for then the Jews prevailed, and the
Romans suffered a total defeat, as is related by Joseph
Ben Gurion. The Roman writers themselves acknowledge evidently this fact; the prophecy, however, was
fulfilled during the time of the first temple (see Isaiah
xxii. 3) " All thy rulers are fled together, they were
bound by the archers; all that were found in thee were
bound together, which fled from a distance." Moreover,
if we say there are two captivities, we must also say
there are two redemptions, viz., the first already effected
at the building of the second temple, and the second
expected at a future period; and what man of sense can
believe that the redemption of the second temple was
a complete redemption, since the Ten Tribes did not join
in the return to Jerusalem? There were only 42,360
men of Judah and Benjamin, who availed themselves of
the permission given by Cyrus, king of Persia, while the
majority still remained in Babylon. Nor can it be said
that those who had returned to Jerusalem enjoyed full
independence, for when settled there, they were tributary to the Medes and Persians, as is related in
Nehemiah ix. 30, " Behold, we are now servants, and
the land which Thou hast given to our fathers to eat the
fruit thereof and its goodly produce; behold, we are
servants in it, and it yieldeth much increase to the kings
whom thou hast set over us, because of our sins, and
also they have dominion over our bodies," etc. Sub-

sequently the cruelties experienced proceeded from the
Greeks, and afterwards from the Romans. Though the
Jews sometimes rebelled, and nominated their own
kings, yet there was no ruler over them of the posterity
of David, on whose house the sceptre will devolve at the
final restoration. The Asmoneans were of the tribe of
Levi, and members of the priesthood; and they were
succeeded by Herod and his descendants until the ruin
of the second temple, as we have mentioned above.

The inferiority of the second temple may also be
judged from the absence of the Ark, the Mercy-seat, the
Cherubim, and the Urim, and the Thummin, and the
Shechinah. The temple was deprived of the Shechinah
(the manifestation of the divine presence); all the prophecies ceased, and the former miracles were no longer
witnessed. Under these circumstances, how can it be
asserted that Israel's redemption was complete? We
must rather acknowledge, that the Lord excited compassion in the heart of Israel's conquerors, and awakened
the mind of Cyrus to grant permission to the Jews to
return to Jerusalem, to rebuild the temple, to serve the
Lord, and to be freed from their bondage.

We thus see that the evil consequences of the original
captivity still subsisted, and the return from Babylon;
though Herod, after committing great bloodshed among
the sages and pious of Israel, built a splendid and mag-
nificent temple, yet it is not a matter of doubt that
Herod was all the time subjected to the Romans, and
held his throne under their authority. All this tends
to shew that the captivity continued from the day
of the destruction of the first temple by Nebuchadnezzar until the present time. The apparent omission in Deut. xxviii. of consolations and the like promises, as are held out in Leviticus at the close of the
maledictions, can easily be explained, since in the former

portion the words of the covenant are not completed; for immediately after the denunciations, Moses assembled the Israelites to establish the covenant with them while they were standing before the Lord; hence we read in Deut. xxix. 12, " That thou shouldst enter into covenant with the Lord thy God and into his oath." Moses adds in this chapter the oaths of the covenant, in addition to what he impressed on them in the preceding chapter; then after laying before them the dread of the calamities, he subjoins the most emphatic consolation and promise of perfect redemption. See Deut. xxx. 1, ' And it shall come to pass when all these things are come upon thee, the blessing and the curse which I have set before thee, and thou shalt call them to mind among all the nations whither the Lord thy God has driven thee," (ver. 2) " And shalt return unto the Lord thy God and shalt obey his voice, according to all I commanded thee this day, thou and thy children, with all thy heart and with all thy soul," (ver. 3) " That then the Lord thy God will turn thy captivity and have compassion upon thee, and will return and gather thee from all the nations, whither the Lord thy God has scattered thee.' (ver. 4) " If any of thine be driven out unto the utmost part of heaven, from thence will the Lord thy God gather thee, and from thence will he fetch thee." (ver. 5) "And the Lord thy God will bring thee unto the land which thy fathers possessed, and thou shalt possess it, and He will do thee good, and multiply thee above thy fathers." Ver. 6, " And the Lord thy God will circumcise thine heart, and the heart of thy seed, to love the Lord thy God with all thine heart and with all thy soul that thou mayst live." Ver. 7, " And the Lord thy God will put all these curses upon thine enemies and on them that hate thee which prevented thee." Ver. 8, " And thou shalt return and obey the voice of the Lord, and do all the commandments which I command thee this day." Ver. 9, " And the Lord thy God will make thee plenteous in every work of thy hand, and in the fruit of thy body, and in the fruit of thy cattle, and in the fruit of thy land for good: for the Lord will again rejoice over thee for good, as he rejoiced over thy fathers." Ver. 10, " If thou shalt hearken unto the voice of the Lord thy God to keep His commandments and His statutes which are written in this book of the law, and if thou turn unto the Lord thy God with all thy heart and with all thy soul." Hence, we see that this prediction is awaiting fulfilment, since the particulars contained in the above quotation did not, during the time of the first or second temple, take place. At the same time, we discover in the said passages every consolation that hope can suggest, for it points out at once both our restoration and the redemption of our souls: a redemption which is the truest deliverance from all troubles, and the boon and summit of all human aspirations. The promise with regard to our future state far surpasses the promise given in Leviticus, which alludes merely to our political restoration. There is certainly a distant allusion to the divine regard and consideration of the second temple; yet, as full liberty never shone upon those who went up, as we have clearly and incontestably shewn, we must necessarily conclude, that the curses, as contained in Deuteronomy, will be succeeded by those superlative and extensive blessings which a future and universal restoration will produce for Israel.

CHAPTER XVIII.

THE Christians offer an objection against the divine law, by stating that the Mosaic code gave no promise to the faithful of bliss in a future state, but limited all reward and punishment solely to our existence here below. They refer us to the 26th chapter of Leviticus, and maintain that on this account no mention is made in the law or in the prophetic writings concerning the condition of the soul in a future state, and that all predictions relate only to worldly prosperity.

Refutation.—The divine law dwells in many passages on our reward in this world, man being a compound of matter and spirit; and agreeably to this division the divine commandments are likewise of a double character, some calling on our physical, others on our intellectual powers. Now, the fulfilment of our duties depends on the co-operation of body with mind. Our material state is open and manifest to all, while our spiritual condition remains imperceptible. On this account, Holy Writ treats with clearness and precision on the dispensations affecting our material condition, and touches but lightly upon those affecting the soul in a future state. We must here call attention to the forcible truth, that the uninterrupted enjoyment of peace and prosperity of our corporeal existence must ever be the prime object of our wishes, and the benevolent design of the Almighty. It is only in the tranquil untroubled state of the body that man has an opportunity to devote himself fully and entirely to the faithful performance of the divine behests. When struggling with malady, or suffering from hunger, or labouring under any bodily affliction, it becomes impossible for us to fulfil many of our religious duties. The law, therefore, holds out the reward to its pious followers, that their bodies shall be free from trouble and disease, so that they may be enabled to conform to the Holy Will of the Almighty, and thereby prepare the soul for eternal bliss. We see clearly in Leviticus (xxvi. 11 and 12), that the law, after promising tem-

poral happiness, adds also the boon of spiritual welfare.
See ibid., " And I shall place my residence among you;
and my soul shall not abhor you, and I shall walk among
you, and I will be your God, and you shall be unto me
a people." Thus was also promised to Abraham and
his posterity worldly success for the performance of the
covenant. Spiritual reward is indicated by the following passage in Genesis (xvii. 7): " I will be unto thee
a God, and to thy seed after thee." In the same chapter
(ver. 8) the gracious addition is made, " And I shall be
unto them a God." The patriarch Jacob, too, when
concluding his vow by saying (Gen. xxviii. 21), " And
the Lord will be unto me a God," alluding to spiritual
welfare, as every thinking man must acknowledge. Not
in this portion alone, but throughout the whole law, we
meet with a variety of passages bearing reference to the
ultimate destination of man, especially where God's
immediate influence and supervision over the conduct
are expressed.

The very ceremonial observances ordered in the law,
and the whole temple service had no other purpose than
to bring the worshipper near the Throne of Mercy, and
to purify and to prepare the soul for a more exalted
state. The closeness with which God, by His covenant,
has bound unto himself the people of Israel, is the
reason He called them " His first-born son," " His chosen
one," " His friend," " His beloved," " His holy one,"
" His portion," and " The bond of His heritage."
The epithet, סגולה (Segulah), commonly rendered " peculiar people," has occasionally the signification of any
object *peculiarly precious and valuable*. This interpretation of the foregoing Hebrew word is confirmed in
Ecclesiastes ii. 8. The announcement of Divine Grace,
or favour, our lawgiver, Moses, communicated to Israel
by denominating them " *Children of the Almighty*," who

are beloved by their Father in Heaven, attached to Him in their present state, and not separated from Him in the life to come. We refer the reader to Deut. xiv. 1, 2, " Ye are the children of the Lord your God; ye shall not cut yourselves nor make any baldness between your eyes for the dead. For thou art a holy people unto the Lord thy God, and the Lord has chosen thee to be a *peculiar* people unto Himself above all the nations that are upon the earth."

The tendency of these passages, is to teach that it is unbecoming to indulge in excess of grief on account of the death of the body, since it is declared that Israel is a nation holy to the Lord and chosen by Him. By the word *chosen*, we understand that the soul is destined to adhere to Him and to enjoy His presence for ever. If earthly distinctions were intended to be the sole purport of human existence, death would be a more severe visitation on the rich than on the poor. Another allusion to a future state, we must refer to Leviticus xviii. 5, " Ye shall, therefore, keep my statutes and my judgments, which if a man do he shall live in them, I am the Lord." It cannot be imagined that this relates to longevity on earth, for we do not find that the pious, who observe the divine law, prolong their existence here below, beyond those who transgress; the passage, therefore, necessarily refers to immortal life.

The opinion of the opponents of Judaism is that the first man, through his rebellion against the word of God, was condemned to spiritual death. They rest their argument on the passage in Genesis ii. 17, " For on the day that thou eatest thereof thou shalt surely die," which death they deem to be that of the soul. Now, by comparing this passage with the preceding quotation, we cannot avoid the conclusion that the curse of Adam will have no effect on those who faithfully obey the divine ordinances set forth in the Mosaic law. We refer the reader, also, to the 5th chapter of St. Paul's Epistle to the Romans, which forcibly corroborates our argument; a careful perusal of the following words, from Deut. xxxii. 46, 47, will likewise justify the view here taken: " Set your hearts unto all the words which I testify among you this day, which ye shall command your children to observe, to do all the words of this law, for it is not a vain thing for you, because it is for your life; and through this thing you shall prolong your days on the earth," etc. Here, two different rewards obtainable through observance of the Divine Law are held out to man. There is a spiritual reward and a temporal reward. Concerning the spiritual, Scripture says, " For it is your life;" and concerning the temporal reward, we read, " And through this thing you shall prolong your days on the earth." The welfare of the soul, on account of its surpassing value, is mentioned first, though in reality it is the last lot of man. Another allusion to the reward of eternal life is made in Deut. xxxiii. 29, in the very last words recorded in the speech of Moses, " Happy art thou, O Israel, who is like unto thee a people saved by the Lord?" This verse conveys the idea that worldly acquisitions, such as dominion, power, conquest and increased wealth do not constitute true happiness, because they can be shared by nations who do not acknowledge God; for true happiness is spiritual salvation, of which no people have been declared worthy excepting the people of Israel, as we perceive in the words, " Happy art thou, O Israel; who is like unto thee, a people saved by the Lord?" A truth confirmed in the words which follow, He is " the shield of thy help," seem to convey the idea, that the boon of spiritual blessings does not exclude temporal happiness; and that those who devote themselves to the Lord, find also their protection in Him in the time of need. The same idea is expressed in the words of the Psalmist, " Trust in the Lord, He is your salvation and shield." The Divine interposition is further illustrated in the sequel of the verse under consideration (viz. Deut. xxxiii. 29), where we see " The shield of thy help," and " Who is the sword of thy glory;" showing, as the Psalmist says, " That not by their *own* swords they inherited the land."

A reference to the punishment of the soul is made in Leviticus xxii. 3; " Say unto them according to your generations, every man of your seed who shall approach to the sanctuary which the Children of Israel shall sanctify unto the Lord while his impurity is upon him, that soul shall be cut off from before me; I am the Lord." The words "*from before me*" relate to the soul which originates from a holy source, and to which it will return if found worthy. A similar allusion to the soul is made, ibid xxiii. 29; " For whatsoever soul it be that shall not be afflicted on the self-same day shall be cut off from her people ;" and again, " and every soul which shall do any work on the self-same day, that soul shall I cause to be lost in the midst of her people;" that is to say: she shall not be gathered to the souls of the pious who are denominated " her people." Thus, we find in Genesis xxv. 8, " And he was gathered unto his people;" that is to say: he was gathered to, and associated with the spirits of pious and Godly men. We will give a further proof that scripture does not treat here on the mere body; for in Deut. xxxii. 50, we read, " And thou shalt be gathered unto thy people, as Aaron thy brother died in the mountain Hor, and was gathered unto his people." Thus, we see that the term *gathering* applies exclusively to the soul. In like manner, Isaiah lviii.: " The glory of the Lord gathereth thee in." Balaam,

though a Gentile prophet, perceiving by the power of his
vision that the Israelites not only stood in this world
under the special supervision of the Almighty, but had
also a blissful end and rich hope after their death; he
therefore prayed for himself to be deemed worthy of par-
ticipating in their spiritual bliss in a future state. See
Numbers xxiii. 10, " May I die the death of the righteous, and my last end be as his."

The theme of beatitude of the soul is constantly reverted to by David in his Psalms, and is the incentive
for keeping the commandments of the Divine law, and
of pouring forth prayers for its attainment. See Psalm
xix.: " The law of the Lord is perfect, restoring the
soul." Psalm xxvii. 13, " Unless I had believed to
see the goodness of the Lord in the land of the living."
Psalm cxvi. 8, 9: " For Thou saveth my soul from death,
my eye from tears, my foot from stumbling; I shall
walk before the Lord in the land of the living." Psalm
xxvi.: " Do not gather in my soul with the sinners."
Psalm xvi. 10, 11: " For Thou wilt not leave my soul in the
grave; Thou wilt not let thy pious men see corruption;
Thou makest us know the path of life; fulness of joy is
in thy countenance; delights are at thy right hand for
ever." Psalm xlix. 15: " But God will redeem my soul
from the power of the grave, for He will take me, Selah."
Psalm xxv. 12, 13: " Who is the man who feareth the
Lord, him shall He teach in the way he should choose,
his soul shall abide in bliss, and his seed shall inherit
the earth." Psalm xxxi. 19: " How great is Thy goodness which Thou hast preserved for those who fear
Thee." Psalm xxxvi. 7, 8, 9: " How precious is Thy
mercy, O God, and the children of men shall be protected
under the shadow of Thy wings; they shall be satisfied
with the fatness of Thy house, and Thou shalt give them
drink from the stream of Thy delights, for with Thee is

the source of life; in Thy light we shall see light."
Psalm lxxiii. 25: "Who will be for me in Heaven, if I
delight not to be with Thee on earth?" And various other
passages of like description occur throughout the Psalms.
Solomon, the son of this sublime poet, has enlarged on
the beautiful representation of the Heavenly fruit: he
says in Ecclesiastes iii. 21: "Who knoweth the spirit
of man which rises on high?" and ibid. xii. 7: "And
the dust goeth to the earth as it was, and the spirit returneth to God who gave it:" and Proverbs xi. 7:
"When the wicked man dies, hope is lost, and the expectation of his exertions is lost." Ibid xiv. 32: "The
wicked man is driven away by his own evil doings; but
the righteous man confideth even in his death." And
ib. xxiii. 17, 18: "Let thy heart not envy the sinner, but
abide in the fear of the Lord the whole day; for surely
there is an hereafter, and thy hope shall not be cut off."
And ibid. xxiv. 14: "Know, then, that wisdom is equally
good for thy soul if thou findest it; and there is an hereafter, and thy hope shall not be cut off." See also
Isaiah xlv. 17, where he says: "Israel is saved by the
Lord with an everlasting salvation," etc. A parallel
phrase occurs in the words of Moses, Deut. xxxiii. 29,
viz.: "Happy art thou, O Israel, who is like unto thee?"

This implies that the spiritual salvation is not a
transitory boon, but an everlasting benefit; therefore
Isaiah says, in chap. lvii., "Ye shall not be abashed and
not be ashamed through eternity." Isaiah remarks, on
the death of a penitent man (chap. v.) "I saw his ways
and I healed him, and led him to his repose, and I
bestowed comfort on him and on his mourners." The
words, "And I saw his ways and I healed him," clearly
indicate the spiritual healing, that is, the pardon for
iniquity. To the same effect we read in Psalm xli. 4,
"Heal my soul, for I have sinned unto Thee." Also in

Isaiah vi. 10, " And he shall return and be healed," (which means after the expiation of his sins) " I shall lead him to his destination, and thereby bestow comfort upon him, and also to his mourners", who will derive consolation from the knowledge that after his death he will partake of that happiness which is reserved for the pious in the world of souls. The grant of a glorious reward of the pious is alluded to in Isaiah lviii. 8, " Then thy light shall break forth like the morning dawn, and thy healing shall spring forth speedily, and thy righteousness shall go before thee, and the glory of thy God shall gather thee, viz., into the place of happiness where the souls of the righteous are received in the bond of endless life." The term light applies to the existence of the soul in the region of spirits, where it enjoys immortal bliss in the presence of the Lord. This is further illustrated by what Abigail said to David (1st Sam. xxv. 29), " And the soul of my lord shall be bound up in the bond of the living with the Lord thy God;" on the other hand she says, with regard to the spiritual punishment of the wicked, " And the soul of thine enemies He shall cast away as from a sling." And Ezekiel says (xviii. 8, 9), " The wicked man who turneth away from all his sins which he hath committed, and observeth all my statutes and does judgment and righteousness, he shall surely live;" and further, " When the wicked man returneth from the wickedness which he hath committed, and shall do judgment and righteousness, he shall live with his soul." " When he turneth from all his transgressions, he shall surely live and not die." And xx. 13, " And I gave to them my statutes, and my judgments are made known to them which if a man doeth he shall live in them." It is perfectly obvious that the prophet speaks of everlasting life wherein no death can occur, and which may justly be denominated true existence with regard to the future state. Elihu says (Job xxxiii. 30), "To bring back his soul from perdition to shine in the light of the living." The prophet, Zachariah speaks on that subject in chap. iii. 7, "Thus saith the Lord of hosts, if thou wilt walk in my ways and keep my observances, and judge also my house and guard my court, I will give thee ingress among those who are standing here," (the ministering Angels.) This promise manifestly shows that the soul, after being freed from the body, obtains a blissful habitation in the world of spirits. We may also quote the words of Daniel (xii. 2). "And many of those who sleep in dust shall awake, some for eternal life and some to shame and everlasting contempt, and they that be wise shall shine as the brightness of the firmament, and they who promote righteousness shall be as stars for ever and ever."

The above verses found in the law, in the Prophets and in the Hagiography form a sufficiency for our faith in spiritual rewards and punishments hereafter. There are many other passages to be met with in the Divine Law and the Prophets, affording additional evidence of the immortality of the soul.

CHAPTER XIX.

MANY Christians oppose us with the opinion that the Mosaic law had not been established for a permanent, but only for a limited period, and was totally abrogated by Jesus, who bequeathed to his disciples and followers a new law which dispensed them from conforming to the ancient statutes and ordinances laid down in the Mosaic code. For (they allege) according to the old law, they (the Israelites) had been given over to the power of death, while the new dispensation was a law of grace and easy

to practise. The commandments given, they say, were
so rigorous that no man could observe them properly.
Hence it came that the fundamental laws, such as circumcision and the observances of the Sabbath, were but
temporary, and continued only to the time of the coming
of Jesus the Nazarene, who immediately substituted
baptism instead of circumcision, and the consecration of
the first day instead of the seventh.

Refutation.—This statement of the Christians is fallacious. The Gospel itself refutes their opinion, for in
Matthew v. 17 to 20, Jesus says to his disciples, " Think
not that I am come to destroy the Law or the Prophets; I am not come to destroy but to fulfil; for verily
I say unto you, till Heaven and earth pass one jot or
one tittle shall in no wise pass from the law till all is
fulfilled;" " Whosoever, therefore, shall break one of
these least commandments, and shall teach men so, he
shall be called the least in the kingdom of Heaven; but
whosoever shall do and teach them, the same shall be
called great in the kingdom of Heaven."

The Christians themselves must admit that Jesus and
his Asostles were circumcised; for we find that Paul
circumcised his disciple, Timotheus, as is recorded in
the Acts xvi. 3, which fact proves, according to their
own statement, that the law was not abolished even
after the existence of Jesus. The seventh day was also
kept sacred by the founders of the Christian religion and
its disciples. The Sabbath was observed (the trans-
later refers to the book of Feasts and Fasts published
1825) for nearly five hundred years after the vulgar
era, when one of the Popes instituted the sanctification
of the first day of the week instead of the proper
Sabbath-day. See the record thereon in Zemach David.

The seventh day is not merely instituted as a ceremonial law, prescribing to us cessation of all labour, but

is to be held universally sacred by the express word of
the Almighty, " Remember the Sabbath-day to keep it
holy," Exodus xx. 8.   See also ibid xvi. 29, "Behold
the Lord giveth you the Sabbath; therefore He giveth
you, on the sixth day, food for two days."   The supply
of manna during the six days of the week, and the
allotment of double the quantity on the sixth day
afford a miraculous confirmation of the sanctity of the
Sabbath.

Therefore the Divine Ordinance of the Sabbath cannot be abrogated; more especially as this command is
included in the decalogue, the authority of which is
acknowledged by all followers of Christianity.   It appears, however, that the Christians have been anxious to
abolish the law of Moses on their own accord and
responsibility, for they have no authority whatever for
doing so from Jesus and his Apostles.   If Jesus had
really absolved them from the commandments contained
in our Bible, wherefore did he urge the observance of a
part of them; as, for instance, the honour due to parents,
neighbourly love and charity?   Wherefore did he warn
them against homicide, adultery, theft, and false testimony?   See Matthew xix.   On what foundation rests
the Apostle's prohibition to abstain from idolatry, incest,
and eating of blood and strangled animals? (See Acts
xv. 20.)   Nor can we comprehend the assertion that the
law of Moses must discontinue because the Israelites
had been guilty of death according to it, but not
according to the law of Jesus, which was called the law
of Grace.   Did not St. Paul order the death of one
marrying his father's wife? (See 1st Cor. v. 1).   Even at
the present day, Christians inflict death on the mur-
derer, the adulterer, and the thief;* while, according to

---

* This was perfectly true at the date when the author wrote.—
TRANSLATOR.

the Mosaic dispensation, pecuniary thefts were not
punished with death. See Exodus xxi. 16, where it is said
" He who stealeth man and selleth him, he shall be put
to death," etc. Equally untrue is it that the law of Jesus
is more easy to practise than that of Moses.   In
Matthew xix. 21, we find, " If thou wilt be perfect, go
and sell that thou hast, and give to the poor." The
same is repeated in Luke xviii. 22.   This shows that it
is required by the laws of Jesus, that man shall dispose
of his property and devote it to charitable purposes;
the law of Moses, however, decrees that only the tenth
part of the harvest shall go for charitable purposes, and
the remainder be enjoyed by the owner.   This proves
that the legislative system of Moses is by no means
oppressive; but on the contrary, serves to benefit both
the body and the soul.   Again, if men have been dispensed from obedience to the laws of Moses, why do
they acknowledge some of the laws on consanguinity,
and prohibit intercourse between the following six
degrees of affinity, namely, with the mother, the father's
wife, the sister, the brother's wife, the daughter, and
the son's wife? With regard to other relations they are
are not guided by the Divine enactments transmitted
to us through Moses; but occasionally they permit
the unlawful, and forbid the legitimate degrees of
intermarriage.

The Christians seem here to abandon the solid foundation on which we rest our hopes, and act from self-
formed opinions.   The Gospel presents no express code
on the points in question, and if these laws are no longer
valid which determine the relationship of consanguinity,
why did not Jesus introduce new regulations in lieu of
the laws of Moses?   In modern days the Christians are
partly guided by the Mosaic code, and partly by human
enactments at various periods.   They make changes

and alterations, accommodating them to the customs of the day, and render established principle subservient to temporary wants and arbitrary innovations. Convinced, as we Israelites are, that the divine revelation proceeds from Infinite Wisdom, and is, therefore, in itself complete and perfect in its aim, we cannot possibly admit of any change, deviation, addition, or diminution. Holy Writ warns us on this point. Deut. iv. 2 : " Every word which I command you ye shall observe and do. Thou shalt not add unto it, and not diminish therefrom." Further (chap. iv. 8), " Where is a nation so great which has such just and righteous statutes as all this law is which I place before you this day ?" Ibid, " If thou wilt obey the voice of the Lord thy God to observe His commandments and His statutes which are written in this book of this law," etc. In the same book (xxxiii. 4) we read, " The law that Moses commanded unto us is an inheritance of the congregation of Jacob." To this we add the words of the Psalmist (Ps. xix. 7—9), " The law of the Lord is perfect, restoring the soul; the testimony of the Lord is faithful, making wise the foolish; the statutes of the Lord are just, rejoicing the heart; the commandments of the Lord are pure, enlightening the eyes; the fear of the Lord is clean, standing for ever; the judgments of the Lord are true and righteous altogether." In the same book (Ps. cxix.) he says, " And I will keep thy commandments for ever and ever." We refer also to the conclusion of the prophecy by Malachi, who says, " Remember ye the law of my servant Moses which I commanded him in Horeb, concerning all Israel (giving them), statutes and judgments." These verses give satisfactory evidence, that the divine law in its sublime perfection and simplicity is not to be enlarged or curtailed, and much less to be abrogated and superseded

by any other code. The immutability of the law is
pronounced in Deut. xxviii. 1, " And thou shalt listen
to the voice of the Lord, and do all His commandments
which I command thee this day." The same is repeated
in a subsequent passage, it being said, " If thou wilt
but listen to the voice of the Lord thy God to observe
His commandments which are written in the book of
this law."

This manifestly proves that the gracious promises and
assurances will only be realised provided we rigidly
follow the precepts prescribed in the books of Moses.
The expression, " this day," points out the impossibility
of a subsequent legislation, and the unchangeableness of
the revealed Will of the Almighty. In a like manner,
we learn from the passage, " The law which Moses
commanded us," is an inheritance of the congregation
of Jacob; that, contrary to the Christian belief, no
period whatever has been assigned to limit the duration
of the Mosaic code. The law of Moses is to remain an
everlasting inheritance to the congregation of Jacob for
ever. " For it shall not be forgotten out of the mouth
of his seed." The term, " congregation of Jacob," (instead of *house* or *seed* of Jacob), shews that the law is
not merely an inheritance to the *children of Jacob*, but
to all who may congregate with them, " from the sons
of the stranger, who join themselves to the Lord to
serve Him, and to love the name of the Lord, and to be
His servants. Every one that keepeth the Sabbath
from polluting it, and taketh hold of my covenant."
" They shall," as Isaiah says (xiv. 1), " be joined with
them, and be included in the house of Jacob." The
expression, " All His commandments are sure, they
stand fast for ever and ever," is no less an evidence of
the eternity of the laws contained in the Pentateuch,

as לָעַד (" for ever"), and לְעוֹלָם (" eternally"), imply an uninterrupted and endless course of time. We meet with an unmistakable use of the two words in the Psalm clxviii. 6, " And He has established them for ever and ever, He has given an ordinance and it shall not be infringed." The passage, " And I will keep Thy commandments continually for ever and ever," alludes to a period unlimited by time. In accordance with this, we find in Exodus xv. 18, the words יְיָ יִמְלֹךְ לְעוֹלָם וָעֶד " The Lord shall rule for ever and ever." So likewise in the exhortation of the last of the prophets (Malachi iv. 4), " Remember ye the law of Moses, which I commanded unto him on Horeb, concerning all Israel (giving him statutes and judgments)," we discover that there will never be any other law besides the law given unto Moses on Mount Sinai. We likewise meet with Gentile authorities, who state that the law of God given to Israel is eternal and perfect—that no succeeding law has ever been given—that those are mistaken who assert that Moses gave the first and Jesus the second law—and that Jesus gave no new law, but merely confirmed the commandments given through Moses. Thus in all these doctrinal points they are found to agree with us.

CHAPTER XX.

" AND many nations shall go and say, Come let us go up to the mountain of the Lord, to the house of the God of Jacob, and He shall teach us in His ways, and we will walk in His paths, for out of Zion shall go forth the law and the word of the Lord from Jerusalem" (Joel ii.) This verse is combined by the Christians with that in Isaiah li. 4: " Hearken unto me, O my people, and give ear unto me, O my nation, for a law shall procced from me, and I will make my judgment for a light of the people." They deduce from it that Isaiah here prophesied that there would be a future covenant, viz., the law of Jesus; the law of Moses having been delivered on *Sinai*, while the new doctrine of Jesus was promulgated in Zion.

Refutation.—The preceding chapter disproves this assertion, we having therein established on incontestable testimony, that the law of Moses is not to be revoked, and that no second revelation is to be added to the former; therefore no inference or support can be derived from the above texts. The verses quoted do by no means declare that a new law was to be given by the Almighty, but that the תורה, which means instruction and improvement, shall go forth from Zion, and shall be communicated through the advent of the true *expected* Messiah. Hence, they shall say, " And he shall instruct us in his ways, and we will walk in his paths." The King Messiah is to be the Instructor. In allusion to him, the prophet says, " And he shall judge among the Gentiles." A passage relating to this we read in Isaiah, " Behold the servant on whom I shall rely, for he as judge and a teacher, shall carry out judgment among the Gentiles, and they shall wait for his instruction." A parallel promise is given in the words, " For the law [i. e. instruction] shall proceed from me, and I will make my judgment rest as the light of Nations." The beneficent activity of the King Messiah is further ex-exhibited in the prediction (Isaiah ii. 4), " And they shall strike their swords into ploughshares," etc.

This justifies the expectation that, in cases where otherwise wars arising from strife and contention would occur, appeals will be made to the King Messiah, who will rule over all nations, and decide which party is in the right, and which in the wrong. Thus, he will estab-

lish peace between them, and thus prevent warfare between nations. The destructive instruments of battle will
no longer be required, but will be converted into imple-
ments of husbandry. " Their swords shall be struck into
ploughshares, their spears into pruning-hooks; nation
shall no longer lift up sword against nation, and they
shall no longer learn the arts of war." We acquire by
this prophecy a manifest assurance that the law which
is to proceed from the Messiah is nothing else but
the instruction and propagation of the most humane
principles. The Hebrew word תורה is very frequently
used for conveying the idea of *instruction*. See Prov.
i. 8, " My son, hear the instruction of thy father, and
forsake not *the law* (or teaching) of thy mother." Further, ibid. iii. 1, " My son, forget not my *laws* (teachings), and let thine heart keep my precepts." And in
the same chapter, "for I give you a good doctrine: do
not forsake my *laws*" (*i. e.* instructions). No person
will venture to assert, that King Solomon alluded to any
new law, written by himself, or any of his contemporaries. Controversial opponents, themselves, must acknowledge, that the word תורה in the Book of Proverbs
has no other meaning but worldly uninspired instruction; and the inference deducible from this interpretation, with regard to the passage under discussion, is so
obvious, that it leaves no ground for vindicating the
existence of a new law, subsequent to the one given
by Moses.

CHAPTER XXI.

Isaiah vii. 14, " Therefore, the Lord shall give unto you
a sign; behold, the *young woman* is with child, and she
will bear a son, and she will call his name Emanuel"

(God is with us). This verse is applied by the Christians as an evidence of their faith. The prophet, they
say, predicted here, that an Israelitish virgin would
conceive, and bare a son (Jesus) under the influence of
the Holy Ghost, as is related in the Gospel of Matthew.

Refutation.—This assertion rests solely on the support of imagination. The word עלמה (young woman)
used in this verse, does not mean *a virgin*, as they maintain, but signifies merely *young woman*. See Gen.
xxiv. 14, where Abraham's servant says, first, "And
there shall be *a damsel* הנערה to whom I say," etc. : and
afterwards, he says, "and there shall be *a young woman*
העלמה who cometh out to draw water," etc. Both נערה
and עלמה can be applied either to a maiden or a married
woman. With regard to a maiden, we find in Gen. xxiv.,
"the young woman run and told her father's household:"
and, in Ruth ii., "To whom belongeth this young
woman ?" (הנערה). In the same way, we meet with the
word עלמה meaning simply young female : for instance,
Exod. ii. 8, "And the *young woman* went and called
the mother of the child." As we express in Hebrew
נערה and עלמה indiscriminately for a virgin or a married woman, so we apply, respecting a young man, both
נער and עלם See 1 Sam. xvii. 58, "Whose son is this
lad?" (עלם)· And in the same chapter, v. 56, "Whose
son is this young man ?" (נער)· The age of adolescency
is likewise expressed both by עלומים and by נעורים. See
Isaiah, liv. 4, "and thou shalt forget the shame of
עלומים *thy youth."* And Jer. xxx., "and the disgrace of
נעורי *my youth."* This proves, that the female in minor
age, whatever her state may be, is denominated alike by
נערה or עלמה in the same manner as the young man in
minor years is styled נער or עלם· The wife of Isaiah,
who was still *youthful*, is termed in Scripture, עלמה
young woman. Moreover, the sense of the chapter is

altogether adverse to the exposition of the Christians. It refers to Ahaz, king of Judah, who had been in great trouble and consternation on account of the confederacy which the monarchs (Pekah, king of Israel, and Rezin, king of Syria,) had determined on, namely, to besiege and subjugate Jerusalem. See Isaiah vii. 2, " And it was told to the house of *David*, saying, Syria is confederate with Ephraim; and his heart was moved, and the heart of the people, as the trees of the wood are moved with the wind." Hence, the Lord sent to him the prophet Isaiah, to give him courage, that his heart should not be dismayed at their approach—since their design would assuredly be frustrated. To convince him of this, the Almighty gave him a sign, or token that Jerusalem would remain unmolested, and that the territories of Samaria and Damascus would soon be abandoned and deserted. Had it been the purpose of inspired writ to announce, as the Christians maintain, the advent of Jesus, how could Ahaz be concerned in a sign that could only be realized many centuries after his death, or how could any promise cheer his heart that was not to be fulfilled in his own days? It is true, there is also a prophecy, in this chapter, relating to calamities suspended over the hostile kings, and which happened within sixty-five years subsequent to the existing danger; " For the head of Syria is Damascus, and the head of Damascus is Rezin; and within threescore and five years shall Ephraim be broken, that it be no people." But the computation of sixty-five years did not commence from the date of the prophecy. At the period when the prophet spoke, his young wife was pregnant, and bore a son, who was first called Emanuel (God is with us), and afterwards, Maher-shalal-hash-baz (speed the plunder, hasten the spoil). " For," says Isaiah, " before the boy shall know how to call father and mother, the riches of Damascus and the spoil of Samaria shall be taken away before the king of Assyria." The fulfilment of this event is thus recorded in 2 Kings xvi. 9. "And the king of Assyria hearkened unto him, and the king of Assyria went up against Damascus, and took it, and carried the captives to Kir, and slew Rezin." In the same book (xv. 29) the fate of Pekah, king of Israel, is described in the following words. "In the days of Pekah, the son of Remaliah, king of Israel, came to Tiglath-Pileser, king of Assyria, and took Ijon, and Abel-Beth Maachah, and Janoah, and Kedeth, and Hazor, and Gilead, and Galilee, all the land of Naphtali, and carried them captive to Assyria." Verse 30, " And Hosea, the son of Elah, made a conspiracy against Pekah, the son of Remaliah, and smote him, and slew him, and reigned in his stead, in the twentieth year of Jotham, the son of Uzziah." The word of the prophet Isaiah ובעוד ששים וחמש שנה " *within* sixty-five years," is to be understood, as at the completion of these years, counted from the time of the prophecy of Amos, who predicted, concerning Damascus (in his book, i. 5), " And I will break the bolt of Damascus, and cut off the inhabitants of the valley, and even the support of the sceptre from Beth-Eden, and the people of Syria shall go into captivity into Kir, saith the Lord." About Israel, the same prophet predicted (ibid. vii. 11), " And Israel shall be exiled from its territory." Hence it appears, that before three years had elapsed after this announcement, the Syrians, and many of the Israelites, with the kings, Rezin and Pekah, were carried into captivity to Assyria. In the twentieth year of Jotham, which was the fourth of Ahaz, Hosea, the son of Elah, killed Pekah, the son of Remaliah, and reigned in his stead.

There is here a variation of statements with regard to these events, twenty years being ascribed to the government of Jotham, while subsequently it is mentioned that the occupation of the throne only lasted sixteen years, so that the four additional years must be considered to belong to the reign of his son Ahaz. We reconcile this discrepancy by the view, that, Ahaz having been a wicked king, Scripture prefers adverting to the departed pious king Jotham than to the reigning monarch, the ungodly Ahaz. Thus the sixty-five years expired in the ninth year of Hosea, the son of Elah, when the complete exile of all Israel took place. The following calculation will shew the historical connection between the prophecy and its fulfilment. Amos prophesied two years before the earthquake, which occurred in the seventeenth year of the reign of Jeroboam, the son of Joash, king of Israel. This king ruled twenty-four years after the earthquake. Then Menahem governed twelve, Pekahiah two, Pekah twenty, and Hosea nine years, which make together the sum of sixty-five years. The seven months of the reign of Zechariah and Shalum are omitted from the calculation, being included in the years of the other kings. This calculation has been adopted by several Christian authors. If our opponents should ask who the young woman was to whom Isaiah alluded when he said, " She is with child, and shall bear a son;" we reply, that she was (as we have before asserted) the prophet's wife. This is proved by Isaiah viii. 3, " And I came to the prophetess, and she conceived and bare a son; and the Lord said unto me, Call his name Maher-shalal-hash-baz." The question may then arise, How could he be called so after the name *Emanuel* had been previously given to him to afford a sign to Ahaz? We answer, by showing that the child received not two but three names, in consideration of the three kings concerned in the prophecy. Referring to the king of Judah he was named *Emanuel* (God is with us), to indicate that from the time of his birth peace would prevail in Judea.

Alluding to the king of Israel, he was called Maher-shalal, and in allusion to the king of Syria he received the name of Hash-baz, pointing out by the two latter names, that those monarchs, with all their possessions, would soon become the spoil of the Assyrian kings. The two names are of a synonymous character, and in perfect accordance with each other. Therefore the prophet says, shortly after mentioning Emanuel (vii. 16), " for before the child shall know to refuse the evil and choose the good, the land that thou abhorrest shall be forsaken of both the kings." In the same style he repeats after the name of Maher-shalal-hash-baz, " For before the child shall have knowledge to call, My father and my mother, the riches of Damascus and the spoil of Samaria shall be taken away before the king of Assyria." See-ing that these two verses are in perfect consonance with each other, the child spoken of must needs be the very same, and he being the son of Isaiah, stands a sign and token to these three kings. The intention to express several events by giving several names to one individual, is evident from the double appellation.

Shear Jashub (i. e. a remainder shall return) is an illustration of the ten tribes who are to remain in their captivity, while the two united tribes of Judah and Benjamin were to return from Babylon to Jerusalem at the expiration of the seventy years. On that account the prophet said, after the second son had been born unto him, " Here I stand, and the children which God has given me for signs and tokens in Israel;" and for this purpose only the Almighty bid him meet Ahaz, accompanied by his son Shear Jashub. Though the latter son was then but very young, his two names with opposite meanings stood as tokens for the future destiny of Ephraim (the ten tribes) on the one hand, and of Judah on the other.

R. David Kimchi has given a forced interpretation to the passage on Emanuel; believing that this individual was not the son of Isaiah, but of the king. The prophet expressing himself (chap. viii. 8), " And the stretching out of his wings shall fill the breadth of *thy land*, O Emanuel;" our expositor supposes, that the possessive, *thy*, could not have been addressed to a person who was not a son of the ruler of the country. But this conclusion is, to me, quite unfounded. We find, frequently, ארצך (thy land), meaning thy *native* land, or country. See, for instance, Gen. xii. 1, " And the Lord spake unto Abraham, go out of thy land." Now, it is well known, that Abraham was not the lord of the land which he was ordered to quit; but that the word *his* land could only be applied to it inasmuch as it was the land of his birth. See also Jer. xii. 15, " And I shall bring them back, every man to his heritage, and every man to his land." Moreover, suppose Emanuel was the son of a king, how could the land of Israel have been called his country, since he did not succeed his father in the government? It appears to me, that when Isaiah prophesied, saying, " Behold, the woman is with child," he was not aware that he spake about his own wife—just as Samuel was not conscious that he prophesied concerning David, when he said to Saul, 1 Sam. xiii. 14, " The Lord has sought unto Himself a man after His own heart, and has appointed him prince over His people." Further, when Samuel said (chap. xv. 28), " The Lord has torn away from thee the kingdom of Israel, and has given it to thy neighbour, who is better than thee;" for being at the house of Jesse, he knew which of the sons he was to anoint for the kingdom; so that when remarking to Eliab, he exclaimed, " Surely,

the Lord's anointed is before Him;" but only when he
came to David, then the Lord told him to anoint him.
With the same ignorance of things unrevealed, in the
moments of inspiration, Isaiah prophesied on the young
woman, until the token given him in the second prophecy rendered it manifest to him; the Lord saying then
to him (chap. viii. 1), " Take unto thee a large scroll,
and write upon it with man's pen, Maher-shalal-hash-
baz." After which Isaiah writes, " I took unto myself
faithful witnesses; namely, Uriah, the priest, and Zechariah, the son of Jebarachiah; and I came near to the prophetess, and she conceived, and bare a son, and the Lord
said unto me, Call his name Maher-shalal-hash-baz." It
was necessary he should take faithful witnesses, in order
to record all the minute parts of the Divine bidding, since
he himself had to fulfil all.

Scripture introduces the words, " And it was told to
the *House of David*," instead of to " Ahaz," etc.   We
account for this by the fact, that Ahaz was a wicked
man; and it was thought proper, therefore, to indicate
that the miracle did not occur for the merit of this king,
but for the merit of his ancestor.   The disputant may
ask, " In what did, then, the sign and miracle consist, if
the prophet predicted merely that a married woman
would conceive and bear a son?"   We reply, that the
sign and the miracle, undeniably, consisted in the assurance of an event that could not be foreseen and foretold
by a profane man.   Conception and birth do not depend
on human will; and many an infant is born that never
sees the light: nor can we know whether the mother will
give birth to a son or a daughter.   Another miracle is,
the prediction that the mother of the new-born child
would call it Emanuel; and this prediction fulfilled,
vouches for the truth of the additional prophecy, that
Judah and Jerusalem would be saved from the attack of

two belligerent kings. Again, it is a miracle, that the child, after its birth, was not to suck from the breasts of its mother, like other sucklings, but would feed on butter and honey. See Isaiah vii. 15, "Butter and honey shall he eat, that he may know to refuse the evil, and to choose the good." This fare, and the abstaining from mother's milk shall endow him with knowledge to avoid the evil and to prefer the good, and make him excel all other children in intellect. The activity of free agency is to commence with him as soon as he can call father and mother—which renders him pre-eminent among other children of his age. The confirmation of this event is in chap. viii. of Isaiah.

The Christians maintain, that if that child had been born from the young woman like other children of men, his name could not have been called Emanuel (God is with us): but that this name was quite applicable to Jesus, who was a compound of the Divine and human nature.

Refutation.—It is the Hebrew idiom to join the name of the Almighty to the proper names of men, and even to inanimate objects; for instance, Samuel, Zuriel, Uziel, Michael, Eliezer, Elijah, Isaiah, Zurishaddai, etc. In Genesis xxxiii., an altar was called, " El-Elohe Israel" (i. e. God is the God of Israel). In Exodus xvii. 15, an altar is called, " The Lord is my banner." We find the application in Jeremiah xxxiii.16, " The Lord is our righteousness." In Ezekiel xlviii. 35, we find the expression, " The Lord is there," which is applied to Jerusalem, the Holy city, as a name which will be given to it at the time of the Messiah, when the glorious presence of the Almighty shall return to it. That, however, Jesus should be called by the name Emanuel is not affirmed by any passage of the Gospel. We only find in Matthew i. 20, that the angel saith to Joseph in a dream, " Fear not to receive Mary thy wife, for

that which is conceived in her is of the Holy Ghost, and
she shall bring forth a son, and they shall call his name
Jesus (ישׁוּע), for he shall save his people from their
sins.   Now, all this was done that it might be fulfilled
which was spoken of the Lord by the prophet, saying,
Behold, a virgin shall be with child, and shall bring
forth a son, and they shall call his name Emanuel," etc.
It is further stated, " And Joseph took unto him Mary
his wife, and knew her not until she had brought forth
her first-born son, and she called his name Jesus."   In
Luke ii. 21, we find, " And when the eight days were
accomplished for the circumcising of the child he was
called Jesus, which was so named of the angel before he
was conceived in the womb."   From this it appears that
Emanuel was a different individual from Jesus, for
Jesus was in no instance called Emanuel—as to the
name Jesus, it was given to him by mere chance, there
were many other Jews named Jesus.   See Ezra ii., iii.,
and x., and the 2nd book of Chronicles xxxi.   The
Jews spell Jesus ישׁוּ, because the ע is omitted in the
pronunciation of the Christians; but suppose the ע is to
be retained, there is no inference deducible from that in
favour of their faith, as Matthew tried to establish for the
Christians, to apply the name of Jesus also to the son of
Sirach, who wrote a book called Ecclesiasticus.

Our disputant may ask, Of whom did Isaiah prophesy in chap. ix. 6, when he said, " Unto us a child is
born, unto us a son is given: on his shoulders shall be
the government: and they shall call him Wonderful,
Counsellor, Almighty God, Father of Eternity, Prince of
Peace.   Of the increase of [his] government and peace
there shall be no end [without end, Heb.] upon the
throne of David and upon his kingdom, to order it and
to establish it with judgment and with justice, from
henceforth even for ever"?

We give the following reply: Those passages refer to Hezekiah, king of Judah, during whose government Israel experienced, through a divine intercession, a signal deliverance from Sennacherib, king of Assyria, who had raised a siege against Jerusalem with an army of a hundred and eighty thousand valiant men. That this great miracle, namely, the fall of the camp of Sennacherib, referred to in the verses under consideration, was occasioned from the regard entertained by the Almighty for " the virtue of the child born unto us," and which, at the time of the prophecy, was *already* " given unto us." For when Ahaz ascended the throne, Hezekiah had already attained his ninth year. The truth of this exposition is borne out by the verses antecedent and subjoined to the passage " for a child has been born unto us." The latter word of the 6th verse of the 9th chapter of Isaiah must be rendered thus: " And he who is Wonderful, a Counsellor and Omnipotent God, a Father of Eternity, he called his (the child's) name *Prince of Peace*." The child born unto Ahaz is entitled the *Prince of Peace* because of the peace granted to Israel in the days of Hezekiah.

The preceding epithets are applied to the Almighty as indications of marvellous occurrences accompanying the life of Hezekiah, " God showed Himself *Wonderful*," causing for his (Hezekiah's) sake, the shade of the sundial to recede; as " Counsellor," the Lord established his own designs, and frustrated those of Sennacherib; as " the Omnipotent God," He evinced His divine attribute by suddenly destroying the immense army of the invading king; as " Father of Eternity," and Ruler of time, who, according to His pleasure, adds to and diminishes from the life of mortals, He manifested His power by prolonging the life of Hezekiah for a period of fifteen years.

The opponent may object to the above translation, by pleading, that he finds in his version of Isaiah the verb (ויקרא) in the passive, viz.: "and his name *was called*, and not, as we are supposed to read, וַיִּקְרָא taking the verb in the active form (he *called* his name), so that the epithets which follow apply to the child, whose name the Almighty called "Wonderful," etc.

We know well that Jerome has made a practice of accomodating Scripture to the notions of his own creed; and has endeavoured to establish an authority for his belief in the Divinity of Jesus. All endeavours, however, have failed. Even after adopting the reading of Jerome, we should be entitled to assign the above epithets to Hezekiah, since we have already proved that the nature of the holy language allows application of the name of the Almighty to human beings, and even to inanimate objects, inclusively. To give to Jesus the above appellations is altogether incompatible with his own history. How can he claim the names "Wonderful" and "Counsellor," when it is remembered, that one of his disciples frustrated his designs, and betrayed him to his enemies? How can he merit the title, "Powerful" or "Omnipotent God," who suffered an unnatural death? How can he be the "Father of Eternity," who did not attain even half of the natural period of human life? How can he be distinguished as the "Prince of Peace?" whereas, no peace existed in his days: and as he himself asserted, by saying, "I am not come to bring peace into the earth, but the sword." The Christians avail themselves of the passage, "to the increase of government, and peace without end," to oppose us with the following question:—"If the intention of the prophet had been to prophesy an earthly kingdom, how could he say that his (the king's) government would be without end?" We reply to this, that the expression, "*without end*," (אֵין קֵץ) is a mere figure of speech. We find, similarly, in Isaiah, ii. 7, " And his land was full of silver and gold, and there was *no end* to his treasures; and his land was full of horses, and there was *no end* to his chariots.'

Thus we find, also, in Ecclesiastes iv. 8, " There is One, and no second, and he has neither son nor brother; and there is *no end* to all his troubles." At the end of the above prophecy, Isaiah says, chap. ix. 7, " On the throne of David, and over his kingdom." This passage is a clear refutation of the Christian doctrine of the Messiah, for Jesus never sat on the throne of David, and never ruled over Israel. Should they interpret the throne of David in a spiritual sense, we must declare that the throne of David never meant anything but in relation to terrestrial government. David sat on a real throne, and his kingdom was a positive reality. Scripture, therefore, treats of it here in that sense only, and does not allude to any visionary kingdom. The expression, to establish it, and support it, " in judgment and righteousness, now and for evermore," shows that his dominion —that is, the dynasty of David—will never perish. And though an interruption has occurred during the time of the captivity, the government, nevertheless, will in the days of the Messiah, return to the scion of David. See Ezekiel xxxvii. 36, " And they shall live in it, and their children, and their children's children, to eternity, and my servant David shall be prince over them for ever." This whole passage refers to the Messiah, as will be shown hereafter. Our opponents may remark, " How can the idea of eternity be understood from the words ' even for evermore,' if the government of the house of David ceased from the time of the captivity?" Our answer to this argument is, that an intermediate cessation destroys not the nature of the perpetual duration; for we find that the commandment of circumcision, was enjoined on the posterity of Abraham, as an everlasting covenant, (see Genesis xvii. 7), "And my covenant shall be in your flesh as an everlasting covenant;" and, nevertheless, the ceremonial was, from sanitary motives, discontinued during the whole period of the journey through the desert. When, however, the tribes had entered the Land of Promise, the practice of that covenant was resumed, and will remain in force, even in the days of the Messiah, as the Prophets have declared to us. See Isaiah lii. 1, "Awake, awake! put on thy strength, O Zion; put on thee the garments of thy glory, O Jerusalem, thou holy city, for there shall never more enter into thee the uncircumcised and the unclean." The prophet Ezekiel likewise says (chap. xliv. 9), "Thus saith the Lord God, Any son of an alien, of an uncircumcised heart and of un-circumcised flesh, shall not enter into my sanctuary." Another instance we find in the covenant which the Almighty made with Phineas to grant the high priest-hood to him and his posterity for ever; a long sus-pension occurred among his posterity, for we learn that Eli, Abimelech, and Abiathar officiated as high priests, until King Solomon ascended the throne; never-theless that dignity reverted to the rightful party, viz., the descendants of Phineas (see 1st Kings ii. 26); where it is related that Solomon deposed Abiathar, and placed Zadok in his office. The same is related in 1st Chron. xxix. 22, "And Zadok they anointed to be priest because he was of the lineage of Phineas; and though another interruption in the dignity of priesthood took place during the time of the captivity, it will be restored at the coming of the Messiah; and the words in Numb. xxv. 13, will be realized, "And it shall belong to him and to his seed after him as an everlasting priesthood." Ezekiel informs us on this point by telling us (chap. xliv. 15), "And the priests, the Levites, the *children of Zadok*, who observed the observances of my sanctuary, while the children of Israel strayed from me, they shall come nigh unto me." This prophecy is connected with the Advent of the Messiah, as will be explained in its proper place. We have now given a full refutation to mistaken assertions of our opponents, and having founded our arguments on prophecy, they can only be opposed by opponents of truth itself.

CHAPTER XXII.

Isaiah lii. 13, " Behold my servant shall prosper, he shall be exalted and extolled, and be very high." In this and the verses that follow until the end of chap. liii. the Christians assert, that the prophecy of Isaiah constitutes a prediction of Jesus, the Nazarene, concerning whom Isaiah has said, " He shall be exalted and extolled, and be very high," because to him alone it is asserted these words can be attributed, " Surely he has borne our sicknesses and our pains. He was wounded by our transgressions and oppressed by our iniquities." For he is said to have, by his death, saved their souls from the power of Satan.

Refutation.—This assertion lacks truth, Scripture having declared, " Behold *my servant* shall prosper, he shall be exalted," etc.; how can these words be made to refer to Jesus, after they (the Christians) inconsiderately represent him to be God? If he were a Divine Being, how could the prophet call him a servant? The Christian disputant may say, that in a corporeal respect he was called servant, and in a spiritual respect he was entitled God." To this defence we object, by referring the reader to chap. x., where we have given comprehensive proofs of the non-divinity of Christ, by shewing that, by the authors of the Gospel, he was not considered to be a

God, and much less so by himself.   This matter shall
again be noticed in the second part of this work; when
we shall refute the several passages of importance
relative to the subject in the Gospel.   We may be
permitted to mention here that the prophetic word, " He
shall be exalted and extolled, and be very high," were
not fulfilled in Jesus, he having been condemned to death
in an inglorious manner, and thus the prophecy was not
realized in him—" He shall see seed and live many days,"
for he had no offspring.   His disciples cannot be called
his offspring, though the word בנים (sons) is applicable to
them, and אבות (fathers) to the teachers.   The word זרע
(seed) is used in the Bible only for bodily heirs; nor do
we find that Jesus reached an old age, for he was put
to death when thirty-three years of age.   We cannot
apply the words, " he shall live long" (English version,
" prolong his days") to a Divine Being, for the term of
longevity is inappropriate to the Deity who is the Prime
Cause of all existence, and whose self-existence is eternal;
moreover, we wish to know to whom will the Christians
attribute the promise, " Therefore will I apportion unto
him spoil among the many, and with mighty men he shall
share the spoil."   Who are the many and mighty men with
whom Jesus is to partake in the spoil? and to whom
refer the words, " And he intreated for the transgressors"?   Did Jesus, who, according to their futile
notions, was styled a God, *pray* for transgressors?   Many
more such queries suggest themselves on this theme,
but we will first examine the true import of the chapter.
The words, " Behold my servant shall prosper," to the
end of the 53rd chapter, concern the people of Israel,
who are still bearing the yoke of this captivity, and are
termed *my servant* in the singular number, which expression is used in many other places; for example
(Isaiah xli.), "And thou, O Israel, *my servant*, Jacob

whom I have chosen, the seed of Abraham, my friend."
Again, " And I say unto thee, Thou art *my servant*."
In chap. xliv. 21, Isaiah says, " And now hear, O Jacob
my servant, and Israel whom I have chosen;" and further
on, " Fear not, *my servant* Jacob;" and " Remember
these things, O Jacob and Israel, for thou art *my
servant*." " I have formed thee to be *my servant*." Ibid.
xlv. 4, " For the sake of Jacob *my servant* and Israel
my chosen one." We find also in the Prophecies of
Jeremiah (xxx. 10), "Fear not, O *my servant* Jacob, saith
the Lord, and be not dismayed, O Israel." The same is
repeated, " Fear not, O Jacob *my servant*, saith the
Lord." Similar expressions occur in the Psalms. Psalm
cxxxvi. 22, " An inheritance to Jacob *his servant*," etc.
All these passages afford an evidence that the term *servant* in the singular is frequently addressed to the whole
people of Israel. The same form of address in the
singular is used in the delivery of the ten commandments, though directed to an assembly of six hundred
thousand persons.

We may be asked, What connexion with Israel has
the following passage in Isaiah liii. 4, 5 : " Surely he
has borne our sickness, and carried our pains, and we
considered him plagued, stricken by God, and afflicted.
And he was wounded by our transgressions, and bruised
by our iniquities. The chastisement for the sake of
our weal came upon him, and by his wounds we were
healed." It may be alleged, that it has never been
known at any period that the people of Israel have
borne the sicknesses, the pains, and the wounds due to the
iniquity of other nations; and whatever afflictions and
troubles Israel have endured, came upon them on account
of their own sins, and not for those of other nations.

In our reply to this objection, we will show, first,
that the prophets frequently designate humiliations and

adversities by the name of sickness and wounds. Compare Isaiah i. 5, 6, " The whole head is sick, and the whole heart faint, from the sole of the foot even unto the head there is no soundness in it, but wounds and bruises and putrifying sores." And again in xxx. 26, " In the day that the Lord bindeth up the breach of his people, and healeth the sore of their wound." In like manner, Hosea vi. 1, " He has torn and He will heal us. He hath smitten and He will bind up." Lamentations ii. 13, "For thy breach is great like the sea, who can heal thee?" Jeremiah x. 19, " Woe is me for my hurt, my wound is grievous, and I said, This is my sickness, and I must bear it." Afterwards he explains the meaning of this fracture, this sore, and this sickness, by exclaiming (ibid. ver. 20), "My tabernacle is spoiled, and all my cords are broken; my children are gone forth from me, and they are not," etc. Ibid. xxx. 12, " For thus saith the Lord, Thy fracture is mortifying, thy wound is exceedingly sore." Soon afterwards the consolation is given in the words in verse 17, " I shall bring relief unto thee and heal thee from thy wounds." The prophet then explains in what the healing and relief are to consist, viz. (ver. 18), " Thus speaketh the Lord, I shall bring back the captivity of thy tents, O Jacob, and I shall have compassion on its inhabitants, and the city shall be built on its ruins, and the palace shall stand in its proper place. There shall again proceed forth from them thanksgiving and the voice of mirth, and I shall increase them, and they shall not be diminished," etc. In chap. xxxiii. 6 to 8, he says, " I bring up into it a remedy and healing, and I shall heal them." Therefore, he explains in what the remedy and healing will consist, in the words, " And I shall bring back the captivity of Judah and the captivity of Jerusalem, and I shall build them as formerly, and I shall cleanse them from all their iniquities which they have committed against me," etc.

From all these verses it appears, that Scripture designates the captivity as attended with calamities, and describes the troubles that took place during the exile under the names of bruises and wounds—but redemption, enlargement, and deliverance, Scripture depicts by the terms of *curing* and *healing*. Now, with the prophecy, " My servant shall be prosperous," we receive comfort, and strengthening of our hearts—although we are lowered deeply, and trodden down to the ground by reason of our captivity, hope is offered us for the future; and through the mercy of the Lord, we shall be raised, and exalted, and promoted to a high degree. When the days of restoration dawn upon us, the Gentile nations, together with their rulers, in witnessing the deliverance of Israel, and their elevation to a most exalted rank, will be greatly amazed—as they previously have been at our degradation during our captivity, when contumely and insult have been our lot from all nations of the earth— so they will express their wonder at our improved condition, and they will say, one to the other, " Now it is manifest to us, that we have all strayed like a flock without a shepherd; each of us has turned his own way; our fathers inherited fallacy and vanity, in which there is no profit; no Divine law, nor any true faith, is belonging to any nation of the world except the people of Israel. The plagues and the torments which the Israelites have borne in captivity have not come upon them on account of their sins: we, ourselves, ought to have borne the trouble and the chastisements on account of the greatness of our iniquity. Surely, the sickness and the pain which ought to have come upon us, came upon them, to atone for our sins: while they were servants under our authority, while they have interceded for our welfare, and the success of our kingdoms—yet we considered it differently—namely, that on account of the greatness of their sin, for inflicting death on our Messiah, who is our God, these great calamities have befallen them." So far will go the words of the Gentiles.

Here we may mention, that the Gentiles are not responsible for their trespasses in the same manner as those to whom the will of God has been revealed. Only when their iniquity is outrageous, when their ill-treatment of righteous Israelites is aggravated, when the enormities inflicted on the Israelites equalled the chastisements imposed upon those who perished by the Deluge, or of those who shared the fate of Sodom and Gomorrah—it will be then the Lord will visit their iniquities, and bring total destruction upon them: though permitting the suffering and persecution of Israel, he will not allow actual extinction. This forbearance towards us is expressed in Jeremiah xxx. 11, "For I am with thee, saith the Lord, to save thee. For I shall make an end of all the Gentiles among whom I have scattered thee; but of thee I shall not make an end; I shall correct thee in measure, but I will not hold thee guiltless." Amos, likewise, notices in his book, chap. iii. 2, "I have known you from all the families of the earth; on that account, I shall visit upon you all your sins:" and in the Proverbs we find "Him whom the Lord loveth, he chastiseth," etc., "and he shall cleave to the house of Jacob." The punishments of Israel are not only for their own good, but also for that of other nations. Hence, Isaiah prophesied concerning the restoration of Israel, chap. xiv. 1, "And strangers shall be joined with them." It is well known that Israel is the chosen nation concerning whom it is recorded in Exodus (chap xix. 5), "And ye shall be unto me a peculiar people from among all the nations; for mine is the earth." All this tends to prove, that the Almighty revealed His law to Israel for the purpose that they should learn to walk in the right way, and to perform righteous deeds. With this distinguished gift for themselves, He has coupled the noble mission that they should become useful to other nations; "For His mercy extends to all His creatures." With a view to Israel's instrumentality in His Divine government, we find (in Exodus xix. 6), "And they shall be unto me a kingdom of priests and a holy nation." And to the same purport says Isaiah (chap lxi. 6), "And ye shall be named the priests of the Lord; ye shall be called the servants of our God." "Ye shall eat the riches of the Gentiles, and in their glory ye shall triumph." In numerous parts of the Scripture, the people of Israel are called *priests*, it being the duty of that class to inculcate religious duties and precepts, and to "teach Jacob judgments, and Israel the Law." Thus, it is our vocation to instruct, in the law of the living God, the Gentiles, among whom we are dispersed; and as the Psalmist says, Psalm xcvi. 3, to "relate His glory among the Gentiles, His wonderful works among the nations."

All future felicity of the Gentiles will proceed from Israel, as has been assured to our patriarchs, (see Genesis xii. 3,) "And in thee all the nations of the earth shall be blessed;" and ibid. xxviii. 14, "And through thee and thy seed all the families of the earth shall be blessed." Here we have an additional testimony that the people of Israel are graciously distinguished, the Almighty having appointed them as His portion and inheritance, (see Psalm cxxxv. 4), "The Lord has chosen Jacob for Himself, and Israel as His distinct," (people), or in other words of Scripture, Deut. xxxii. 9, "For his people are the portion of the Lord, Jacob is the lot of his inheritance." The law has, therefore, been given to us, with the intention that we should teach to other nations the ways of the Lord. When the guide-pursues the right road those who follow will safely reach the end of the journey, while the stragglers will undoubtedly lose their way altogether. Therefore must those who wish to arrive at their destination keep close to their leaders; and thus, at a future day, according to the prophecy of Zech. viii. 23, " Ten men from the Gentiles of various tongues shall take hold of the garment of the Jew, saying, We will go with you, for we have heard that God is with you." The felicity of Israel will be shared by those who associate with them in the same manner as Jethro (and his descendants who settled in Palestine) shared in the welfare of our people according to the promise of Moses, Nunbers x. 32, "And it will come to pass, if thou will go with us, that all the good which the Lord will do unto us we will do unto thee." In Jeremiah xxxv. 19, there is a further evidence that the promise given by Moses was fulfilled. The prophet says, " There shall never be wanting to Jonadab, the son of Rechab, a man to stand before me." Here the words, " to stand" mean to endure, to last, in conformity with the phrase used in Isaiah lxvi. 22, "As the new Heavens and the new earth shall *stand* before me, saith the Lord, so shall stand your seed and your name."

Returning again to the examination of Isaiah liii. we have to notice, that, at the time of the restoration, the followers of the Jews will escape unhurt from all the troubles incident to wandering strangers. The Jews will resemble those warriors who, standing foremost, are exposed to the most imminent perils, and nevertheless, when the enemies shall be conquered, those who are in the rear shall equally share in the spoil, although not exposed to the same amount of danger. Hence Isaiah liii. 5, says, metaphorically, " He is pierced for the sake of our transgressions, he is bruised for the sake of our iniquity, the chastisement for our good comes upon him, and through his sore we are healed." The prophet, proceeding (ibid ver. 12), in the same figure of speech, alludes to the spoil allotted to the front ranks of the divine army of the Israelites, and says, " Therefore will I give him his portion among the many, and with the mighty he shall divide spoil, because he has exposed himself to death, and has been counted among sinners, and has borne the iniquity of many, and interceded for transgressors."

From previous as well as subsequent verses, the reader is enabled to judge that the inspired writings treat solely on the calamities which Israel has to endure during the captivity, and that compensation will be granted to them from the time of their redemption from the captivity. See, for instance, Isaiah lii. 1, " Awake, awake, put on thy strength, O Zion, put on the garments of thy glory, O Jerusalem, thou holy city, for there shall no more enter thee the uncircumcised and the unclean." Now this passage is succeeded by the words, " For not speedily shall ye go forth; ye shall not go in by flight, for the Lord is going before you, and the God of Israel is gathering you." Then follow these words, "Behold, my servant shall prosper." Chapter liv. 1, commences, " Rejoice, thou barren woman who hast not borne;" and the verses which follow equally indicate Israel's final redemption. All these Divine promises are strictly connected with the gracious assurance laid down. Ibid li. 22, " Thus saith thy Sovereign, the Lord my God, who pleadeth the cause of His people; behold, I have taken out of thine hand the cup of trembling, even the dregs of the cup of my fury, thou shalt drink it no more." The same harmony is evident between the expression, " No uncircumcised and unclean shall enter there," and the oath contained in chap. liv. 9, 10, " For this is as the waters of Noah unto me; for as I have sworn that the

waters of Noah should no more go over the earth, so
have I sworn that I would not be wroth with thee. For
the mountains shall depart, and the hills be removed,
but my kindness shall not depart from thee; neither
shall the covenant of my peace be removed, saith the
Lord, that hath mercy on thee." ¡Having now dwelt
generally on the prophecy relative to the restoration of
Israel, we shall examine, more closely, each particular
expression.

Isaiah lii. 13, "Behold my servant shall prosper, he shall
be raised and exalted, and be very great."

The word יַשְׂכִּיל "he shall prosper," is found again
in the 1st Samuel xviii. 14, "And David *was pros-*
perous in all his ways." "My servant shall prosper,"
relates to that period when Israel shall leave the
countries of its captivity, and be elevated to the highest
degree of happiness. "As many were *astonished* at
thee, so was his appearance deteriorated more than that
of any man, and his form more than that of the sons of
men." The word *astonished* expresses the surprise which
will be felt, and is used in the same sense in Ezekiel
xxviii. 19, "And all who knew thee among the nations
were astonished at thee." The astonishment is to be felt
by those who are to consider " thy (Israel's) deep humiliation, and the duration of thy captivity; and they shall
say one to the other, " Truly, his appearance is deteriorated more than any man, and his form more than that
of the sons of men." And indeed it has become pro-
verbial among the Gentiles, to exclaim, at the wretched
appearance of their neighbour, " he looks as miserable
as a Jew."

" Thus, he shall startle many nations, the kings shall
shut their mouths against him, for what has not been
told them they have seen, and what they have not heard
they have understood."

The prophet Isaiah means to say, that in the same

manner as the Gentiles formerly were amazed at the
depth of humiliation into which we had been thrown,
they shall, at a future period, be astounded at the height
of distinction at which we shall arrive; and they shall
then say to each other, "who would have believed the
report brought to us?" etc. The kings themselves shall
remain dumb and speechless. The verb יִקְפְּצוּ they
shall keep (their mouths) closed or shut, is similarly
used in Job v. 16, וְעֹלָתָה קָפְצָה פִּיהָ "and wickedness
closed its mouth." With the above prophecy of Isaiah
agrees, also, the prophet Micah, chap. vii. 10, "Gentiles
shall see it, and be ashamed, in spite of all their strength;
and they lay their hands on their mouths when perceiving that our distinctions shall surpass every description and prediction: " *Who would have believed the report we have heard ; and to whom has the arm of the
Lord been revealed?*" This shall be said by the Gentiles at the sight of Israel's prosperity. "We (shall
they exclaim), we have put no faith in the hearsay that
reached us through the prophets, and now we perceive
with our own eyes that more has been done than we had
heard; for how could we conceive that the omnipotence
of the Almighty would manifest itself especially on behalf of such an insignificant and disregarded people!"

"He grew up before him like a sucking babe, like a
root on parched land, without form, without beauty that
we might look at him, without comeliness that we might
find pleasure in him."

The purport of this is, that the Gentiles shall declare
the rise of Israel is just as preternatural as if a branch
were to grow from parched ground. "While groaning
under the yoke of his captivity, how could we suppose
that he could endure the burdens imposed on him?
When we consider their wasted body, and saw them
groping their way like the blind, we did, indeed, not

envy and covet their lot; but on the contrary, we vili-
fied and spurned them.   Isaiah liii. 3, " He was despised
and the least of men; a man of pains, and acquainted
with disease, and as one from whom man hideth his
countenance, he was despised, and we esteemed him not."
This means, How should we (Gentiles) have envied
his (the Jew's) lot who was the most despised and ab-
ject of the children of men ; who was accustomed to
load himself with all the troubles and torments of his
exile, which may be compared to pains and diseases. On
account of his extraordinary inferiority and degradation
we despised him, hiding our faces from him, being unwilling to notice him.   " However, he hath borne our
diseases, and carried our pains, and we esteemed him
smitten of God and afflicted."

This means—The Gentiles after having perceived, by
ocular evidence, that he (the Jew) has the truth on his
side, they shall say: " We have all wandered like sheep,
the miseries and persecutions of the captivity have not
befallen him on account of his own iniquity, but ought
to have come upon us on account of our iniquity; and
while we believe that he underwent trials and chastisements in retribution for his rebellion to God, he (the
Jew) suffered in consequence of the transgressions of
the Gentiles.   "And he was tormented on account of our
transgressions; he was bruised on account of our iniquities; the chastisement of our peace was upon him,
and by his bruises, we were healed." The word מחלל
(afflicted) is related to חיל (pain as women in labour).

The phrase " the chastisement of our peace was upon
him," indicates that this life presents a world of change
and vicissitude, no enjoyment is complete and perfect;
there is no state of peace without struggle; there is no
quietude without an intermixture of strife and contention, and there is no gladness and enjoyment without

sorrow and contrition. All pleasures and delights are intermingled with evils. Hence we (Gentiles) see clearly that "the chastisement of our peace has come upon him;" that is to say, we (Gentiles) have acquired a state of peace, but the struggles by which it was obtained fell to his (the Jew's) lot. Thus he (the Jew) received wounds and bruises, as results of his captivity, while we derived from his vicissitudes healing and restoration, viz., prosperity and dominion. The word נרפא (healed) is used in an analogous sense, in Exodus xv. 26, "For I the Lord am He *who healeth thee*," which sentence accords with the preceding words, "All the diseases which I put upon the Egyptians, I shall not put upon thee."

The word וּבַחֲבֻרָתוֹ means " by his bruises." The omission of the Dagesh, in the second radical letter, has led some to interpret it " in his society." Those expositors compare the word with that occurring in Hosea iv. 17, viz., חבור עצבים אפרים " Ephraim is associated with Idols," etc. In that case, it would seem that we (Gentiles) praying to God in society, or in conjunction with them (the Jews), the Almighty listened to our entreaties and sent us relief from our afflictions. Isaiah liii. 6, " We all strayed like sheep, each of us turned to his own way; and the Lord visited on him the iniquity of us all."

This means—The Gentiles will make confession of their guilt, by acknowledging that the Lord is truly and entirely with Israel, and that they (the Gentiles) strayed like a shepherdless flock, every man following his own way, and each people worshipping his peculiar god: " but now," will they say, " now we know that our idols are not gods."

In corroboration of this we find, in Jeremiah xvi. 19, 20, " To thee nations will come from the corners of the earth, and they will say, Surely our fathers inherited falsehood, vanity in which there is no profit." Moreover

we read there, shall a man make gods unto himself, and
they are no gods? (shall the Gentiles continue in their
accusation) " We have deserved a most rigorous punishment, but the Lord visited and cast our punishment
upon Israel.   He has hitherto laboured for our sake
and borne our yoke and our tribulations, henceforward
we will freely and cheerfully labour for him, and subject
ourselves to him."

Therefore Isaiah says, lxi. 5, " And strangers shall
stand forth and feed your flocks," etc.   With the same
view that prophet says (chap. xlix. 23), "And kings shall
be thy nursing fathers, their queens thy nursing
mothers; they shall bow down their faces to the ground
before thee, and they shall lick the dust off thy feet,
and thou shalt know that I am the Lord, and that those
who hope in me shall not be put to shame."

Isaiah liii. 7, " He was oppressed, and he was afflicted,
yet he opened not his mouth; he is brought as a lamb to
the slaughter, and as a sheep before its shearers is dumb,
so he openeth not his mouth."   For (will the Gentiles
say concerning the Israelites) while that people was
held captive under our power we extorted from them
contributions under various pretexts, and by means of
false accusations.   We inflicted on them bodily torments,
yet they shewed patient endurance under them, and
remained silent and calm like the lamb when led to the
slaughter, and like the weak defenceless sheep submitting
to the shearers.

This condition of Israel is prefigured in the complaint
in Psalm xliv. 11, " Thou givest us away like the
sheep that is to be consumed."   A similar comparison is
made by Jeremiah (chap. l. 17), " Israel is like a scattered
flock, the lions have chased them away : first, the king of
Assyria has devoured them; and lastly, Nebuchadnezzar,
king of Babylon, has crushed them.   Isaiah liii. 8, " He

was taken away from prison and severe judgment, and who shall speak of his generation? for he was cut off from the land of the living, and through the transgression of my people he was stricken."

This means—That by this time the Israelites will have escaped the direful oppressions to which they had been subjected during their exile ; and it will then be manifest that no human language can supply an adequate description of the incessant afflictions endured by the Jews, and of their unswerving belief in the only One God. Then will the Gentiles acknowledge that the visitation which befell the Jews tended less to illustrate the sinfulness of the victims, than the depravity of the persecutors. The word "transgression" is followed by the expression, "my people," for each nation will attribute to itself the consequences of the malignity to which Israel had been exposed.

Isaiah liii. 9, " And he made his grave with the wicked and with the rich his tomb, although he had done no wrong, and no guile had been in his mouth."

This means—That, in honour of his religion, the Israelite used to expose himself freely to martyrdom, as is confirmed by the above-cited allusion to it in Psalm xliv. 22, " For on account of thee, we are slain all the day, for we are considered like sheep for slaughter, for we have constantly been attacked by false accusation, through which they sought to inflict on us the retributions due to the guilty."

In all such cases the persecuted parties were not offenders, and we Gentiles felt incensed because the Israelites would not conform to our ill-founded dogmas, and "would not hold deceit in their mouths." For even to escape death the Israelites would not make a confession with their lips to which their hearts must give an utter denial. Ibid, 10, "And it pleased the Lord to humble him. He afflicted him with ailment. Since his soul has offered itself as a sacrifice, he shall see seed and live long, and the delight of the Lord shall prosper in his hand."

This means— Since Israel has so firmly adhered to the divine law, and has subjected himself to death under religious persecution, we [Gentiles] see no other object for the infliction and chastisements, except that the Almighty visits him with punishments in order to humble and to try him with a view to compensate him for his submission: therefore, in sharing his grave with the Israelite he shall see seed, that is to say, become exceedingly numerous. This elliptical mode of omitting the word expressive of excess and largeness occurs also in Numbers xiii., where we find אנשי מדה " Men of size," that is, men of large or gigantic size. Other prophets also contribute their testimony to the future increase of Israel. See, for instance, Zech. x. 8, " I will hiss for them and gather them, for I have redeemed them, and they shall increase as they have increased."

In the same chapter the prophet foretells: " I will bring them into the land of Gilead and Lebanon, and it shall not be large enough for them" (English Version, "no place found for them"). Ezekiel xxxvi. 37, has on the same subject the following prophecy: " I will increase them with men as a flock." The words " he shall live long" have a parallel in Isaiah lxv. 22, " For as the days of the tree shall be the days of my people." Zechariah says, in chap. viii. 4, " And every man (shall sit) with his staff in his hand for very age."

The Almighty in afflicting and humbling us during our captivity purposes, therefore, to bring to pass our ultimate benefit, and to strengthen our number in the time of our restoration. This is confirmed in Deut. xxx. 5, " And He will make thee better and more numerous than thy fathers were." So far go the words which convey the restoration of Israel. The last two verses of the chapter contain the promise added by the Almighty (Isaiah liii. 11), " He shall see of the travail of his soul, and shall be satisfied. By his knowledge shall my righteous servant make many righteous, for he shall bear their iniquities." The words, " by his knowledge," are thus illustrated in Jeremiah xxxi. 34, " For they all shall know me, from the least of them unto the greatest of them." " He shall make many people righteons," means that Israel shall impart its knowledge of righteousness to the Gentiles. See on this point Micah iv. 2, " And many nations shall come and say, Come and let us go up to the mountain of the Lord, and to the house of the God of Jacob, that He may teach us His ways, and we will walk in His paths; for the law shall go forth from Zion, and the word of the Lord from Jerusalem." Hence, Israel, the servant of the Lord, shall, by his righteousness, remove the wickedness of the Gentiles, and through his righteousness peace and happiness shall reign among mankind at large. Isaiah liii. 11, " Therefore will I divide him a portion among the great, and with the mighty he shall divide the spoil; because he poured out his soul unto death, and he was numbered with the transgressors, and he bare the sin of many, and prayed for the transgressor."

This means—I shall allot him a portion and a reward among the greatest and worthiest men that lived on earth, viz., among the patriarchs and holy prophets.

The allotment will consist in spiritual beatitude which far surpasses all corporeal well-being. The translation of רַבִּים (great) is justified by the occurrence of וְרַב in Genesis, " And the greater [in the English Version, the elder] shall serve the younger." But worldly prosperity is likewise promised in Isaiah's prophecy, as he says,

" And with the mighty he shall divide the spoil." " The mighty" are the hosts of Gog and Magog, and the nations who will come to carry on war with Jerusalem, and who will be removed by sudden death. See Ezekiel xxxviii. 22, " I will plead against him with pestilence and with blood, and I will pour down floods of rain upon him, and upon his bands, and upon the many people that are with him," etc. Israel shall then partake of the spoil and property in retribution of the extortion and depredation formerly practised towards Israel. See Zech. xiv. 14, " And the wealth of all heathen shall be gathered together, gold, and silver, and raiment in great abundance."

Thus Israel shall be compensated for the bodily and mental suffering heaped upon them during their exile.

In that epoch, life shall be ransomed by life and property by property. This is intended by the words, " Because he poured forth his soul unto death." The verb הֶעֱרָה " he poured forth" (from the root עָרָה) is synonymous with the expression in Genesis xxiv. 20, "And she poured forth her pitcher," etc.

"And he was numbered with the transgressors" is analogous to the sentence, "And he made his grave with the wicked." That is to say, the gentiles treated Israel as a wicked, ungodly race, and, therefore, these exuberant blessings shall now be bestowed unto Israel which are reserved for the upright and God-fearing men, and those who revere His name like the holy patriarchs and the prophets of our people. " He bore the sin of many" means, he was not only free from the wickedness imputed to him by the gentiles, but through his piety he bore their sins and suffered for their iniquity. At the same time he prayed for those nations who had inflicted on him heavy sufferings, and besought the Almighty to grant prosperity and abundance to the kingdoms of the gentiles. See Jeremiah xxix. 7, " And seek the peace of the city whither I have caused you to be carried captive, and pray unto the Lord for it.," etc. With the same tolerant spirit our Rabbins admonish us thus: " Pray for the prosperity of thy native country." The prayers we offer up to the Almighty are an evidence of our submission to this precept. We pray for the long life and happiness of our gentile rulers, and we address other prayers all tending to prove the interest we take in the welfare of other nations; we pray for the fertility of their land and for the plentiful supply of food required for the nourishment of all.

CHAPTER XXIII.

ISAIAH lxiv. 5 (in the English version, ver. 6), "And we are all as an unclean *man*, and all our righteousnesses are as a rotten garment and as a leaf, and our iniquities take us away like a wind." A Christian once addressed me in the following terms:—" That there is not one man on the earth who does good and sinneth not. Yea, ye must know well that there is not one man capable of observing all the commandments prescribed in the laws of Moses; and that your righteous acts have not enabled you to attain the end you seek. How inefficient, then, must the prayers and the actions of the wicked prove ?"

Reply—We must certainly admit that no man can obtain salvation through his own acts alone; but man must combine with his piety a total submission to the mercy and loving-kindness of the Lord. Jeremiah announces it clearly (chap. xxx. 21), "And I will cause him to draw near, and he shall approach unto me, for who is he whose heart is emboldened to approach unto me ?"

The Psalmist says, in the same manner (Psalms lxv. 4), " Blessed is the man whom thou choosest and causest to be near unto thee, that he may dwell in thy courts." Therefore, he prays (in Psalm lxxix. 9), " Help us, O God of our salvation, for the sake of the glory of Thy name, and deliver us and forgive us our sins, for the sake of Thy name." In Psalms xxv. 2, the sacred poet says, " For the sake of Thy name forgive us our iniquity, for it is great." Again in Psalms cxv. 1, " Not unto us, O Lord, not unto us, but unto *Thy* name give glory, for the sake of *Thy* mercy, and for the sake of *Thy* faithfulness." Again in Psalms cxliii. 11, " For the sake of Thy name thou shalt quicken me; for the sake of *Thy* righteousness thou shalt bring my soul out of trouble." In Psalms xliv. 26, he exclaims, " Arise and deliver us for the sake of Thy loving-kindness, in the greatness of Thy mercy blot out my transgression." And in Psalms lxxx. 3, he implores the Almighty, " Return unto us, O God, and cause *Thy* countenance to shine (upon us) and we shall be saved." Thus says, also, the prophet Jeremiah xiv. 7, " If our iniquities testify against us, then grant, O God, for the sake of Thy name;" and further, " For the sake of *Thy* name do not rebuke us." In the Lamentations v. 21, he says " Cause us, O Lord, to return unto Thee and we shall be turned." Daniel, in his prayer, ix. 18, 19, uses similar language, " *For not on account of our* righteousness we pour out our supplications before Thee; but on account of *Thine* abundant mercies, O Lord, hear them; O Lord, forgive us; O Lord, hearken and grant them; delay not, O God, for *Thine* own sake, for Thy name is called upon *Thy* city and *Thy* people.' Numerous other passages might be quoted all conveying the same idea.

Hence the Almighty has given us the assurance, through His prophets, to deliver us from our captivity, and to blot out our sins and iniquities, not for our sake but for His own sake.   Thus Isaiah says, xlviii. 11, " For my sake, for my own sake will I do it." In chap. xliii. 25, the same prophet says, " I, even I, am he who blotteth out thy transgressions for my own sake, and thy sins I will not remember."   This is expressed, also, by Ezekiel, xxxvi. 22, " Not for your sake, O house of Israel, am I dealing thus, but for *my* holy name." We find in the same book, chap. xx. 44, "And ye shall know, that I am the Lord, by my dealing for the sake of my name, and not according to your evil ways and your corrupt actions, O house of Israel, saith the Lord God."   We may cite here, also, the words of Jeremiah xxxi. 37, " Thus saith the Lord, If the heavens above shall be measured, or the foundations of the earth be searched, I will also rebuke the seed of Israel for all they have done."   This divine declaration clearly confirms our opinion that our salvation does not solely depend on our imperfect individual merit and righteousness, but on the mercy of the faithful God, who will never change although we may be found undeserving before him.

The expression of the prophet, " We are all unclean, and all our virtues are like a rotten garment," has reference to such religious works as are performed through vain-glory and selfish motives, in order to create envy among our neighbours, it is evident enough that the best actions must displease the Almighty when they originate from base motives; " For the Searcher of hearts," say our sages, " regards the intentions only." Hence the admonition in Deut. xv. 10, " Thou shalt supply him liberally, nor shall thy heart be vexed while thou givest." And in chap. xxviii. 47, we read, " Because thou didst not serve the Lord thy God in joy, and with a cheerful heart." The above passage, " We are all unclean, and all our righteousness is like a rotten garment," relates, therefore, to the objectionable conduct and impure intentions of those who selfishly labour in the cause of the Almighty, and, as the leaves dropping from the tree are carried away by the wind, so we, in consequence of our sins, are dispersed throughout all the quarters of the globe.

CHAPTER XXIV.

JEREMIAH iii. 16, " And it shall come to pass, when ye be multiplied and increased in the land, in those days, saith the Lord, they shall say no more, The ark of the covenant of the Lord, neither shall it come to mind, neither shall they remember it, neither shall they visit it, neither shall that be done any more." From this the Christians argue that the law of Moses, which was deposited by the side of the ark, would at a future period be annulled.

Refutation.—In chap. xix. we have already proved by unmistakable evidence, and especially by their own Gospels, and even by allusions to their theological writers, that the law of Moses is eternal, and that no new revelation will ever supplant our old law. Having then sufficiently proved the feebleness of the opinions adverse to this view, we confine ourselves here to the above quoted explanations : every reader of the Scriptures knows the passage in 1 Kings viii. 9, " There was nothing in the ark but the two tables of stone." These tables having been called the tables of the covenant, the ark, as the receptacle of those tables, was named " the ark of the covenant." The Christians themselves admit that the contents of the tables of the decalogue are immutable, and that no man can hope for the salvation of his soul who repudiates the Ten Commandments. We shall have to return to this subject on reviewing some passages in Matthew xix. So much is certain, that the Christians are enjoined to follow the Ten Commandments, although they have arbitrarily altered the day appointed for the celebration of the Sabbath, and, although no sanction for so doing was given either by Jesus or his disciples; consequently, the Christians have no right to plead that the ark of the covenant of the Lord, and the two tables with their contents, will ever be forgotten; nor are they justified in the assertion, that the law of Moses will be abrogated: and not be remembered any longer by Israel, since the scriptural passages cited by them do not afford any evidence in support of their argument, particularly as Malachi, the last of the prophets (chap. iv. 4), gives the divine admonition, " Remember the law of Moses my servant, which I commanded him on Horeb, enjoining it on all Israel with the statutes and judgments." This prophet clearly demonstrates that the divine law will certainly not be abolished at any future time; on the contrary, that the dignity of Israel and the dignity of Jerusalem will be augmented at a future day. Hence he alludes to those days when Israel shall have increased and multiplied in the Holy Land, and when the Gentile nations shall come to seek the Word of the Lord at Jerusalem. To this effect says Isaiah (chap. ii. 2), " And all nations shall flow unto Him." Those nations shall not profanely ask after the divine covenant, and intrude into the resting-place of the Holy Ark, for they shall be too fully impressed with the sanctity of the house of God, where the throne of judgment will be re-established. The temple will then not be the exclusive locality to which the Gentiles shall flock, but *all* Jerusalem will be a residence of divine knowledge, whither the Gentiles shall resort in order to call upon the name of the Lord, and to serve

Him with one accord; and the sacred and godly duties
of man will not be limited only to the precincts of the
temple. See Joel iii. 17, " And Jerusalem shall be holy,
and strangers shall not pass through it." Here we learn
that the holiness of Jerusalem will prevent aliens from
entering it for the purpose of desecrating it. The unworthy among the Gentiles, and the unclean among
Israel, will in like manner be kept away through awe of
the Holy City; but the city of the Lord shall spread its
conversion and enlightening influence to the remotest
distance. The Gentiles, following the wholesome minis-
tration of the chosen race, will be deemed servants
of the Lord like the children of Israel. The prophet,
therefore, says, " And many nations will join the Lord
and shall be my people." In chap. lvi. 6, 7, Isaiah predicts, " Also the sons of the strangers that join themselves to the Lord to serve Him, and to love the name
of the Lord, to be His servants: every one that keepeth
the Sabbath from polluting it, and taketh hold of my
covenant, even them will I bring to my holy mountain, and make them joyful in my house of prayer:
their burnt offerings and their sacrifices shall be accepted upon mine altar; for mine house shall be called
a house of prayer for all people."

This shows that, at the time of the Advent of the
Messiah, all nations will pay homage to the holiness of
the land of Israel, and the entire land of Palestine will
assume the sacredness of the city of Jerusalem; and the
city of Jerusalem will again partake of the sanctity of
the Divine Temple.

CHAPTER XXV.

JEREMIAH xiv. 8, " Hope of Israel, the Saviour in the

time of trouble, why shouldst thou be as a stranger in
the land, and as a wayfaring man that turneth aside to
tarry for the night?" I was once asked by a Christian
the meaning of the expression, "Hope of Israel, the
Saviour in the time of trouble." I replied, the prophet here addressed the Almighty, as in chap. xvii. 13, "O
Lord, the Hope of Israel, all who forsake thee shall be
ashamed." The same Deity is the Saviour of Israel in
the time of trouble, and there is no other Saviour besides
Him. See also chap. xiii., "And there is no Saviour
besides me." My interrogator said thereupon, You ought
to bear in mind that the prophet, speaking about this
Saviour, says, "Why shouldst thou be as a stranger and
as a wayfaring man, that turneth aside to tarry for the
night? Does not this prove to you, by means of those
prophetic words, that the saving Divine Being would
dwell like a stranger on earth, as our Saviour Jesus
actually did? why then do you withhold from him your
belief after the prophet gives his testimony about him?"
I replied to this, "You Christians are accustomed to
establish your objections to our faith, and the evidences
of your faith, on detached biblical passages, without
regard to the leading idea, and with the preceding and
subsequent words of the text, nor do you make unbiassed
comparisons with the parallel sayings of other prophets;
for your object is not to expose absolute truth, but to
confirm, by means of subtleties and specious reasonings,
your preconceived notions."

The true object of Jeremiah will be found on the
perusal of the adjoining passages. Jeremiah having a
prescience of the famine which was about to take place
in the Holy Land (see the commencement of chap.
xiv.), when he saw that the severity of the dearth would
exceed all bounds, and the consternation of Jerusalem
would put up a cry to heaven; when he noticed that

the calamity would be so universal that the very brutes
of the field would suffer under its scourge, he made the
confession recorded in the words, " If our iniquities bear
witness against us, O Lord, then deal with us according
to Thy name." By this he declared, that the trouble
had not come upon our people by way of chance, but as
a consequence of our misdeeds; for the famine did not
prevail anywhere else except in the Land of Israel;
therefore, he implored of the Almighty to grant relief
for the sake of His Holy Name: that is to say, God,
as proclaimed in His supreme unity by our nation, is on
that account called " the God of Israel," whilst we are
denominated " His people and the flock of His pasture."
When He chastises us, He acts in accordance with
justice, since our derelictions are numerous, and since
we so frequently strayed in the pursuit of idolatry, the
perpetration of violence, and in listening to false prophets. Jeremiah having thus made confession of our
sins, exclaims, by way of entreaty, " Thou Hope of
Israel, and its Saviour in the time of trouble !" The
prophet hereby implies, that, although they have departed from Thy paths, they (the Israelites) still hope
that Thou wilt save them from the present distress, and
as Thou hast delivered them in every generation, so wilt
Thou also now have mercy on them, and not suffer
them to be consumed by famine. Then the prophet
continues, " Why wilt Thou be like a stranger and like
a traveller who has turned aside to pass the night." By
this we have to understand, " That Thou, O Lord, wilt
hide Thy face from us and have no compassion on us,
it will appear as if Thou wert not the Lord of the Earth,
but as if thou wert a stranger in a foreign country,
without power therein to afford relief from trouble." In
a similar manner said Moses (Numbers xiv. 15, 16),
" And if Thou wilt kill all the people like one man, then

the nations who have heard Thy fame will say, Because
the Lord had not the power to bring this people," etc.
So prays also the Psalmist, " Arise, why wilt Thou sleep;
O Lord, awake, why wilt Thou abandon us for ever;"
or, in other words, Permit it not to appear as if Thou
wert unmindful of our misery and of our affliction.   In
fact, all the prophets address the Almighty in an
anthropomorphical manner, in order to convey their
ideas more intelligibly to their audience.

The reason that Jeremiah compares the Almighty
with a stranger is threefold.   1st. A sojourner in a
foreign land, one passing merely through a foreign city,
is unable to rescue the oppressed from the hand of the
oppressor, or the poor and the needy from the hand of
the depredator. For though such strangers or travel-
lers be of high rank, their authority is too inconsider-
able, when in a foreign land, to afford any assistance to
those around them.   Thus the Sodomites said about
Lot: " This one man came to live here as a stranger,
and now he will be even a judge." 2ndly. Though a
man be a native or an established settler, he may be
unable to give assistance in times of trouble, being
deprived of the requisite influence and presence of mind.
Bewildered about his own safety, he is utterly incapaci-
tated to extricate others from their unfortunate state.
3rdly. Even he can only grapple with those who are
inferior in valour and strength, but when met with a
superior force he must either desist or submit.   Hence
the prophet says, " Why wilt thou be like a mighty man
who is unable to save."

In order, however, at the same time, to teach that
such a condition is totally incompatible with the divine
nature of the Almighty, and to show that the Almighty
is really the God of the heavens and of the earth, and at
the same time dwells among us, the prophet, by the

addition, " But Thou art among us," refutes the imputation that the God of Israel is a stranger, and rather
proves that *He* is established where we sojourn, and that
we are the strangers and not *He*; that we have, therefore, the best founded expectation that *He* will save us.
The same declaration, " Thou art in the midst of us,"
stands in just opposition to the question, " Why wilt
thou be like a bewildered man?"   The prophet suggests
that the Almighty, far from being perplexed by the
suddenness of terrific occurrences, rather manifests himself as an incomparable and omnipotent deliverer.   In
like manner we see in the words, " And Thou art among
us," a repudiation of the idea that " Thou art like a
strong man who cannot deliver," when resisted by a
superior force; for the prophet now acknowledges, " And
Thy name is called upon us, for Thou hast long been
adored by us as the God of Israel.   Thou hast brought
us out from the land of Egypt with a strong hand, and
an outstretched arm."

The very words of the Decalogue connect the divine
unity with the deliverance from Egypt, since it is said,
" I am the Lord thy God who hath brought thee out of
the land of Egypt."   It is a notorious fact, that Scripture in various places points out the condescension of
God, who allied His name with Israel, by saving them
from various troubles.   See, for instance, Leviticus xxii.,
" Who hath brought you out of Egypt, in order to be
unto you a God."   When the subjects of King Hezekiah
were rescued from the hand of Sennacherib, king of
Assyria, the Almighty was also acknowledged as God of
Israel.   See 2 Kings xix. 20, " Thus saith the Lord
God of Israel, Since thou hast prayed unto me concerning Sennacherib, the king of Assyria, I have heard thee."
The prayer here alluded to was received favourably,
because it expressed unconditional submission to the

all-powerful Being who alone rules the destinies of His creatures. Further views of the faith of Israel in the salvation by the Lord, may be obtained from Deut. iii. 24, where we read, "For who is a God in heaven or in the earth, who could perform anything like unto Thy deeds and Thy mighty works?" Isaiah says, (chap. xiv.) " Truly Thou art an invisible God, the God of Israel and its Saviour." Jeremiah (chap. iii.) says " Verily in the Lord our God is the salvation of Israel; our trust, our reliance is therefore in Thee, and Thou wilt neither abandon nor forsake us." Thus we understand the quotation from Jeremiah, which is placed at the heading of this chapter, and which is totally misapplied when referred to on account of his having been a stranger on earth.

CHAPTER XXVI.

JEREMIAH xvii. 4, "And I will cause thee to serve thine enemies in the land which thou knowest not; for ye have kindled a fire in mine anger, which shall burn for ever."

Christian expositors have explained this verse by the assertion that Jeremiah here predicted an everlasting captivity, from which no redemption is to be hoped.

Refutation.—The Hebrew words עַד עוֹלָם occur in Scripture in three significations. First, in application to an existence unlimited by time. Thus, we have in 2 Samuel vii. 26, " That Thy name may be magnified for ever, by saying The Lord of Hosts is the God of Israel." In 1 Chron. xvii. 24, we also find, " In order that Thy name may be magnified for ever, by saying, The Lord of Hosts is the God of Israel." The second meaning of עַד עוֹלָם for ever, relates to man's limited existence on earth, (see 1st Samuel i. 22), " That he

may sit here for ever." And 2nd Samuel xii. 10, David
is thus forewarned, "The sword shall *never* (עד תסור לא
עולם) depart from thy house." The word *never* merely
relates to David's lifetime. In the third place, the
Hebrew expression עד עולם stands distinct from the
forenamed two meanings, and relates to a period finite
in the prescience of the Almighty, but unlimited
according to the knowledge of men. See Isaiah xxxii.
14, " Because the palaces shall be forsaken, the multitude of the city shall be left; the forts and towers shall
be dens *for ever*, a joy of wild asses, a pasture of flocks."
The limitation of the words *for ever* is shewn in the verse
immediately following, "Until the spirit be poured
down upon us from on high, and the wilderness be a
fruitful field," etc. The destruction decreed to last *for
ever* will, nevertheless, give way to restoration as soon as
the spirit, that is to say the favour of the Lord, shall
descend on us. The term it shall burn *for ever*, refers
to the third signification; but it cannot mean the infini-
tude of eternity as some Christians would have us
believe, because all the prophets have predicted a complete restoration to the whole house of Israel. What
can be more explicit than the following passages:—
Isaiah, in chap. lxvi. 20, says, "And they (the Gentiles)
shall bring all your brethren a gift from all nations as
a gift unto the Lord, on horses and in chariots," etc.
Jeremiah xxx. 8, says, " Strangers shall no more enslave
them (the Israelites.") Ezekiel xxxix. 6, 29, says, "And
they shall know that I am the Lord their God, since I
have caused them to be exiled among the Gentiles; and
I will gather them into their land, and I will not suffer
any of them to remain behind, and I will no more hide
my countenance from them, as I have poured out my
spirit over all the house of Israel, saith the Lord God."
Such well defined promises admit of no contradiction,
or they have all proceeded from the same divine source.

CHAPTER XXVII.

JEREMIAH xviii. 7, " In an instant I shall speak concerning a nation and concerning a kingdom, to pluck up and to pull down and to destroy it."

From this and the ensuing verses, Christians have concluded that the Jews vainly expect the fulfilment of those promises which refer to a prosperous futurity. They tell us (Jews), your hopes must be disappointed. Sinfully you have acted, yea sinfully in the sight of the Lord, for all the promises of the prophet, whether for good or for evil, are given conditionally. The Almighty ordains a propitious future for a people or for an individual; and if the people or the individual, by evil acts, become unworthy of such a benefit, it is withheld, and the Almighty substitutes evil for the intended good; and when the people or the individual again repent and improve, the imminent punishment is withdrawn, a favour is bestowed instead, as has been exemplified by the history of Jonah in Nineveh. The Christians interpret, therefore, the above passage from Jeremiah thus—"At one instant I decree the destruction of a people or of a kingdom, etc. When, however, the people or the kingdom amend their conduct, I withhold the threatened calamity. At another instant I resolve to deal out benefits. When, however, the people offend me, and act disobediently, I recall my decrees of grace." To this the Christians add the following imputation:—The Almighty has, time after time, released Israel from the tyranny of their enemies. Admonition after admonition He sent to them through His prophets to induce them not to follow the instigations of a corrupt heart, and He imposed on them the duty of obeying His commandments and statutes. The Israelites, however, whenever they felt the soothing help of the Lord, hardened their hearts again, and neglected the biddings of the Almighty. This has induced Him to abhor them and to reject them altogether.   And He will never again favour them. See 2 Kings xvii. 20, " And the Lord rejected all the seed of Israel and afflicted them, and delivered them into the hand of spoilers until He had cast them out of His sight."

Thus says also Jeremiah (chap.xv. 1), " And the Lord said unto me, If even Moses and Samuel were to stand before me, my mind would not be towards this people; cast them out of my sight and let them go forth."

Refutation.—It is a false accusation to allege, that we Jews expect the fulfilment of the divine promises so long as we persevere in evil doings, and commit sins like depraved men, and still expect a reward as if we were true and zealous servants of God.   Far be from us any such presumption.   But we do profess with an unshaken confidence that we shall one day cling to the Lord with an undivided heart, and that the Almighty will receive us in mercy, subdue our misdeeds, and then bring to pass all the glorious predictions given by the prophets.   We rely on the words pronounced in Deuteronomy iv. 30, " When thou shalt be in trouble, and when all these things shall have befallen thee, in the latter days thou shalt return to the Lord thy God and hearken to His voice; for the Lord thy God is a merciful God, He will not suffer thee to be weakened, nor will He destroy thee, nor will He forget the covenant with thy fathers which He swore unto them." We may also advert to chap. xxx. 1—7, of the same book, " And it shall come to pass, when all these things shall have come upon thee, the blessing and the curse which I have set before thee, and when thou shalt have taken it to heart among all the nations among which the Lord thy God shall have

banished thee, that thou shalt return with all thine heart
and with all thy soul to the Lord thy God, and obey His
voice according to all that I command unto thee this
day, thou and thy sons. And the Lord thy God shall
bring back thy captivity, and gather thee from among
all the people whither the Lord thy God shall have
scattered thee. Even if thine outcasts be at the end
of the heavens; even from thence shall the Lord thy
God gather thee, and even from thence shall He take
thee, and the Lord thy God shall bring thee into the
land which thy fathers inherited; and thou shalt inherit
it, and He shall do good unto thee, and He shall make
thee more numerous than thy ancestors. And the Lord
thy God shall circumcise thy heart, and the heart of thy
seed, to love the Lord thy God with all thy heart, and
with all thy soul, for the sake of thy life. And the Lord
thy God shall bring all these imprecations upon thine
enemies, etc., when thou shalt return to the Lord thy
God." The prophets have also announced the constancy
of our future adherence to the Lord, and have made the
fulfiment of the good promised dependent on our full
repentance. See Isaiah xliv. 22, " I have blotted out
thine iniquities like a thick cloud, and thy sins like a
cloud; return unto me, for I have redeemed thee." Also
Jeremiah (iii. 14) says, " Return unto me, ye backslid-
ing children, saith the Lord, for I am married unto you,
and I will take you one from a city, and two of a family,
and I will bring you into Zion." See also Ezekiel xxxiii.
11, " Say unto tHem, As I live, saith the Lord God,
I have no pleasure in the death of the wicked, but that
the wicked turn from his way and live: turn ye, turn
ye from your evil ways, for why will ye die, O house
of Israel?" In like manner, says Hosea (xiv. 1, 2),
" Turn, O Israel, unto the Lord thy God, for thou hast
stumbled through thine iniquity. Take with yourselves

words, and turn unto the Lord, and say unto Him: Thou
who forgivest every iniquity, receive us graciously, and we
will render the calves of our lips" (i. e. thanksgivings).
Zechariah, in chap. i. 3, says, " And thou shalt say unto
them, Thus saith the Lord of Hosts: Return ye unto
me, saith the Lord of Hosts, and I will return unto you,
saith the Lord of Hosts."

To the same effect, says Malachi iii. 7, " Since the
days of your fathers ye have departed from my statutes,
and ye have not observed them: return unto me, and I
will return unto you, saith the Lord of Hosts." Similar
passages abound among the prophets, which tend to
prove that repentance is the fundamental condition on
which all our hopes hinge, for no human being escapes
the commission of sin. See Ecclesiastes vii. 20, " For
there is no righteous man in the earth who doeth good
and sinneth not." Therefore our All-gracious Ruler
has taught us the means of repentance, and the ways to
avoid the snares of depravity. David had committed
many transgressions, and subjected himself with sincere
submission to the divine chastisements: his sins were,
therefore, forgiven him, and his good works were accepted in favour of him and his posterity. See Isaiah
xxxvii. 35, " And I shall protect this city to save it for
my sake, and for the sake of my servant David." King
Manasseh affords another instance of pardon having been
obtained through sincere repentance, although he had
exceeded his predecessors in the indulgence of an iniquitous conduct; yet the Lord was pleased with his contrition, and reinstated him on his throne. Consequently
we thus interpret the passage, " At an instant I shall
speak," etc. The reparation of Israel's conduct is the
only condition of their escape from the infliction of condign punishments; therefore the prophet continues the
divine message in the following manner: " Now go to,

speak to the men of Judah and to the inhabitants of Jerusalem, saying, Thus saith the Lord, behold I frame evil against you, and devise a device against you; return ye now every one from his evil way, and correct your ways and your doings." Nor are we disposed to imagine that we should suffer less for our sins than our fore-fathers did for theirs. On the contrary, we are admonished to be equally vigilant as our ancestors in the avoidance of sin; and when our frail human nature betrays us into sinful acts, it becomes our imperative duty to resort to sincere repentance, for only then the Lord receives us and casteth our sins into the abyss of oblivion. See Ezekiel xviii. 21, " But if the wicked will turn from all his sins that he hath committed and keep all my statutes, and do that which is lawful and right, he shall surely live, he shall not die. All his transgressions that he has committed, they shall not be mentioned unto him; in his righteousness that he hath done he shall live."

We may mention here, also, that the many divine predictions and promises which are of a cheering character have been given in the unconditional and irrevocable form of an oath; for instance, Ibid xxxvi. 7—12, "Thus saith the Lord God, I have lifted up mine hand, (which is the symbol of an oath) that the Heathens that are around you shall surely bear their shame. But ye, O, mountains of Israel, ye shall shoot forth your branches and yield your fruit to my people of Israel, for they are at hand to come. For behold I am for you, and I will turn unto you, and you shall be tilled and sown. And I will multiply men among you, O, all ye house of Israel, even all of it; and the cities shall be inhabited, and the wastes shall be builded, and I will multiply among you men and cattle, and they shall increase and bring fruit, and I will settle you after your old estates, and will do better unto you than at your beginnings, and ye shall know that I am the Lord; yea, I will cause men to walk among you, even my people Israel; and they shall possess thee, and thou shalt be their inheritance, and thou shalt no more bereave them of men."

Thus the Almighty communicates to us in Ezekiel's prophecy, that he will prosperously re-establish the Holy Land in its primitive condition, and even enlarge His bounty upon it, so that it shall no longer consume Israel, its inhabitants.

The disputant cannot raise an objection and maintain that the prophecy of restoration is merely given conditionally, for there an oath is expressed, *lifting of the hand*, which does not admit of any condition whatever. See Deut. xxxii. 40, where we read, " For I lift up my hand unto the heavens, and I say, As true as I live for ever." Nor can it be asserted that this assurance merely relates to Israel's exit from Babylon, for at that period the Lord did not raise Israel to its pristine state, and then the whole of Israel did not return to their land; the ten tribes of Israel were omitted, and no more than 42,360 men of the tribe of Judah and Benjamin actually came back. Neither was Israel at that time spared from affliction, as it will be at the future redemption, which is clearly demonstrated by the contents of the above prophecy, and other passages, (see Ezekiel xxxvi. 22—28). In fact, the whole concluding part of the chapter speaks in an unconditional tone. And this is quite natural; for where the Almighty has given predictions relating to the glory of His name, and not that of our name, no conditional language could be applied. We have, in other similar passages decided and unconditional assurances (see, for instance, Isaiah liv. 9, 10), "For this is as the waters of Noah unto me; for as I have sworn that the waters should no more go over the earth, so have I sworn that I would not be wroth with thee. For the mountains shall depart and the hills be removed; but my kindness shall not depart from thee, neither shall the covenant of my peace be removed, saith the Lord that hath mercy on thee." Thus we find, ibid chap. lxii. 8, 9, " The Lord hath sworn by His right hand, and by the arm of His strength: Surely, I will no more give thy corn to be food for thine enemies, and the sons of the strangers shall no more drink thy wine for which thou hast laboured. But those that gather it shall eat it and praise the Lord, and they that have brought it together shall drink it in the courts of my holiness."   See also Jeremiah xxxi. 35, 36, 37, " Thus saith the Lord, who giveth the sun for a light by day, and the ordinances of the moon, and of the stars as a light by night, who divideth the sea when the waves thereof roar: The Lord of Hosts is His name.   If those ordinances depart from before me, saith the Lord, then the seed of Israel shall also cease from being a nation before me for ever. Thus saith the Lord, If the heavens above can be mea-sured, and the foundations of the earth searched out beneath, I will also cast off the seed of Israel for all that they have done, saith the Lord."   When our oppo-nent takes into consideration all these passages, how can he maintain that the Almighty has cast off and disowned Israel, and will no more vouchsafe to His people a re-demption from this captivity?   Surely the restoration will at last take place; then His anger will no more visit us, then His loving-kindness and His covenant of peace will no more be drawn from us, then He will no more cast us away, and no more deprive us of establishment as a nation.   Our past sins will then no longer be remembered, but He will graciously pardon all our former errors and transgressions.   For Jeremiah

has, in the above prophecy, expressly announced in the
name of the Lord, " I will pardon their sins, and remember their iniquity no more." Neither can the
argument be founded on the words occurring in 2 Kings
xvii. 20, " And the Lord rejected all the seed of Israel,
and afflicted them, and He gave them into the hands of
spoilers, until He cast them out of His sight." This
rejection and casting away is only a temporary punishment limited to the period of the captivity, but is not
final and perpetual; consequently it is not a dissolution of the ancient covenant. See, on this, Leviticus
xxvi. 44, " And yet for all that, when they be in the
land of their enemies I will not cast them away, nor will
I abhor them to destroy them utterly, and to break my
covenant with them, for I am the Lord their God."
The periods for their removal are fixed by the Almighty,
and only known to Him, who, by means of frequent
chastisements, desires to remove from them all that is
unbecoming and objectionable. See Isaiah i. 25, " And I
will turn my hand upon thee, and purely purge thy dross,
and remove all the base metal; and I will restore thy
judges as at first, and thy counsellors as at the beginning; afterwards thou shalt be called the City of Righteousness, the faithful city." Similar to this prophecy
are the words of Ezekiel xxii. 15, " And I will scatter
thee among the heathen, and disperse them in the countries, and will consume thy filthiness out of thee." All
this tends to prove the object of our exile as solely to
purify us, to rid us of inherent imperfections, and to
free us from the pollution of our sins. Hence the prophet, with a view to our ultimate purification, says, in
Lamentations iv. 22, " Thy iniquity, O daughter of
Zion, is ended; He shall no more cause thee to be a
captive." Now, we will show that no argument can be
established against us, from the words of Jeremiah

xv. 1, " And the Lord said unto me, Though Moses and Samuel stood before me, yet my mind would not be toward this people; cast them out of my sight, and let them go forth."

These words were addressed to Jeremiah after the Lord had charged him thrice not to intercede on behalf of Judah and Benjamin, that they might be led into captivity like the other ten tribes. For the Lord had said to Jeremiah, chap. vii. 15 16, " And I will cast you out of my sight as I have cast out all your brethren, even the whole seed of Ephraim: therefore, pray not thou for this people, neither lift up a cry or prayer for them, neither make intercession to me, for I will not hear thee." Now the Lord explained to him the reason why He would not listen to his intercessions, and he says (in verse 17, 18), " Seest thou not what they do in the cities of Judah and in the streets of Jerusalem? The children gather wood, and the fathers kindle the fire, and the women knead their dough, to make cakes for the queen of heaven, and pour out drink offerings unto other Gods that they may provoke me to anger." In the same book, chap. xi. 11, He says, " Therefore, thus saith the Lord, Behold, I will bring evil upon them, from which they shall not be able to escape; and though they shall cry unto me I will not hearken unto them." Also here the reason is pointed out why the Almighty would refuse to grant his prayer (ibid v. 13), we find, " For according to the number of thy cities were thy Gods, O Judah," etc. And in the same chapter we have a second warning of the Almighty that Jeremiah should not intercede (Ibid. v. 14), " Therefore, pray not for this people, nor offer up a cry or supplication for them, for I will not hearken in the time that they cry unto me in their trouble." For how could the Almighty be favourable to a petition for mercy while they con-

tinued in the sin which caused the infliction: nor could
impenitent sinners find grace with Him. Hence the
words, Ibid., " And they shall cry unto me, but I will
not hear them." The imminent evil relates to sword,
pestilence, and famine. See chap. xiv., " For through
the sword, pestilence, and famine, I destroy them."
When, therefore, Jeremiah perceived that the prayer
for the house of Judah was in vain, he prayed
(chap. xiv. 7), " O Lord, though our iniquities testify
against us, do it for thy name's sake." The prophet
then concludes with the words, " We are called by Thy
name; therefore, forsake us not." Upon this follows the
reply of the Almighty: " Thus saith the Lord unto this
people, Thus have they loved to wander, they have not
refrained their feet, wherefore the Lord doth not accept
them; He will now remember their iniquity and visit
their sins." Hereby is meant—Since the Jews have
mistrusted me, and have preferred to seek their protection among the Egyptians and the Assyrians, in order
to escape the danger of adversaries, and since the Jews
have not refrained from following profitless objects, I
will remove them and render them the captives of their
enemies. But, before I shall lead them into exile, I will
remember their iniquity by famine, and visit their sin
by the sword and by pestilence.

After having acquainted the prophet that his people
had no hope of deliverance from the evils decreed upon
them, the third injunction was given to Jeremiah not to
offer up a supplication for the deliverance of the people
(see Ibid. chap. xiv. 11, 12), " Then said the Lord unto
me, Pray not for this people for their good; when they
fast I will not hear their cry, and when they offer burnt
offering and an oblation, I will not accept them, but I
will consume them by the sword, and by the famine, and
by the pestilence." Here again, allusion is solely made

to their prayers coming from an impenitent heart, and offered up during their perseverance in wickedness.

The present passage reminds us of the one in Isaiah i. 15, 16, " And when ye spread forth your hands, I will hide mine eyes from you; yea, when ye make many prayers I will not hear; your hands are full of blood; make you clean; put away the evil of your doings from before mine eyes; cease to do evil." The verses we have quoted demonstrate that favourable reception of prayers is only denied so long as those evil deeds continue which bring the punishment to pass, but the supplications meet with grace when the supplicant renounces his sinful conduct. The pious prophet Jeremiah seeing, then, that his influence was insufficient among the unfortunate transgressors, appealed once more to the Almighty not to reject them and not to abhor them, for the sake of His holy name, since the Lord had been acknowledged on earth as the God of Israel. He prayed also to the Almighty not to suffer Jerusalem, known as the seat of the glory of the Lord, to be reviled; moreover, not to break His covenant made with the Israelites when he brought them out of Egypt. Hence, he says in Jeremiah, xiv. 21, " Do not abhor us for Thy name's sake, do not disgrace the throne of Thy glory; remember us, and break not Thy covenant with us." Thereupon the Lord replies, that the prayer of Jeremiah would not avail to rescue the Israelites from the calamities of the evil ordained for them on account of their iniquities; and even if Moses and Samuel, who were superior prophets, were to raise their voice in the behalf of the transgressors, to avert the punishment of the sword, pestilence, and famine, their prayer wil not avail. To this Divine resolve these words refer—" Cast them out of my sight (presence), and let them go forth. And it shall come to pass, if they say unto thee, Whither shall we go forth?

then thou shalt tell them, Thus saith the Lord: Such as
are for death, to death; and such as are for the sword,
to the sword; and such as are for the famine, to the
famine; and such as are for the captivity, to the captivity." So that all instigators to sin will meet with the
fatal sentence assigned for them, while those who have
been betrayed into sin will have to go into captivity,"
and save nothing but their lives. For the Lord desireth
not to exterminate them altogether. See Jeremiah v.
18, " And even in those days I will not make an end of
you." Nor were the prayers of Moses of any avail when
the Israelites first sinned in worshipping the golden
calf, nor on their giving way to the insinuations of the
spies sent from the desert to search the Land of Promise;
also when the instigators of sin were punished with
death, and the survivors who had yielded to the bad
example were visited with the merited punishment.
The intercession on behalf of the transgressors would
have proved fruitless unless the instigators had been first
removed by sword, pestilence, and famine. But as soon
as the necessary chastisement would be inflicted, and
the remaining sinners would have expiated their sins by
the miseries attending the exile, He will graciously
receive them at the epoch of the restoration, and although
they should not then be purified entirely from their
sins, He will have compassion on them for the sake of
His name, as is said in 1 Samuel xii. 22, " For the Lord
will not forsake His people on account of His great
name, since the Lord has vouchsafed to make you His
people." The same is said in Isaiah xlviii. 9, 10, 11,
" For my name's sake I will defer mine anger, and for my
praise will I refrain for thee, that I cut thee not off.
Behold I refine thee, but not with silver. I have chosen
thee in the furnace of affliction. For mine own sake,
even for mine own sake, will I do it, for why should my

name be polluted, and I will not give my glory unto
another." The re-establishment of the Holy City is an
inducement to exalt us as His own people. See Isaiah
lxii. 1, "For Zion's sake, I will not delay, and for
Jerusalem's sake I will not rest, until her righteousness
shall go forth like a bright light, and her salvation like
a brilliant flame." Nor will the Almighty ever be
unmindful of the covenant made with our ancestors.
See Leviticus xxvi. 44, "And even in the land of their
enemies I will not reject them, nor rebuke them to consume them, and to destroy my covenant with them, for I
am the Lord their God." This promise was subsequently repeated in the prophecy of Ezekiel xvi. 60,
" And I will remember my covenant made with thee in
the days of thy youth, and I will establish unto thee an
everlasting covenant." Again, ibid. ver. 62, "And I
will establish my covenant with thee, and thou shalt
know that I am the Lord, in order that thou mayest
remember me, and feel shame; but thou shalt open thy
mouth no more on account of any degradation of thine,
while I shall forgive thee for all thou hast done, saith the
Lord." This last quotation clearly shews, that, although
we have rebelled in the eyes of the Lord, he, nevertheless, will grant us forgiveness for His own sake, and for
the sake of His covenant.

The promised favour will not be withheld from us,
and we shall have passed through all our ordeals; we
shall, at the appointed time, be planted again on our soil
enjoying the perfect favour of the Almighty, and He
will fulfil the promise given in Jeremiah xxxii. 41,
"And I shall rejoice over them to do good unto them,
and I will in truth plant them in their land, with all my
heart and with all my soul." We have thus had an
opportunity to demonstrate that the threatened evils
will finally be counterbalanced and replaced by benefits.

CHAPTER XXVIII.

Jeremiah xxxi. 15, " Thus saith the Lord, A voice is heard in Ramah, lamentation and bitter weeping, Rachael is weeping for her children, refusing to be comforted on account of her children, because they are not to be found."

The Christians adduce this passage as a prophecy relating to their creed, and as if Jeremiah had here predicted the slaying of the children in Bethlehem, decreed by King Herod. For that king is said to have learnt that in Bethlehem of Judah a child had been born that was intended to be in future a king of the Jews, and as he could not ascertain who the future pretender was and where to be found, he ordered all the children under the age of two years, in and about Bethlehem, to be massacred. To this event the words quoted above refer, as the reader will find by examining Matthew ii.

Refutation.—We have, on a former occasion, shown that the Christians support the doctrine of their religion by sentences dissevered from their contexts and connection, without regard to the concurrence of the entire paragraph from which their quotations are taken. If, according to their suppositions, Rachel, was weeping for the ruthless slaughter committed among the children of Bethlehem Judah, the question arises, why was not Leah represented as the grieving mother, since it was from her that those victims of the tyranny of Herod were descended ? Another question arises: what connection has the bereavement there spoken of with the consoling promises given by the Lord? (Jer. xxxi. 17), "And they shall return from the land of their enemy, and the children shall return to the boundary." The following explanation of the passage will, however, produce

conviction : — The prophet speaks here allegorically.
The children alluded to here are the ten tribes in exile.
These ten tribes are comprised under the designation of
Ephraim (the tribe descended from Rachel); therefore
she is weeping for her children who are banished from
their country by the kings of Assyria.   The ten tribes
were called *Ephraim*, because their first king, after
their defection from the king of Judah, was Jeroboam,
the son of Nebat, from the tribe of Ephraim.   This is
confirmed by the prediction in Jeremiah vii. 15, " And
I shall cast you away from my presence, as I have cast
away all your brethren, the whole seed of Ephraim."

The last Hebrew word in the verse cited in the
beginning of this chapter (Jer. xxxi. 15), is איננו which,
in reality, does not mean they are not (to be found);
but *he* (or *it*, is not to be found), because the singular
relates here to the word עם (people), which is implied;
for when the tribes of Judah and Benjamin returned
from the Babylonian captivity, the ten tribes did not
return with them, nor was the place of their settlement
fully known; for this reason the whole number of the
missing children (or people) is expressed in the singular.
Alluding to the restoration of the whole people in the
days of the Messiah, the prophet Jeremiah continues, in
the name of God (ibid. xxxi. 16, 17), " Refrain thy
voice from weeping, and thine eyes from tears, for thy
work shall be rewarded, saith the Lord.   And they
shall come again from the land of their enemies.   And
there is hope in thine end, saith the Lord, that thy children shall come again to their own border." These verses,
which are all connected with one another, give the most
intelligible proof that the prophet did not allude to the
death of the children of his people, but to their dispersion.   By this interpretation we can make sense of
the 18th verse of the same chapter, " I have heard

Ephraim lonely bemoaning himself thus: Thou hast chastised me, yea, I was chastised as a young bullock untrained to the yoke." Again, ibid. ver. 20, "Is Ephraim my dear son, is he my darling child"? And again, ibid. ver. 21, " Set thee up waymarks, make unto thee high heaps, set thine heart towards the highway, even the way towards which thou wentest; turn again, O Virgin of Israel, turn again towards thy cities." These words refer to the return of the captives of Israel. The ultimate and complete return of the tribes of Israel was also predicted by Ezekiel xxxvii. 19, " Thus saith the Lord God, I will take the stick of Joseph which is in the hand of Ephraim, and the tribes of Israel his fellows, and will put them with him, even with the stick of Judah, and make them one stick, and they shall be one in mine hand." This chapter points out the gathering of the ten tribes, and their re-union with the tribes of Judah and Benjamin, as also their subordination under one king in the days of the Messiah.

We have already, in a former part of this work, noticed that the restoration of the ten tribes was not intended to happen at the return from the captivity of Babylon, and that altogether only 42,000 went back to the Holy Land.

Certain Christians have asserted that the name of Israel, mentioned in particular parts of Scripture which relate to the restoration, is restricted to the ten tribes; but this is not true, for it is written, that Israel shall be remembered by the tribe of Judah. See chap. xxx. 18, " And I shall bring back the captivity of Jacob's tents;" and in the same book, chap. xxiii. 6, we find, " In his days shall Judah be saved and Israel shall dwell in safety." Amos ii., speaks first of the three transgressions of Israel, and then of those of Judah, meaning by those of Israel, the ten tribes. But when the name,

Israel, alone occurs, it includes also the two tribes of Judah and Benjamin, it being the collective name of the whole people.

CHAPTER XXIX.

JEREMIAH xxxi. 31, " Behold the days come, and I will make a new covenant with the house of Israel and with the house of Judah." The Christians assert that the prophet Jeremiah here foretold the giving of a new law for the people of Israel—viz., the Gospel of Jesus of Nazareth.

Refutation.—Scripture does not allude here to the substitution of a new law for the old one, but merely the making of a new covenant, a covenant independent of the law. Thus we find in the history of Phineas (Numbers xv. 12), " Behold I give him my covenant of peace." The covenant thus made could not possibly mean the emission of a new law intended for Phineas alone. In Leviticus xxvi. 42, we meet with a like mention of a covenant, " And I shall remember my covenant with Jacob, my covenant with Isaac, and also my covenant with Abraham will I remember," etc. From this mode of expression, nobody would venture to infer that the Almighty gave a special law to each of the patriarchs. Covenants also are made between man and man. Thus we find, in Genesis xxi. 32, " They two [Abraham and Abimelech] made a covenant with each other." Returning now to the true sense of the verse at the head of this chapter, we find that the Almighty has reserved for Israel the bestowal of a new covenant of protection when they shall be restored to their land, a covenant which, unlike the former one, will never be dissolved. On that account the prophecy continues (in

Jeremiah xxxi. 31 and following verses); that the
future covenant will not be according " to the covenant I made with their fathers in the day that I
took them by the hand to bring them out of the
land of Egypt, which covenant they broke," etc. After
this introduction, the prophet proceeds, " But this
shall be the covenant that I will make with the
house of Israel; I will put my law in their inward
parts, and write it in their hearts, and will be their God,
and they shall be my people." These quotations suffice
to show, that the Almighty had not intended to issue a
new law, but to impress His ancient divine law on their
hearts, that it never should be forgotten throughout all
time. The reader, on referring to chap. xix., will find
that we demonstrated there the perpetuity of the divine
law as it was given on Sinai; consequently the promul-
gation of a new law supplanting the former cannot
possibly take place.

CHAPTER XXX.

HOSEA ii. 11, " And I will cause all her mirth to cease,
her feast days, her new moons, and her Sabbaths,
and all her solemn festivals." From this passage the
Christians argued, that, on the coming of Jesus Christ,
the dispensation of the laws for keeping Sabbaths, new
moons, and festivals, was revoked, and the Lord found
no more any pleasure in Israel's observance of those
days; as was declared in Isaiah i. 14, " Your new moons
and your appointed seasons my soul hateth.'

Refutation.—The prophet here merely announces that
during the severe adversities resulting from the exile, the
rejoicing formerly attendant on the festive seasons, will
cease, and affliction come in its stead. This may be
seen on referring to the accompanying verses, and is

confirmed by the subsequent events. After the desolation of the temple, when the Israelites were prevented from the due observance of their religion, the obligation of the Sabbath and the enjoyments of the festivals were forgotten. See Lamentations ii. 6, " The Lord has caused the solemn days and the Sabbaths to be forgotten in Zion," which took place because " He hath increased to the daughter of Judah, mourning and lamentation." Had it been the intention of the prophets Isaiah and Hosea to predict the cessation of the Sabbaths and festivals, how could they and later prophets so emphatically urge the strict observance of these solemn days? See for instance, Isaiah lvi: Nor does it follow from the expression, " Your new moons and your appointed festivals my soul hateth," that the Almighty was weary of the sacred observances, and desired to have them abrogated; but it is obvious, that the evil-doers of that period assembled at the sanctuary for idolatrous purposes. Their celebration of the Sabbaths and festivals could not be acceptable while they worshipped idols, and not the true, Divine Being, as appears from the context of the first chapter of Isaiah. Were the Christian interpretation true, that the abolition of the sacred days is expressed in the first chapter of Isaiah why then, does the very same book conclude with the following prophecy which is to be fulfilled at the coming of the Messiah? " And it shall come to pass that from one Sabbath to another, and from one new moon to another, all flesh shall come to bow down before Me, saith the Lord." In like manner, Zechariah prophesied in the last chapter of his book, ver. 16, " And it shall come to pass, that every one who is left of all the nations which came up against Jerusalem, shall even go up from year to year to worship the King, the Lord of Hosts, and to keep the feast of tabernacles."

This shows that the festivals are to continue even at the time of the Messiah, when not only the Jews, but also the Gentiles then in existence, will solemnly observe the days of Holy Convocation. We have, moreover, to refer the reader to the nineteenth chapter of this work, where we remarked that even Jesus and his disciples held the Sabbath holy, and that, only several centuries after his death, a pope ordered the first day of the week instead of the seventh to be kept as the day of rest. Thus we prove that this innovation runs counter to the very doctrines inculcated by Jesus.

CHAPTER XXXI.

AMOS ii. 6, " Thus saith the Lord, For three transgressions of Israel, and for four I will not turn away the punishment thereof ; because they sold the righteous and the poor for the value of a pair of shoes."

Some Christian writers have attributed this prophecy to the fate of Jesus, who was sold for thirty pieces of silver; and they have asserted that the fourth transgression being the sale of their righteous One will never be pardoned to Israel, and the consequence of this sin has been our present captivity.

Refutation.—The interpretation betrays a want of due appreciation of the connecting sentences, and the parallel sayings by other prophets. The above verse means, that a casual concurrence of the three crimes— idolatry, incest, and homicide—was not the primary cause of Israel's expulsion from the Holy Land, but the chief cause was the universal depravity that *prevailed throughout the nation*, of which the mercenary leaders of the people gave the iniquitous example. The prophet Amos says, therefore (chap. v. 12), " They persecute the just, they take a bribe, and oppress the poor in the

gate." The word צדיק (righteous) used there has no
reference to the man who leads a godly life, but only to
the man whose cause is unimpeachable before the tribunal of justice, and in whose favour the sentence of the
judges ought to be given. The word צדיק here is of
the same signification as in Exodus xxiii. 8, where it
is said, that the bribe given to the judge, " perverteth
the words of the righteous." The expression, " for they
oppress the needy for a pair of shoes," means, that the
judge, for the most insignificant bribe, turns the scale of
justice, and deprives the poor hapless man of his right,
by pronouncing in favour of the guilty who offers the
bribe. The prophet also inveighs against rich sinners.
Amos viii. 4, " Hear this, O ye who swallow up the
needy, even to make the poor of the land to fail, saying,
When will the new moon be gone that we may sell the
corn, and the Sabbath that we may set forth wheat,
making the ephah small and the shekel great, and falsify-
ing the balances of deceit: that we may buy the poor
for ourselves, and the needy for a pair of shoes, yea, and
sell the refuse of the wheat?" This passage is, in wording and sense, closely related to that of chap. ii., and
both convey the idea of an iniquitous proceeding in
buying and selling. We notice, in the above quotation, that the new moon was then more strictly
observed, and ordinary pursuits were suspended, and,
judging from the admonitions of the prophets, it
would appear that they indulged in convivial and
social entertainments. Compare with this 1 Sam. xx. 5,
beginning with " To-morrow is new moon," and the
second book of Kings ii. 4, " Why goest thou to-day to
him [to the prophet], since it is neither new moon, nor
Sabbath;" as the injustice described in the Book of
Amos relates merely to the mercenary conduct of the
superiors in legal decisions, and to the grovelling dispo-

sition of buyers and sellers in their several dealings, it must be deemed utterly futile to construe those words of Amos as alluding to the history of their Saviour. Besides, if the prophet had intended to make any allusion to Jesus, he ought to have ascribed the transgression to the tribes of Judah and Benjamin, who alone resided in the Holy Land in the days of Jesus, while the ten tribes were scattered among their enemies, and could take no part whatever in the proceedings against Jesus.

Nor can it be asserted that the expression, " And for the fourth transgression will not turn aside the punishment thereof," conveys the announcement, that Israel will never be pardoned for the sale of Jesus, for we find the very same mode of expression applied to the transgressions of Damascus, Gaza, Tyre, Edom, etc., who had no concern whatever in the sale of Jesus. When we read Scripture with proper attention we arrive at the very opposite conviction to the opinion of the Christians respecting our eternal condemnation. See, for instance, the following passages: Psalm cxxx. 8, " And He will redeem Israel from all their sins." Jeremiah xxxiii. 8, " And I will cleanse them from all their iniquities which they committed against me, and I will pardon all their iniquities with which they sinned and rebelled against me." In the same book (chap. l. 20) we read, " In those days and at that time, saith the Lord, the iniquity of Israel shall be sought for, and not be seen; and the sins of Judah, and they shall not be found; for I shall forgive all whom I shall cause to remain."

CHAPTER XXXIII.

Amos v. 2. " The virgin of Israel is fallen: she shall no more rise; she is forsaken upon her land; there are none to raise her up." From this verse it has been argued, that the downfall of Israel is determined for ever, that our captivity will never terminate, and that we have no chance of redemption.

Refutation.—It appears from other words of the same prophet that this prediction does not relate to the perpetual condemnation of Israel; for he says, at the close of his book (chap. ix. 14, 15), " And I will bring back the captivity of my people Israel, and they shall build the waste cities, and inhabit them, and they shall plant vineyards and drink the wine thereof, and they shall also make gardens and gather fruit of them. And I will plant them upon their land, and they shall no more be rooted out of their land which I have given them, saith the Lord thy God." Since a contradiction in the prophetic promises cannot be admitted, the above passages can only be explained in the following manner. The prophet, after having related the evils which await Israel on account of their iniquitous conduct, reproaches them in chap. iv. 6, of the same book, five successive times, " And ye have not returned unto me, saith the Lord."

He continues, in the same chapter 12, " Thus I will do unto thee, O Israel! and because I will do this unto thee, prepare to meet thy God, O Israel"! which implies penitence and good deeds; for then He will do good unto thee and change thy sufferings into happiness, for He is thy God who dispenses evil and good according to your doings." In order to represent Him to the mind as the universal Disposer of Events, the prophet goes on to say (Ibid. iv. 13), "For lo! He that formeth the mountains, and createth the wind, and declareth His purposes unto man, that changes the morning into darkness, and treadeth upon the high places of the earth, the Lord, the God of Hosts, is His name." As Creator of the world He is cognizant of everything, He is the

Maintainer and Supporter of all things, the most distant events He inspects clearly; and He, through His
prophets, acquaints man with His designs. As He makes
light and darkness alternate for the benefit of His
creatures, He makes also the good and the evil to effect
His will among the children of men. Thus He is to be
worshipped under the name of God of Hosts as the
God of the whole Universe. Thus He does, as Supreme
Judge, dispose us to submit to His decrees; and
although we may occasionally suffer in consequence
of our errors and failings, we still feel that His protec-
sion extends over us in strict accordance with His
goodness. This idea is conveyed by the whole tenor of
the fourth chapter of the book of Amos, and forms an
appropriate introduction to chap. v. which begins thus,
"Hear ye the word which I take up against you, even
a lamentation, O house of Israel! The virgin of Israel
is fallen; she shall no more rise," etc. He speaks here
of the virgin of Israel, and announces that the physical
energies of the people are exhausted by the tyranny of
strangers and by the loss of those sent into exile; their
own kings and rulers had no longer power to effect the
repentance required, and therefore a Divine intervention
was necessary to accomplish their restoration. The
prophet therefore, Ibid. v. 3, brings the sad message,—
" For thus saith the Lord, The city that went out by a
thousand shall leave a hundred, and that which went
forth by a hundred shall leave ten to the house of
Israel." According to the prophet, the calamities contingent on the fall of Israel would be fearful, for they
would be cast down by the sword, or decimated by
famine and pestilence, and only a small portion would
be spared for the captivity. Against such national
prostration the prophet points out the sole remedy, consisting in sincere repentance. The terrifying announce-

ment of Israel's destruction is, therefore, entirely miti-
gated by the Divine counsel, Amos v. 4, " Thus saith
the Lord unto Israel, Seek ye me, and ye shall live."
It is well understood that the term *to seek*, means to
become penitent. Isaiah, in lv. 6, 7, uses a similar
expression, " Seek ye the Lord, while he is yet to be
found." He explains there his admonition by saying,
" The wicked man shall leave his way, and the iniquitous
man his thoughts, and return unto the Lord, and He
will have compassion on him." This shows that the
prophet Amos has not predicted the irretrievable ruin
of Israel, but that it may hope to obtain, through
penitence, its restoration and revival, as a nation.

CHAPTER XXXIII.

Micah v. 2, " But thou, Bethlehem Ephratah, though
thou be little among the thousands of Judah, yet out of
thee shall come forth unto me a ruler in Israel, whose
goings forth have been from everlasting." This verse
has been designated by the Christians as confirming their
faith ; and they assert that the prophet meant to say that
their Messiah would be born at Bethlehem, and they
declare that it is impossible for Israel to expect that the
Messiah will be born there, seeing that the city of
Bethlehem has already been destroyed.

Refutation.—For three reasons it is impossible to
vindicate this prophecy in favour of Jesus, setting aside
the numerous other unsubstantial arguments they allege
to prove that he was the true Messiah. First,—The
above scriptural passage has no special allusion to
him. The birth of Jesus in Bethlehem does not
entitle him to the claim of being the Messiah, for
hundreds and thousands of children were born at
Bethlehem, and that casualty did not constitute

them Messiahs. Secondly,—We read there, " From
thee shall come forth unto me a ruler." Now, as to
Jesus of Nazareth, he was by no means a ruler. On
the contrary, the people ruled over him, as is evinced
by the mode of his death. Thirdly,—It is not said that
Bethlehem would be the birth-place of the Messiah, for
we find that the prophet adds there, " And his going
forth shall be of olden times." But the sense of the
verse is this: Thou Bethlehem, although one of the
minor localities among the cities of Judah, from thee a
man shall come forth (*i. e.*, trace his descent back to
thee), who shall be a ruler in Israel, and that same man
will be the King Messiah who will be a descendant of
David who came from Bethlehem. See 1 Sam. xvii. 12,
where he is termed " The son of an Ephrathite from
Bethlehem Judah." The words "since olden times,"
relate to the great space of time elapsed between the
reign of David and the coming of the Messiah. We
must also call the attention of the reader to the chapter
preceding and the passages following the verse on which
we are treating, and it will then be perceived that
the whole prophecy is applied to the terrific convul-
sions predicted to happen at the epoch of the "latter
days." In connection with this prophecy must be read
the announcements of Ezekiel xxxviii. and xxxix., and
Zechariah xiv.: We must not be deterred from the
adoption of this interpretation by the frequent recurrence in Amos iv. of the particle which, by its signification "And now," may be considered to indicate, that
the subject of the prophecy is close at hand, for we
frequently find the same עַתָּה (now) is used merely to
make an event present to the imagination, which event
may, nevertheless, be exceedingly remote from its actual
fulfilment.

See, for instance, Isaiah xliii. 19, " Behold I am doing

a new thing, *now* it shall spring forth." This prophecy
treated of an event to be fulfilled long after the time in
which the prophet lived, ibid. xlix. 19: " For *now* thou
[O land] art straightened, and without inhabitants, but
those who swallow thee up are yet far away." See also
Ezekiel xxxix. 25, " Now I shall bring back the captivity of Jacob, and have mercy upon all the house of
Israel." And ibid. xliii. 9, " *Now* they shall remove
from me their lewdness and the carcasses of their kings."
Thus we have also an allusion to the days of the Messiah
in Micah v. 4, " For now he shall be magnified to the
ends of the earth." In the same sense must be viewed
the concluding words of chap. iv. (in the English version ver. 1 of chap. v.), " Now gather thyself in troops,
O daughter of troops, He hath laid siege against us.
With a rod they shall smite the cheek, even Him who is
the Judge of Israel." The last words are borne out by
Zechariah xiv. 2, " And half of the city shall go into
captivity." For then the judges and leaders of the
people will be exposed to the most mortifying humiliation, in order to purify the remnant of Israel by the
trials of persecution. See ibid. xiii. 9, " And I shall
bring the third part into the fire, and I shall purify
them as silver is purified, and try them as gold is tried,
etc." Having now shown that the verse cited at the
commencement of the chapter must be interpreted in
connection with the preceding passages, we will discuss
it in relation to the subsequent verses. We have in
Micah v. 3, " Therefore, he will give them up until the
time that she who travaileth has given birth." The
meaning of this verse is, that Israel, compared with a
woman in the pain of labour, shall suffer until the
period of the delivery (*i. e.*, redemption), and ultimately
obtain the looked-for consolation. In like terms, says
Jeremiah, in chap. xxx. 7, " And it is a time of trouble

for Israel, and it shall be delivered therefrom." Thus says also Daniel in chap. xii. 1, of his book, "And it shall be a time such as never had been since it became a nation, and at this time thy people shall be rescued." The words in Micah v. 3, "And the remnant of his brethren shall return with the children of Israel," mean the remnant of the brethren of the Messiah—viz., the children of Judah and Benjamin who are scattered among the nations, shall return to their own land, together with the ten tribes of Israel. The word עַל in this verse has the same signification as עִם meaning *together with*. In the same sense it occurs in Exodus xxxv. 22, "And the men came *together with* the woman." This prophecy of Micah is identical with that given in Hosea ii., "And the children of Judah and the children of Israel shall assemble together, and they shall make unto them a chief, and go up from the land." Returning again to Micah v. 4, we further read, "And he shall stand and feed in the strength of the Lord," etc. This must naturally be attributed to the King Messiah, who will be endowed with extraordinary powers. Then "they shall abide," which means they shall then continue in the land in undisturbed peace. With this we compare chap. iv. 4, "And every man shall abide under his vine tree, and under his fig tree, and none shall make him afraid," for the awe of the Messiah shall prevail throughout the whole earth. The following words in Micah v. 5, "And this shall be the time of peace, when Ashur (*i. e.*, Assyria) shall come into our land," are equivalent to the words in Zechariah ix. 13, "And he shall speak of peace to the nations." Ashur represents the enemy who brought terror into our country: such enemies shall, in the times of the Messiah, be utterly impotent. "We shall set up near him seven shepherds and eight principal men." The rendering of עָלָיו "by or near him," is justified by the occurrence of the same Hebrew word in that verse in Numbers ii. 20, " *And near him*, or *together with him*, in the tribe of Manasseh."

The words *shepherds* and *principal men* (or princes of men) relate to the leaders who will be appointed by the King Messiah. The numbers " seven and eight must be taken as indefinite signs of number, meaning only *many*, as we find in Ecclesiates, " Give a portion unto seven and also unto eight." The word *shepherds* (*i. e.*, pastors) is synonymous with principal men (or, literally, princes of men), and means therefore overseers of the people. Micah, chap. v. 5, 6, continues, " And they shall lay waste the land of Ashur with the sword."

The word וְרָעוּ (and they lay waste) occurs in the same sense in Jeremiah xi. 16, " And they shall break his branches"; and Ibid. ii. 16, " And they *shall break* the crown of thy head." Micah then speaks of the land of Nimrod, which was Babel, as is clear from Genesis x. 10, " And the beginning of his kingdom was Babel." Thus the Messiah shall deliver us from the Assyrians when they come into our land, and when they break in upon our borders. The King Messiah will rescue us from the power of arbitrary tyrants, so that we shall no more be molested by invading enemies. Ashur and Babel are selected by Micah as examples of Israel's enemies, because those two powers destroyed the Holy Land. The prophet then gives the consolation, Micah v. 7, " And the remnant of Jacob shall be in the midst of many nations as dew from the Lord, as the showers upon the grass, that tarrieth not for man, nor waiteth for the Son of Man." This verse means that those who escape the tyranny of the enemies shall be placed under the special protection of the Almighty, and no human power shall prevail against the remnant of Israel. As the descent of dew is beyond human influence, so Israel shall be beyond the reach of human

influence. The prophet then introduces a second comparison and says, " And the remnant of Jacob shall be
among the Gentiles in the midst of many people, as a
lion among the beasts of the forest." Israel is thereby
compared with the most powerful creature unto which
all other animals are inferior, and therefore he resumes,
Micah v. 9, " Thine hand shall be exalted above thine
adversaries, and all thine enemies shall be cut off."
This prophecy is in connection with the following:
Micah v. 10, " And I will cut off thy horses out of the
midst of thee, and I will destroy thy chariots, and I
will cut off the cities of thy land, and throw down all
thy strongholds." For at that period Israel will attain
a supremacy which will render war needless, and all
hostile preparation will be superseded by universal
peace. Hence Zechariah says, chap. ii. 4, "And Jerusalem shall be inhabited as a town without walls."

The whole tendency of the prophecies we have now
treated on, shows evidently that unfulfilled events are
spoken of relating to the time of our Messiah when we
shall be gathered together to the Holy Land, and when,
after the overthrow of the opposing powers, universal
peace shall reign on earth. No man can argue that
those promises were fulfilled by Jesus of Nazareth, or
his disciples. For the founders of the Christian religion
passed their lives in unmitigated trouble, nor can it be
asserted that an allusion to the Eternal God is implied
by, " And his coming forth is from ancient time from
the days of old." We cannot possibly attribute to the
Infinite Being a "coming forth"; moreover, we shall
have occasion to show, from our refutation of the
Gospels, the total impropriety of giving Jesus the title
of God, and from what we have advanced hitherto, it is
quite evident that Jesus was just as far from being a
Messiah, as he was from being a Divinity.

CHAPTER XXXIV.

HAGGAI ii. 9, " The glory of this latter house shall be greater than that of the former, saith the Lord of Hosts, and in this place will I give peace, saith the Lord of Hosts." Christians have raised the question, In what did the glory of the latter house consist, seeing that the Jews, during the time of the first temple, were independent, and during that of the second temple they were vassals of the Persians, Syrians, and Romans, the last of whom ultimately destroyed the temple and banished the Jews. They therefore interpret it to signify that the existence of Jesus, during the time of the second temple, constituted its glory.

Refutation.—The word כבוד (glory) has two significations. In the first place, it means worldly distinction and opulence. In this meaning, we find it in Genesis xxxi. 1: " And from what belongeth unto our father, he has gotten all this הכבוד (wealth)." The same is meant in Proverbs iii. 16, " In his left hand are riches and *glory*." In the second sense, כבוד means the real or spiritual distinction. For instance, in 1 Samuel iv. 21, we have " the glory hath departed from Israel." See also Psalm lxxxv. 9, " That glory may dwell in our land"; and Zechariah ii. 5, " And for glory I shall be in the midst of her." Some commentators have assigned this second sense to the passage under consideration, and they say that the superior glory of the second temple consisted in the entire absence of idolatry; some have said that the word כבוד relates to the first or fictitious kind of glory, because Herod is said to have decorated the temple in the most gorgeous style. But such an interpretation is set aside by the non-fulfilment of Haggai's prophecy (chap. ii. 9), " And in that place

will I give peace, saith the Lord of Hosts." For during
the existence of the second temple no peace reigned in
the land; but according to Daniel, "the street and the
entrenchment were to be built amidst the troubles of the
times." Much less can it be said that the glory of the
temple was reserved for the days of Herod, for from his
house contention never departed, and after his death sufferings never ceased with the Jews, until their final overthrow. Nor can we admit that the glory of the second temple
consisted in its longer duration—a point discussed in the
Talmud (Baba Bathra), for Scripture makes no mention
of the glory being attributable to the length of the time
during which the temple was constructed or lasted.
And even if the duration of the second temple had exceeded by double the time that of the first temple, the
word *glory* could not have been assigned to this distinction. Besides this, we must also notice that the peace
promised to reign in the latter times, did by no means
prevail during the existence of the second temple. The
real object of the prophecy under consideration is to
show, that the human labour displayed in rearing the
second temple was esteemed but insignificant by the
Almighty, for the prophet announces a complete change
of heaven and earth. See ibid. ii. 6, "For thus saith
the Lord of Hosts, There is one thing yet which is a
little matter with me, that I shake the heavens and the
earth, and the sea and the dry land." Then also will
the prophecy be fulfilled, "and the valuable things of
all nations shall come" (as contributions to the glory of
the house of God). Hitherto such an event has not
yet come to pass; but it will take place when all the
nations of the earth, who are adverse to the Jews (and
who are termed in Scripture, Gog and Magog), shall be
subjugated and pacified. See Ezekiel xxxviii. 19, 20,
"In my jealousy, and in the fire of my wrath have I

spoken, Surely in that day there shall be a great shaking in the land of Israel: so that the fishes of the sea and the fowls of the heaven, and the beasts of the field, and all the creeping things that creep upon the earth, and all the men that are on the face of the earth, shall shake at my presence," etc. The restoration of the latter temple has, on that account, been brought into connection with the battle of Gog and Magog (i, e., the ultimate cessation of all warfare). At that time the temple will be erected in surpassing splendour, and testifying all is the Lord's according to the expression by Haggai, that " the gold and the silver belong unto Him." At that time the true glory of the house of God will be made manifest, and will excel that of the preceding temple. The Shechinah (the Divine presence) will re-appear there, and there everlasting peace will take up its abode. To this alludes Haggai, by saying at the end of his book, chap. ii., v. 21, 22, " Speak to Zerubbabel, governor of Judah, saying, I will shake the heaven and the earth; and I will overthrow the throne of kingdoms, and I will destroy the strength of the kingdoms of the heathen, and I will overthrow the chariots and those who ride in them: and the horses and their riders shall come down, every one by the sword of the brother." A similar vision seen by the prophet Zechariah, is also unconnected with the second temple, but relates to events to come in the latter days; for after fearful collisions of the last hostile kingdoms, the Messiah, descendant of Zerubbabel, will come, and He will be the perfection of all rulers. Hence Haggai says, in the concluding words of his book, chap. ii. 23, " And I will make thee—Zerubbabel—as a signet, for I have chosen thee, says the Lord of Hosts." The fulfilment was not to take place in the immediate times of Zerubbabel, for He remained during all His life in the same position as Governor of Israel, without being ever raised to that exalted rank of which Haggai speaks.

But we find in Scripture similar promises, which were to be accomplished among a later posterity. Thus, for instance, the Almighty said to Abraham, when He made a covenant with him to give him the Land of Canaan as an inheritance (Genesis xv. 7), " I am the Lord who hath brought thee out of Ur of the Chaldeans to give thee this land for an inheritance."

This prediction undoubtedly related merely to the posterity of Abraham, as is set forth in the very same chapter (v. 18), " In that day the Lord made a covenant with Abraham, saying, Unto thy seed have I given this land," etc. We must, therefore, of necessity explain the prophecy of Haggai as referring to the third temple, of which Ezekiel, in chap. xl. and in subsequent passages, *et passim*, has given such an elaborate and distinct description. He has given us the express announcement that the Divine presence would reveal itself there in its fullest glory. See Ezekiel xliii. 4—7, " And the glory of the Lord came into the house by the way of the gate which faces the east. So the spirit took me up and brought me into the inner court, and behold the glory of the Lord filled the house. And I heard one who was speaking unto me, and a man stood by me. And he said unto me, Son of Man, The place of my throne and the place of the soles of my feet where I will dwell in the midst of the children of Israel for ever, the house of Israel shall no more defile my Holy name," etc. This prevalence of universal peace will form the superior glory of the latter temple. The inferiority of the second temple may also be argued from the absence of the Holy ark, of the mercy seat, of the Urim and Thummim, etc.; but in the third temple, which is to be raised at a future day, all the tokens of Divine glory will be restored and serve as a pledge for the endurance of perpetual peace. Hence the prophet Haggai says, "And in this place will I grant peace, saith the Lord of Hosts." Utterly untenable is also the assertion of the Christians, that the glory of the second temple consisted in the event of the birth of Jesus. For, when he was born, the temple was fast approaching its dissolution and lacked that peace expressly promised. Besides this, Jesus himself admitted, that his object was not to afford peace; for he says in Matthew x. 34, " Think not that I am come to send peace on earth, I came not to send peace, but a sword." This forms a positive evidence that the promise of universal peace remains still to be accomplished.

CHAPTER XXXV.

ZECH. ix. 9, " Rejoice very much, O daughter of Zion. Shout, O daughter of Jerusalem. Behold thy king cometh unto thee; He is just and has been saved; He is poor and riding on an ass." On the authority of St. Matthew xxi. 5, the Christians maintain that the prophet, on pronouncing this prediction, had in view the entrance of Jesus into Jerusalem on the back of an ass.

Refutation.—The whole prophecy from which the above portion is taken, bears internal evidence to the fallacy of this interpretation; for the prophet speaks solely of the ingathering of Israel and of the advent of the Messiah in the latter days. To arrive at this truth, the verse must be read in its relation with the antecedent and subsequent verses. Refer to the commencement of Zech. ix. 1, where we read, " The burden of the word of the Lord upon the land of Hadrach and Damascus, his resting place." The letter ב occurring in this verse

in the word בְּאֶרֶץ means *upon*, concerning, or relating
to. It occurs in the same sense in Isaiah xxi. 13, " The
burden *upon* Arabia," and the same meaning has the בּ in
many other passages of Scripture.

The lands of Hadrach and Damascus shall, in the time
of the Messiah, be united with the land of Israel, and be
termed the resting-place of the Divine glory, just as the
ancient and more limited country of Israel was designated the resting-place of the Divine Glory.

In this mode, the Psalmist says in Psalm xcv. 11,
" Unto whom I sware in my wrath, they should not
enter into my rest;" or, as we find this expression more
largely expanded in Deuteronomy xi. 12, it is the land
" which the Lord thy God inquireth after; the eyes of
the Lord thy God are continually upon it."   Now, in
the times of the Messiah, the eyes of the Lord will rest
favourably on the lands of Hadrach and Damascus,
because all worship displeasing to the Divine Being will
give way to the acknowledgement of pure truth.   In the
same way, many will also, in the other countries adjacent
to our ancient fatherland, be incorporated in the possession of the House of Jacob, and according to the
expression of Zechariah ix. 1, " The eye of man shall
be directed unto the Lord, as the eyes of all the tribes
of Israel shall be towards the Lord; for all nations will
say unto the men of Judea, " We will go with you, for
we have heard that God is among you."   The words of
Jeremiah xxiii. 17 fully bear upon this subject, " Now
they say unto my scorners, the Lord hath said, *Ye shall
have peace,* " etc.

Zech. ix. 2, " Also Hamath borders thereon, and also
Tyre and Zidon, yet they were wise."   Those towns,
though considered as foreign countries (See Amos vi. 2),
will, in future, form only one empire with that of Israel.
As to the wisdom of Tyre and Zidon, it is often alluded

to by the prophets, as may be seen in Ezekiel xxviii. Such wisdom, available in worldly matters, will not prove of advantage against the supremacy of Israel. For, although " Tyre did build herself a strong-hold and heaped up silver as the dust, and fine gold as the mire of the streets, the Lord will cause her to grow poor." Zech. ix. 3. In rendering the words וְרִשָּׁנָה, " He will cause her to grow poor," we are guided by the terms occurring in 1 Samuel ii. 7, " The Lord maketh poor and maketh rich." Zechariah ix. 4, further says, "And He will smite her power in the sea, and she shall be devoured with fire." This shows that temporal means will be utterly disregarded, and that confidence in perishable substance will be lost with the disappearance of the substance itself. Grand structures shall become insignificant, the towers of refuge and the walls of protection shall be demolished, and devouring fire shall demonstrate that man can never raise a bulwark against the will of the Lord, and that he can only fortify himself with the firmness of faith.

Again, we read in Zechariah ix. 5, " Ashkelon shall see it and fear, and also Gaza be much afraid; and Ekron too, for He hath put to shame her trust." Terror shall emanate from the consciousness of their former unworthiness, and terror shall be followed by humiliation and desolation, as the natural consequences of depraved conduct. Therefore Zechariah says in the same chapter, ver. 6, " The outcasts shall dwell in Ashdod, and I will cut off the glory of the Philistines, and I will take away the guilt of blood out of his mouth, and his abominations from between his teeth." All this part, which is introductory to the verse at the heading of this chapter, shows that a total conversion from ungodly feelings and practices will take place in the countries adjacent to Palestine, and that they will be spared only to become faithful followers of our God, and like the Jebusite of former days, to be subjected to Israel. The various nationalities will then be joined into one faithful body; all will serve with equal ardour the God of Israel, saying in the words of Zechariah viii. 23, " We will go with you, for we have heard that God is with you." The multitude of worshippers will abundantly increase so that the land of Israel will not be able to contain them, and therefore the boundary will, according to Divine promise, be enlarged, and Palestine extend in proportion as the faith of the followers of Judaism shall spread; for to speak with Isaiah liv. 1, " The children of the desolate wife are greater than the children of the married wife," that is to say, the children returning from captivity will far exceed those who once left their native land. Hence Isaiah says, ibid. ver. 2, " Enlarge the place of thy tent, and let them stretch forth the curtains of thine habitations : spare not, lengthen thy cords, and strengthen thy stakes; for thou shalt spread to the right and the left," etc. Jeremiah, too, affords a picture of the future enlargement of Jerusalem. See chap. xxxi. 38, " Behold days shall come, saith the Lord, and the city shall be built unto the Lord from the tower of Hananeel to the gate of the corner," etc., and he concludes this prediction with the assurance, " it shall not be destroyed, nor shall it ever be broken down." As at that time the temple of the Lord will consequently be larger than it had been in former days, as is testified by Ezekiel xl. and in subsequent parts. The peace which will at that time rule in Palestine will be fairly established, so that no man shall have to apprehend any danger from abroad. Zechariah therefore predicts, chap. ix. 8, " I will set up an army for my house, of those who proceed towards it, of those who return from it; and no oppressor shall move against them any more, for now I have seen it with mine eyes." With this prophecy we may compare Zechariah ii. 5, " For I, saith the Lord, will be unto her a protecting wall of fire round about." The expression, "for now I have seen it with mine eyes," relates to the time of the fulfilment, when the Jews will find relief from all tribulation; and then the Lord, who had turned his countenance from us, will again look upon us in mercy. In the same sense, we find in Exodus ii. 25, " And God saw the children of Israel," by which is meant, " He looked upon them graciously." This forms a suitable introduction to the words, " Rejoice very much, O daughter of Zion, shout, O daughter of Jerusalem." The occasion for such joy is afforded by the concurrence of blissful events promised to happen in the days of the Messiah. Zion or Jerusalem is here addressed, individually, as the most important part of the Holy Land. Then He says, " Behold, thy King cometh unto thee ; He is righteous, and is saved;" for the King Messiah will be a righteous Man; and, through his righteousness He will be saved from the destructive attacks of his assailants.

The Christians have perverted the sense of נוֹשָׁע he is saved, and have rendered it as if it were מֹשִׁיעַ a Saviour. The authors of the English version have, with consistent faithfulness, taken an opportunity for perverting the sense by translating it ambiguously, and with more ingenuity than honesty, " and having salvation," instead of " having been saved." Such subterfuges do not strengthen, however, the cause of religion. We must notice, at the same time, that the word מֹשִׁיעַ would not aid their interpretation, for we find this word also in the passive sense, for instance, וְעָלוּ מוֹשִׁיעִים וכו' and "the saved ones shall go up to judge the mount of Esau." The word עָנִי, occurring in the verse at the beginning of this chapter, means *meek* and *modest*. A similar description of the character of the Messiah is given in Isaiah xlii. 2, " He shall not cry aloud and not raise himself up, and not make his voice to be heard abroad; a feeble reed He shall not break," etc.   The appearance of the Messiah on the back of an ass is to indicate his disdain of all vain display, and also that, at the time of his advent, the use of horses for battle will no longer be required.   This is amplified in the announcement, " And I will cut off the chariots from Ephraim and the horses from Jerusalem, and the bow of warfare shall be cut off."   Thus is also the message given by Hosea ii. 18, " And the bow and the sword I will break from the land; and I shall cause them to lie down in security."

Still more forcibly this is predicted in Isaiah ii. 4, "And they shall beat their swords into ploughshares and their spears into pruning hooks.   Nation shall no more lift up the sword against nation, and they shall no more learn the art of war."   For this reason Zechariah says, "And He shall speak peace unto the nations." This shows again that the Messiah will conciliate hostile nations, according to Daniel vii. 27, " All rulers serve Him and obey Him."   Thus Zechariah ix. 10, says, " And His dominion shall be from sea to sea, and from the rivers to the ends of the earth."   Then the Prophet continues (chap. ix. 11), " Thou also who art in the blood of thy covenant, I have sent thy prisoners from the waterless pit."

In these words he addresses Israel, who will be saved through the blood of Abraham's covenant, to which we have adhered in spite of all temptation during the captivity, which is denominated a pit without water.   We come now to verse 12, of the same chapter, " Turn ye to the stronghold, ye prisoners of hope, even to-day do I declare, that I will render double unto thee."   This

may be interpreted in the following manner:—Israel,
ye prisoners, ever hopeful of your ultimate salvation, ye
shall return to God, who is the stronghold and the tower
of strength to those who trust in Him, for to-day I tell
you again, you shall receive a double portion of all joys
lost during the toils of your captivity; and thus I repeat
the promise conveyed to you through the prophet Isaiah
(chap. lx. 17), " Instead of the silver I shall bring gold,"
etc.; and again (chap. lxi. 7), " For your shame, ye
shall have double, and in return for confusion, they shall
rejoice in their portion; therefore, in their land they
shall possess the double," etc.

The object of the word, "double," is merely to express
that God will abundantly bestow his gracious favours:
hence the word מִשְׁנֶי is not confined to the literal sense
of *twice* or *twofold.* Thus we have in Jeremiah xvii. 18,
" And I will destroy them with *double* destruction."
Thus the word " double" signifies merely a frequent
recurrence of the same thing. In chap. ix. 13, Zechariah
continues, " For I have bent thy way, O Judah, towards
me. I have filled the bow, O Ephraim, and raised thy
sons, O Zion, against thy sons, O Javan (*i.e.* Greece),
and made thee as the sword of a mighty man."

Here he alludes to the days of the Messiah when all
Judah and Ephraim, that is to say, all Israel, will return
to their land. For we have already shown, in a former
part, that, at the return from Babylon, only a small
portion of the Jews again settled in their own country.
Now, in the time of the Messiah, *all* will take their
abode in the land of their inheritance, and they will be
no more divided into two kingdoms. This may be
fully seen on referring to Ezekiel xxxvii. The prophet
there tells us, that the children of Zion will prevail over
the children of Javan.

Sometimes we find in Scripture Gog and Magog as

expressive of the opponents of the Jews, for both Javan
and Magog appear in the genealogical enumeration of
nations in Genesis x. 1, 2, as brethren and as sons of
Japheth.

Having now shown that this chapter affords no
foundation for the claims of Jesus to be the Messiah,
since in his days those significant predictions remained
altogether unfulfilled, we proceed to sum up the points
we have discussed.

1. In the days of the Messiah, will take place the
gathering of Judah and Ephraim, that is, of all Israel.

2. Many nations will join Israel as the people of the
Lord.

3. Gog and Magog, that is, the powers opposing
Israel, will be overthrown.

4. Undisturbed peace will then reign throughout the
world.

5. The King Messiah will have dominion over all the
world.

On the other hand, we have shewn that, in the days
of Jesus, not one of those favourable events occurred,
but indeed the reverse took place. The King Messiah
is to declare cessation of warfare and permanent peace,
while Jesus the Nazarene says, in Matthew x. 34,
" Think not that I am come to send peace on earth; I
come not to send peace, but the sword."

The true Messiah is to have his dominion from sea to
sea and from the river to the ends of the earth; but Jesus,
the Nazarene, had no worldly power over the smallest
territory; for he says in Matthew xx. 28, " The Son of
Man (*i.e.* Jesus) came not to be served, but to serve,"
etc. From all this it is obvious that the Christians have
no foundation on which to establish their dogma of a
Messiah.

CHAPTER XXXVI.

ZECHARIAH xii. 10, "And I will pour upon the house of David and upon the inhabitants of Jerusalem the spirit of grace and supplications, and they shall look up to me whom they have pierced, and they shall mourn for him as in the mourning for an only son, and be in bitterness for him, as is the bitterness for the first-born."

The Christians cite this verse as a testimony of the regret which Israel will feel at a future time for having pierced and slain Jesus, who combined human and Divine nature; therefore the Israelites will mourn for him, as one mourns for an only son.

Refutation.—On an unprejudiced perusal of the whole prophecy, of which the above forms part, our Christian brethren would have perceived that the contents are solely referable to the confusion of empires during the latter days, or, as we are accustomed to call that era, the appearance and fall of Gog and Magog. We will elucidate this by taking an attentive view of the entire chapter. It commences with the warning, "Behold, I will make Jerusalem a cup of trembling unto all the people round about." "The cup of trembling" means the confusion and terror which will seize all nations at that period, "and also Judah who shall be engaged in the siege against Jerusalem." For the foreign nations invading the Holy Land, in order to conquer its capital, will coerce and compel the children of Judah to assist in the siege of Jerusalem. In that time, says Zechariah xii. 3, "I will make Jerusalem a burdensome stone for all people; all that burthen themselves with it shall be cut in pieces, though all the people of the earth be gathered together against it." The ill fate formerly attending the warfare of the Jews will now befall the Gentiles; for the prophet continues, " In that day, saith the Lord, I will smite every horse with terror, and his rider with madness, and I will open mine eyes upon the house of Judah, and I will smite every horse of the nations with blindness."   This supernatural intervention of the Almighty will bring the Jewish leaders to reason, on seeing the extraordinary power displayed in behalf of Jerusalem. "And the governors of Judah shall say in their heart, The inhabitants of Jerusalem are too strong for me, through the Lord their God." The leaders of Judah will then no longer side with the devourers of their people, but will pour out their wrath on the enemies of the Jews, for the Almighty has declared, Ibid. v. 6," In that day will I make the governors of Judah like a hearth of fire among the wood, and like a torch of fire in a sheaf; and they shall devour all the people round about, on the right hand and on the left, and Jerusalem shall be inhabited again in her own place, even in Jerusalem."   For during the troubles of our captivity, the ancient city of the Lord has become like an exile from her own soil; in the future, however, she will be restored to herself again, in her pristine glory.   The Lord will then show mercy even to those, who, in their forgetfulness of duty and national affection, have risen against the metropolis of that people and their faith; and He will spare the Jews who first assisted in the siege, as He will spare the inhabitants of Jerusalem who suffered from the siege. The prophet therefore says, " The Lord also shall save the tents of Judah first, that the inhabitants of Jerusalem may not magnify themselves against Judah." The success attending the cause of the Jews will be granted in such a manner as not to disturb the unanimity and brotherly feeling so indispensably requisite for the restoration of our people. The Jews will, at that time, be invested

with new vigour: " And he that is feeble among them
at that day shall be as David;" that is to say, the
weakest among the Jews shall be distinguished as a
hero, and be equal in courage to David. " And the
house of David shall be godly as a messenger of the
Lord before them." The Messiah himself will act as a
messenger of the Lord, and in his own person will lead
his subjects to battle against the hostile nations. Now
the prophet proceeds by saying, Ibid. chapter xii. 9, 10,
"And it shall come to pass in that day, that I will seek to
destroy all nations that come against Jerusalem. And
I will pour upon the house of David, and upon the
inhabitants of Jerusalem, the spirit of grace and of
supplications, and they shall look upon me whom they
have pierced," etc.

The prophet having, in this manner, alluded to the
great superiority of the Jews in the latter days, says
now, that they will look to him in humility and contrition, on account of those who have been pierced and
killed in war. The Jews will be so assured of the
Divine assistance in their restoration, that they will
feel afflicted on account of those who shall become the
first victims of their warfare with the Gentiles. Thus
Joshua and the Israelites were afflicted when first
beaten by the inhabitants of Ai. That leader of the
Israelites then exclaimed, (Joshua vii. 7), " Wherefore
hast thou caused this people to pass over the Jordan,"
etc. And again (ver. 8), " O Lord, what shall I say, after
Israel have turned their backs before their enemies"?
In the same manner, the people shall, in the days
of the Messiah, look up in contrition to God, and im-
plore pardon on account of their having pierced (*i. e.*,
destroyed) the innocent. The term את אשר is equal to
the term בעבור on *account of*, or *because*, and does not
mean "*whom*," as it has been generally rendered. In

Ezekiel xxxvi. 27, we have את אשר in the same sense, "And I shall do it *on account* of your walking (or because ye shall walk) in my statutes." The interest in the life of a fellow-man will be deeply felt during the latter thirty days that the Jews shall mourn for any man slain in the battle, as one is who mourns for the loss of an only son, and they shall be in bitter grief for him, as if it were for a first-born child. The comparison, with the loss of a first-born son, gives, in a few words, a picture of the intensity of grief. The subsequent comparison with the mourning of Hadadrimmon, we cannot further explain, there being no mention on record of the cause and circumstances of that mourning. The prophet then shows how each family in Israel will partake in the affliction caused by the report of the fallen in war; and as it is a well-known fact, that the mournful tidings vibrate more keenly in the hearts of feeling women, than in the hearts of interested men, the prophet draws a distinguishing line between the mourning of the two sexes; and, speaking of the high families of Israel, he says, "And the land shall mourn, each family separately, the family of the house of David separately, their wives separately," etc. The description given here of the belligerent parties, and of the result of their actions near and at Jerusalem, evidently relates to a time not yet recorded in the pages of history. The Christians have therefore no basis, on which to rest their religious theory of the death of Jesus. Were there only a shadow of truth in their pretension, that the grief predicted by the prophet was to emanate from the mode in which Jesus met with his end on the cross, the prophecy ought to be worded, "And they will mourn *for me*, and be in bitterness *for me*." The fallacy of the assertions of the Christians, with regard to this prophecy, is not only to be proved from this detached part, but is also to be considered from what we demonstrated in the preceding parts. See, for example, chap. x., where we have treated on the inconsistency of considering Jesus as the Messiah, and of the absolute impossibility of acknowledging him as the Godhead.

CHAPTER XXXVII.

ZECHARIAH xiii. 7, "Awake, O sword, against my shepherd, and against the man who is my fellow, saith the Lord of Hosts; smite the shepherd, and the sheep shall be scattered, and I will turn my hand against the little ones."

According to the opinion of the Christians, the prophet meant Jesus by the "Man who is my fellow," and the disciples of Jesus by the expression, "Smite the shepherd and the sheep shall be scattered." This assertion rests on what we read in St. Mark xiv. 27.

Refutation.—The explanation given by the Christians to the above passage, is devoid of truth. The context to which the above verse belongs, relates exclusively to the downfall of the kings of Palestine and to the dispersion of Israel. Simultaneously with that event the destruction of idolators was to take place, and the righteous alone were to be saved from utter annihilation. The command given to the sword to "smite the shepherd who is my fellow," merely signifies that those kings shall be punished who oppress the Jews, and who, in their delusion, believe they are doing a godly work in persecuting a religious people, and, in their inordinate conceit, imagine that they are the vicars and associates of the Almighty, whereas in the minds of those men the serpent of temptation whispers, as it did to our first parents, "And ye shall be like unto God, knowing good and evil."

This conceit we have met with among the rulers in Asia and Africa, where enlightenment has made less rapid strides than in Europe; and on that account humiliation is most needful to the uninstructed in order to teach them to know the littleness of pride and the superiority of meekness. " Smite the shepherd and the sheep shall be scattered." This passage indicates that the rulers of the Gentiles, who boast of their iniquitous government, shall be overthrown; and, from their fall, the deliverance of Israel will arise. There are many shepherds that must be struck prior to Israel's entire deliverance ; for, unlike the ancient captivity in Egypt, the Jews are now scattered throughout numerous states and kingdoms. The return of our people to the inheritance of their fathers will, therefore, not take place in one collected body, but in numerous detached hosts. The term וּתְפוּצִין of the above passage occurs also in the form of a noun in Isaiah xi. 12, " And he shall gather the *dispersed* (נְפֻצוֹת) of Judah. " And I will turn my hand against the little ones." This passage likewise alludes to the subdued and powerless princes who shall be visited with humiliation according to their demerits. The Almighty will lend His help to those who have been the victims of malice. The inhabitants of the earth shall be awfully roused from their delusion, obeying the call of Isaiah, who says (chap. xxxiv. 1, 2), " Come near, ye nations, and listen, for the Lord will execute judgment on the cruel persecutors of His people."

CHAPTER XXXVIII.

MALACHI i. 11, " For from the rising of the sun to the going down of the same, my name is great among the Gentiles ; and in every place incense is offered up unto

my name, and a pure offering, saith the Lord of Hosts."
The Christians maintain that this prophecy bears upon
their faith, which has been so extensively diffused in the
world.

Refutation.—We do not discover in these words of
Malachi any allusion to the faith of Christianity, which
had no existence at the era of the prophet.   We know
well that Haggai, Zechariah, and Malachi, were contemporaneous, and lived about three hundred years
anterior to Jesus.   At the time of the last prophet, the
Gentiles were worshippers of the heavenly constellations,
and of idols representing those constellations.   It was
not, however, the intention of Malachi to expatiate on
the abominations of Idolatry, but he merely delivered a
reproof to the sinners of Israel who offered up loathsome
sacrifices, and thereby profaned the name of the
Almighty.   Hence he says (chap. i. 12), "But ye are
profaning it by saying, The table of the Lord is polluted,
and the fruit thereof, even the meat, is contemptible."
Subsequently the prophet reproaches the people, and
says, " And ye *bring an offering* which has been stolen,
and the lame and the sick."   Whoever reads with
attention the lesson of the prophet, will find that he
rebukes the Israelites for their having acted worse in
their sacrifices to God, than the Gentiles towards their
idols."   In this repreof he accords with Ezekiel v. 7,
"And ye have not dealt in the fashion of the Gentiles
that are around you."   While the Israelites neglected
to imitate what was laudable in the worship of the
Gentiles, they blindly followed their reprehensible practices, and, therefore, Ezekiel blames his people by saying
(chap. xi. 12), " In my statutes ye have not walked,
and after my judgments ye have not acted, but ye have
acted after the customs of the Gentiles that are around
you."   " And in every place incense is offered up unto

my name." Hereby a comparison is made between the sordidness in the sacrifices of the Israelites and the greater liberality of the idolators in their offerings to their false gods. For if the latter had been asked to whom they paid those tokens of reverence, they would have answered, to a Divine Power that governs the destinies of mankind, and, therefore, they were filled with awe and devotion, in spite of all their errors. But although those Gentiles had not a pure and an elevated idea of the Supreme Being, they were able to act agreeably to his revealed will; and, therefore, the prophet was justified in declaring in the name of the Lòrd, " For my name is great among the Gentiles." But since a worship cannot be approved in which a creature is put on an equality with the Creator, the Gentiles would only find favour by acquiescing in the sublime belief of an omnipresent and omnipotent Deity; for such a belief alone affords real gratification to the reasoning mind and to the wishful heart. Hence Malachi iii. 4, goes on to say, " And the sacrifices of Judah and Jerusalem shall be pleasant unto the Lord as in days of old, and in former years." The means of finding favour in the eyes of the Almighty will only then increase when religious obstacles shall be removed. The favour of the Lord is therefore contingent on the purity of His worshipper, consequently Malachi declares (chap. iii. 3), " And he shall sit as a refiner and as a purifier of silver; and He shall purify the sons of Levi, and purge them as gold and silver, that they may offer unto the Lord an offering in righteousness." It is natural, that the sons of Levi and the priests should be prominently noticed in this prophecy, for those spiritual guides of the people were the very men who were designated " as the despisers of my name." Those who lead the way to sin must also by their example naturally be the first to meet with punishment.

The verse which heads this chapter has a beautiful parallel in Psalm cxiii. 3, " From the rising of the sun to the going down of the same, the name of the Lord is praised. The Lord is high above all nations." It could not be said, that David included all contemporaneous Gentile nations in the adoration of the God of Israel; and that he considered all the heathen to be believers in the same Deity. For he condemns the practices in the worship of the heathen in the very same book, saying (Psalm cxv. 4—9), " Their idols are of gold and of silver, the works of the hands of man; they have mouths and speak not, they have eyes and see not, they have ears and hear not, they have noses and smell not, they have hands and feel not, feet and walk not, they speak not with their throats. Like unto them are those that make them, yea, all those that trust in them. Let Israel trust in the Lord, He is their shield and their help." Nearly the same terms are used in Psalm cxxxv. 19. We see, then, that the Gentiles, with all their errors, wished to adore a First Cause of all existence; yet the Psalmist, as well as the prophet spoken of above, deemed the faith and the observances of Israel as those strongholds by which the mind of man obtains true eminence and consolation; consequently there is not the slightest motive to forsake the path which our religion points out to its followers, and to adopt a faith so manifestly at variance with our ancient law.

CHAPTER XXXIX.

MALACHI, at the end of the book, saith, " Behold, I will send you the prophet Elijah before the coming of the great and awful day."

It has been asserted by Christian interpreters of this

passage, that we Jews vainly expect the fulfilment of
this prediction, because it has already been realized in
the person of John the Baptist, who in spirit was equal
to Elijah; it being said in Matthew ii. 10, that Jesus
declared that John was the Elijah predicted by Malachi.
They particularly cite chap. xvii. of Matthew, where
Jesus is made to affirm (ver. 12 and 13) " But I say
unto you that Elijah is come already, and they know
him not, but have done to him whatever they listed."
Thus his disciples were led to believe that Elijah and
John were identical in the above prophecy.

Refutation.—How can they deny the personal identity
of the Prophet, mentioned in chap. iv. 5? Who would
venture to affirm that any other person is signified than
the real Prophet Elijah, a truth equally manifest in the
following passages: 1 Kings xviii. 21, " And Elijah
drew near."—2 Chronicles xxi. 12, " And a writing of
Elijah the prophet reached him." If the prophecy
under consideration had had reference to an indefinite
individual, it would have been communicated in such
terms as the following, " Behold, I shall send a man
like the Prophet Elijah." Besides, he might have said,
in terms which could not have failed to produce conviction, " Behold, I shall send you John." What
necessity to have called him Elijah? Our argument
gains in strength by the very statements contained in
the Gospel of St. John i. 21, " And they asked him
[John], what then, art thou Elias [Elijah], and he
said, I *am not*."—" Art thou that Prophet? and he
answered, *No*." Comparing this passage with an assertion made in Matthew, we find a most glaring contradiction in the two Gospels. See Matthew xvii. 10 to 13,
" And his disciples asked Him [Jesus], saying, Why
then say the Scribes, that Elias [Elijah], must first
come? And Jesus answered and said unto them, Elias

[Elijah] shall first come and restore all things. But I say unto you that Elias [Elijah], is come already, and they knew him not, but have done unto him whatsoever they listed; likewise shall also the Son of Man suffer of them. Then the disciples understood that he spake to them of John the Baptist." It is utterly unnecessary to illustrate any further similar expressions bearing so visibly the stamp of human invention; and we are fully prepared to estimate the value of the interpretation given to this discrepancy by the Christian commentators, who maintain that John declined the title of " Prophet Elijah" out of pure humility. Humility will not allow us to utter an intentional untruth in order to establish our superiority. Faithful prophets have openly avowed their missions and the object of their appearance before the world. We dismiss, therefore, the claim of the Christian interpretation as totally unsatisfactory and unfounded.

CHAPTER XL.

Psalm cx. 1, " The Lord said unto my lord, Sit thou at my right side, until I make thine enemies thy footstool."

I heard once a Christian scholar plead that this passage can only have reference to Jesus, who was the combination of divinity and humanity; for of whom else could David have spoken as "my Lord" sitting at the right hand of the Almighty?

Refutation.—To this I made the following reply:— We attribute to David the composition of the 137th Psalm, commencing, " On the rivers of Babylon we sat and wept," a Psalm obviously treating of the Babylonian Captivity, which took place about four centuries after the death of David. An allusion to so distant a period could only have been made by a holy and an inspired writer.

There are also many passages in the book of Psalms which relate to the poet himself, as, for instance, Psalm ii. 7, " I will declare it as a law.   The Lord spoke unto me, Thou art my son, to-day I have begotten thee."   In the same light must be considered many other subsequent Psalms.   There are Psalms of another character, the object of which is to describe the period of the Jewish exile; to this class belongs the above-mentioned Psalm cxxxvii.   Of the like prophetic character is Psalm lxxix. 1, commencing, " O God, the heathen have come into thine inheritance, they have defiled thy holy temple."   In a similar sense we take Psalm lxxiv. 10, " Wherefore, O God, hast thou for ever forsaken us ?" All such Psalms were composed for the captives of Israel through inspiration.   We find other Psalms which have a still more remote bearing, and take within their range the gathering of the captives, and the days of the Messiah.   See, for instance Psalm xcvi. 1, commencing, " Sing unto the Lord a new song," etc.   This and other Psalms were dictated by holy inspiration, and originated most likely from some occurrence which urged the mind of the poet to enlarge upon the future restoration of Israel.   Sometimes the cause of the production of such Psalms is recorded and pointed out by expressions more or less definite.   See, for instance, Psalm xx. 1, " The Lord shall answer thee on the day of trouble," in which David spoke first of his own sorrow, and then passed over to those awaiting the children of Israel while engaged in hazardous warfare.   In the same category stands the Psalm, " God said unto my Lord (master), Sit thou at my right-hand until I make thine enemies thy footstool."   Firstly, David speaks concerning himself, perhaps taking occasion to treat on this subject when his men had sworn "that he should no longer go with them to battle," on account of the danger to which he had so repeatedly exposed his life in conflict with the Philistines. See 2 Samuel xxi. 17, " Then the men of David swore unto him saying, Thou shall no longer go out with us to battle, that thou quench not the light of Israel." The psalm in question seems to have emanated from the impression made on the poet, while his men were anxious to prevent him from exposing his life any more in battle, and speaking, as it were, in their name, he makes them utter an appeal to himself in the following words, " God saith to my Lord, Sit thou at my right hand until I make thy enemies thy footstool." Now, whether David was or was not the author of this appeal, we must allow that in any case this emphatic exhortation was well calculated to work a powerful effect on the mind of a man so pious as King David. Being thus assured of the protection of God, as confirmed by the words, " The Lord shall send the rod of thy strength from Zion," which is, that " He will send thee help from his sanctuary, He will support thee from Zion," as that holy city was the distinguished locality which " the Lord chose for his abode," the words which follow, " Thy people shall be willing on the day of thy power," mean, Thy subjects, O King, will freely offer their lives to spare thine, while thou keepest away from danger. The passage, " Thou art my priest for ever according to the word concerning Melchizedek," means, Thou shalt, during all thy life, be unto me like Melchizedek, king of Jerusalem, who was denominated king and priest of the most high God. See Genesis xiv. 18, "And Melchizedek, king of Salem, caused bread and wine to be brought out, and he was a priest of the most high God." That David's sacred compositions rendered him worthy to be adorned with the title of *priest* appears evident enough from Scripture, as is exemplified in the Second Book of Samuel, where we read, that David built an altar, offered up burnt offerings and peace offerings, which, accompanied by prayer and entreaty, "were accepted by the Lord, and the plague was stayed in Israel." The words על דברתי in the passage in the psalm in question, mean "according to." We find it in the same sense in Job x. "*according to* thy knowledge." The letter י in דברתי is paragogic as the י in רבתי (Lamentations i. 1). We must mention here, by way of digression, a misinterpretation given to the passage, "And Melchizedek brought out wine and bread." The Christians believe, that the bread and wine were offered as articles of sacrifice, but plain sense compels us to believe that the presentation of these things was merely for the entertainment of his guests. The tenth part given by Abraham to Melchizedek, qualified the latter to be denominated priest of the Most High God. Hence we see that the Psalmist meant none but himself, in the composition we have been treating of, while, on the other hand, he alluded to the future condition of the dispersed people, when in his inspiration he proclaimed (Psalm xcvi. 6), "Sing ye unto the Lord a new song, let the whole earth sing unto the Lord." Thus he says also in the subsequent psalm, "The Lord reigneth; let the earth be glad, many isles shall rejoice." Those psalms, as we said above, allude to the still unfulfilled ingathering of Israel. It appears to be a most unjustifiable assertion of the Christian expounder of the psalms to maintain that the phrase, "To sit at the right hand of God," applies to an actual son of God, for the Bible contains numerous proofs that the metaphor, "the right hand of God," solely signifies "Omnipotence of the Deity." What other interpretation could be assigned to the following sentences (Ps. cxviii.

verse 16), " The right hand of the Lord is exalted, the right hand of the Lord worketh mighty things." Exodus xv. 16, " Thy right hand, O Lord, is glorified in strength; thy right hand, O Lord, crusheth the enemy." Even when speaking of man, " the right hand " implies strength and exertion. See for instance Psalm cxliv. 7, " And *their hand* is the *right hand* of *falsehood*." To take the word in a narrow and literal sense, must involve the expounder in the glaring fallacy of applying corporeality to one whom he believes to be the Son of God. To a Jew, it would almost appear blasphemy literally to ascribe a right or a left hand to the Deity, a spiritual being to whom no attribute of corporeality can be absolutely ascribed. When the believer is urged to place himself on the right hand of the Lord, he can only understand that it is his duty to seek the protection of the Omnipotent. The more we read of Scripture, the more proofs we find that many parts of the Bible have been misinterpreted in order to favor a certain religious dogma. The psalm we are treating of has the expression, " The Lord hath sworn, he will not repent," which phrase has been considered as alluding to a new dispensation by which the sacrifices of flesh and blood should cease, and be substituted by oblations of bread and wine. But it has not been borne in mind that the Deity never changes his views. " He is not a man that he should repent." Ordinances once given must be binding upon us, and upon all succeeding generations. We have already disposed of this subject in chapter xix. to which we refer the reader.

CHAPTER XLI.

DANIEL vii. 13, " I saw in the night visions, and, behold,

one like the Son of Man came with the clouds of heaven, and came to the Ancient of days, and they brought him near before him." The Christian expositors of Scripture ascribe the object of this prophecy to the advent of their Messiah, who, according to their view of this prophecy, was to be a superhuman being; otherwise how could he come with the clouds of heaven?

Refutation.—The prophet speaks here of a dream, in which things are meant to be represented in their literal sense. If the dream exhibits preternatural visions, the interpretation does not require a preternatural fulfilment. Daniel mentioned in the same chapter the destruction of the four kingdoms, and predicted that an enduring dominion will be granted to no other than the people holy to the Most High God. See ibid. verse 18, " And the holy ones of the Most High shall receive the dominion, and possess the kingdom for ever and ever, even for ever and ever." Again, verses 26, 27, " And the judgment shall sit, and they shall take away his dominion to consume and to destroy it unto the end. And the kingdom and the dominion, and the greatness of the kingdom under the whole heaven shall be given to the people of the saints of the Most High, whose kingdom is an everlasting kingdom, and all kingdoms shall serve and obey him."

The clouds of heaven mentioned in the quotation at the head of this chapter, bring to mind the heavenly rule which ordains changes on high, in the region which lies beyond the reach and influence of man. He that raises clouds, and makes them descend again to fructify the soil, must be acknowledged as the same supreme agent, and disposer of the fate of man. The idea is familiar to other prophets also. See for example Jeremiah xiv. 22, " Are there among the vanities of the heathen any that send down rain, and do the heavens yield them abundant showers?" " Is it not thou who art our God, and surely we will hope in thee; for thou doest all these things." The fleet clouds are often used as symbols of the swiftness with which God carries out His decrees. See Isaiah xix. 1, " Behold, the Lord riding on a light cloud, and He is come to Egypt." Jeremiah iv. 13, " Behold, like unto a cloud he rises up; like a whirlwind are His chariots. Isaiah lx. 8, " Who are those that are flying like a cloud, and like doves to their windows?"

The superhuman powers developed in the divine dispensations are pointed out by Daniel ii. 34, " Thou sawest that a stone was cut out, but not by any hands, which smote the image on his feet." In a like manner he mentions in the same chapter the aid that will be afforded by God (ver. 44), " And in the days of these kings shall the God of heaven set up a kingdom which shall never be destroyed, and the kingdom shall not be left to other people," etc. Thus the last kingdom on earth will be exalted beyond the others, by enjoying the special protection of heaven, and divine help shall descend upon the empire of the chosen ones, "as rain descends upon the earth blessed by the Lord."

Christians argue that the government spoken of by Daniel must belong to a Divine Being, because we read, " His dominion shall be an everlasting dominion." But we take those words in the sense that the kingdom shall be a perpetual and an inalienable inheritance, descending from father to son without interruption. Hence Daniel says, " And his kingdom shall not pass away." And again in chap. vii. 27, " And all rulers shall serve and obey Him." The last-mentioned prediction is most decidedly not realised in the person of Jesus, for the

Jews, the Mahommedans, and many other nations are not subject to the dominion of Jesus.

Christians may perhaps plead and say that the expression "*all rulers*," refers to a great number merely, and is applied here as in Genesis xxiv. 10, "And he had in his hand *all* the goods of his master." But the connecting words must ever be our guide in cases of doubtful interpretation. Hence the word *all*, here and in any other similar case, cannot be taken in a limited sense; for the prophet Daniel says, "And the kingdom, and the dominion, and the greatness of the kingdom which is *under all the heavens* shall be given to him." Moreover, he expressly states in chap. ii. 44, "I shall break in pieces and consume *all* those kingdoms, and it shall stand for ever." The same prediction we find in Isaiah lx. 12, "For the nation and the kingdom which shall not serve thee shall perish; yea, those nations shall be utterly destroyed." The above-mentioned quotation, page 196 *ante*, "And the saints of the Most High shall obtain the kingdom," has sole reference to the children of Israel. A few citations from Scripture will show that the title *saints*, or *holy ones*, is frequently given to Israel. Exodus xxii. 31, "And ye shall be unto me a holy people. Deut. vii. 6, "For thou art a holy people unto the Lord thy God, the Lord thy God has chosen thee to be unto him a nation distinct from all the nations on the face of the earth." Isaiah lxii. 12, "The holy people, the redeemed ones of the Lord." Daniel vii. 21, 22, "And I beheld the same horn made war with the saints and prevailed against them, until the Ancient of days came, and judgment was given to the saints of the Most High, and the time came that the saints possessed the kingdom." And again, ver. 25, "And he shall speak great words against the Most High, and shall wear out the saints of the Most High, and think to change times and laws, and they shall be given into his hand until a time and times and the dividing of time." Ibid. viii. 24, " And his power shall be mighty, but not by his own power shall he be mighty, and he shall destroy wonderfully, and shall prosper and act, and shall destroy the mighty and the holy people." And ibid. xii. 7, " It shall be for a time, times, and a half, and when he shall have accomplished the scattering the power of the holy people, all these things shall be finished."

As Israel is called in Scripture the holy people of the Lord, so on the other hand is the Almighty represented as the Holy One of Israel. See Isaiah xii. 6, " For great is the Holy One of Israel in the midst of thee." Ibid. xxxvii. 23, " And thou hast lifted up thine eyes against the Holy One of Israel." Ibid. xli. 14, " I have helped thee, saith the Lord, and the redeemer, the Holy One of Israel." Jeremiah l. 29, " For he rebelled against the Lord, against the Holy One of Israel."

The appellation, in Daniel, *Most High*, which the Christians have endeavoured to appropriate to Jesus, is attributable to Israel, as will be seen on examining other parts of the Scriptures. See Deuteronomy xxvi. 19, " And to make thee *most high* above all the nations which He hath made for His praise, for His name, and for His glory; and that thou mayest be a holy people unto the Lord thy God as He hath spoken." Ibid. xxviii. 1, " And the Lord will make thee most high above all people of the earth."

From all these passages, it is evident that Israel could not yield to any other nation the title given to it in holy writ, and it must be acknowledged that the saints of the Most High God can only be of that people which is declared to be most high among the nations of the earth.

The prophecies, showing that the wicked Gentiles shall

perish, and that the righteous shall unite with Israel, are sufficient evidences to prove, that also the present prophecy relates solely to the chosen people, for surely no expounder could reason away the lucid and simple announcement made by Isaiah iv. 3, " And all that shall be left in Zion, and that remain in Jerusalem, shall be called holy." And again in lx. 21, " And thy people, altogether righteous, shall inherit thy land for ever."

Thus we see that Daniel had no other object in view than to represent in his prophecy the final glory of Israel.

CHAPTER XLII.

DANIEL ix. 26, " And after threescore and two weeks shall an anointed man be cut off, and shall have nothing, and a noble people cometh that shall destroy the city and the sanctuary, and its end shall be in a flood, and until the end war is ordained to devastate." It is asserted by Christians that this verse reveals the fate of Jesus, who is to be cut off childless.

Refutation.—In order to see how untenable is the position of the interpreters who rest their faith on such grounds, we must follow again the only just rule that can be adopted, and explain the verse from its context. We find in the same chapter (ver. 24), " Seventy weeks are determined upon thy people, and upon the holy city, to make an end of sins, and to make a reconciliation for iniquity, and to bring to everlasting righteousness, and to seal up visions and prophets, and to anoint the Holy of Holies." The seventy weeks are evidently a given period of time elapsing from the destruction of the first to the destruction of the second temple. See Jeremiah xxix. 10, " For thus saith the Lord, that after seventy years be accomplished at Babylon, I will visit you, and perform my good word towards you, in causing you to return to this place." And Lamentations iv. 22, " The punishment of thine iniquity is completed, O daughter of Zion, He will not again lead thee into captivity." According to the vision of Daniel mentioned in chapter vii. of his book (the seventh and following verses), he saw that the fourth animal (indicating Rome) would persecute Israel for a great length of time ; and he meditated on the visions which were not clear to him, because he had not received a special revelation concerning the latter captivity of the Jews. Hence he says, at the conclusion of the seventh chapter, " As for me, Daniel, my cogitations much troubled me, and my countenance changed in me, but I kept the matter in my heart." The same prophet had similar doubts regarding his visions when he heard the announcement (spoken of in chap. viii.) of the cessation of the continual sacrifice, and of the destruction of the sanctuary, and of the overthrow of the people (see chap. viii. 13, 26). He then thought that the predicted length of Israel's captivity related to that state into which his people then were precipitated; he therefore was told, " Conceal this vision, for it shall be for many days." This communication the prophet found at variance with the one made to Jeremiah, that the captivity would last for seventy years only. We have to explain on this occasion the meaning of " the evening and the morning," mentioned in the original Hebrew of chap. viii. 14.* This expression is illustrated in Zechariah xiv. 7, " And in the eventide there shall be light." The prophet Daniel perceived in this that the darkness of Israel's troubles would be dispelled by the light of Salvation. See, in addition to

---

* It is singularly remarkable that these words, upon which the prophet laid peculiar stress (see *ibid*, ver. 26), are omitted in the English version.

this Jeremiah xxx. 7, " And it is a time of trouble for
Jacob, and he shall be saved from it." The reverse
state of destruction is depicted by gloom and darkness.
See Amos viii. 9, " And I shall darken the earth on a
day of light."

Chapter viii. ver. 13, 14 of Daniel, amply show that the
prophet laboured originally under the opinion that the
intended protraction of the captivity was owing to the
iniquity of the people, and that they would pine in the
state of banishment for two thousand three hundred days
(signifying years); therefore he prayed to God to remove
His wrath and anger. Neither did the angel of the
Lord acquaint him of the actual termination of the last
captivity. Daniel was only given to understand, that the
cessation of prophecy would extend to the whole length of
time necessary for the expiation of the sins of his people,
for then would be fulfilled the prediction mentioned
at the close of Lamentations iv. 22, " Thy iniquity, O
daughter of Zion, is ended ; He shall no more cause thee
to be led into captivity." Regarding the last exile of
Israel, the prophet Ezekiel has recorded similar expressions in his book (chap. xxii. 15, " And I will scatter thee
among the heathen, and disperse thee in the countries,
and will consume thy filthiness out of thee." The complete restoration, which we expect during the latter days,
will be crowned with " everlasting righteousness" (see
Daniel ix. 24). This is confirmed by the agreement of
many prophecies. See Isaiah li. 6, " And my salvation
shall be for ever, and my righteousness shall not be
abolished." Jeremiah xxiii. 5, " And I will raise up
unto David a righteous scion, and a king shall reign and
prosper, and he shall do justice and righteousness in the
earth." Isaiah xi. 4, 5, " And he shall judge the poor
with righteousness, and righteousness shall be the girdle
of his loins." And at that time all Israel will be desig-

nated by the term *righteous.* See Isaiah lx. 21, " And thy people will altogether be *righteous.*" Again, ibid, chap. lxi. 3, " And men shall call them *oaks of righteousness.*" The Psalmist likewise affords a testimony, since we find in Psalm lxxii. 7, " In his days the *righteous man* shall flourish, Jerusalem will then be called, the abode of righteousness, the holy mount." We shall then say, in the words of Jeremiah (chap. xxiii. 6), " The Lord our righteousness." The Messiah himself, according to the same prophet (chap. xxiii. 6), will assume the title, " The Lord our righteousness," as we have already shown in the Chapter xix. of this work.

The words of Daniel (chap. ix. 24) may be taken in the following sense:—" And vision [prophecy] shall be sealed up," that is to say, it will be finally determined and confirmed, for we find a repetition of the same words with the same signification in Job xxxiii. 16, " And he sealed up the chastisement." It cannot, therefore, be pretended that prophecy will then discontinue altogether, for we read in Joel ii. 28, " And it will come to pass afterwards that I shall pour out my spirit upon all flesh, and your sons and your daughters shall prophecy." The epoch of the restoration will thus completely restore the forfeited boon of Prophecy.

We return now to the explanation of the conclusion of verse 24, in Daniel ix. " And to anoint the Holy of Holies," which means that at the restoration of Israel, the Holy of Holies, or the Temple, will receive its new consecration after having lain desolate during the whole period of the captivity. An extensive description of that solemnity is to be found in the prophecy of Ezekiel, chapter xliii.

The seventy weeks spoken of in Daniel ix., are enigmatic terms, conveying the various epochs of Israel's fate during their second occupation of the Holy Land and their subsequent exile. The first epoch, designated in chap. ix. verse 25, expressed by *seven weeks*, is evidently in allusion to Cyrus; for it is said there, "Know and understand that from the giving forth of the word to restore and rebuild Jerusalem, until the anointed prince there shall be seven weeks." Now, we know well from the prophecy in Isaiah xlv. 6, that Cyrus was called the *anointed king*, for we find there, "Thus saith the Lord to his anointed king" (to Cyrus), etc.; and in the same chapter the Lord announces, "he shall build my city and send back my captives." The termination of sixty-two weeks is remarkable for the cessation "*of an anointed king*," that is to say, Israel is according to that prophecy to be bereft of his last ruler. "And there is none for him, there is no anointed ruler for the people of Israel." The cessation of a ruler over Israel is simultaneous with the fall of the Temple, and, consequently, alluded to the conquest by Titus, when Israel ceased to exist as a nation, and was deprived of its Temple, its ruler, and its country. If the Christians take an impartial view of this chapter of Daniel, they cannot possibly imagine that it alludes to Jesus, who suffered on the cross nearly half a century before the exile of Israel.

The contradictory remarks made by Christian expositors on this chapter, afford ample proof of the scanty notions they have of its real signification. Scientific readers who are anxious to obtain a view of all the contradictions which beset the path of the Christian expounders of Daniel, will find an interesting account given in Abarbanel's commentary on the book of Daniel, which bears the title *Mangne Hayeschunyah* (the Shields of Salvation).

With this chapter, we shall conclude the elucidation of Scriptural passages cited by Christians in support of their faith.

CHAPTER XLIII.

SOME small portion of Christians have reproached the Jews with the disbelief in the Apocryphal books; but such persons have been confuted by scholars of their own creed. The works comprised under the collective title " Apocrypha," were composed at a late period after the dispersion of Israel, when prophecy was totally extinct, and when inspiration no longer elevated the compositions of religious writers. The Apocrypha has, therefore, no claim on our religious reverence. Some of those books may have an historical foundation, others are based on fiction and mere invention; and the whole of the Apocrypha was composed in the Greek language, which language does not bear the stamp of authority in the mind of the Jew; we may therefore dismiss this subject without entering into further detail.

CHAPTER XLIV.

I OBSERVED to some Christians, that after the advent of the Messiah, there will be but one faith and one religion throughout the world. See Isaiah xlv. 23, " I have sworn by myself, the word is gone out of my mouth in righteousness, and shall surely not be recalled, that before me every knee shall bend, and by me every tongue shall swear." Zephaniah iii. 9, " For then shall I turn (restore) unto all the people a pure tongue, that they shall call upon the name of the Lord, and serve him with

one accord." The Christians themselves must admit that
there will take place a union of faith, since John acknowledges in his Gospel, chap. x. 16, that there will be " One
shepherd and one flock." Now, since the doctrine of
unity of faith is admitted on all sides, it is not necessary
to argue which of the three principal creeds will prevail,
whether the Jewish, the Christian, or the Mahommedan,
for surely if one of those is to be adopted, the other two
will of necessity fall. When we peruse the statements
of the prophets, we must undoubtedly acknowledge that
Israel's faith is intended to survive all others, See for
instance, Isaiah lii. 1, " Awake, awake, put on thy
strength, O Zion, put on the garments of thy glory,
for neither the uncircumcised nor the unclean shall ever
enter again into thy gates." Scripture evidently designates the Christians by the name of *uncircumcised*, and
the Mahommedans, in despite of their frequent ablutions,
deserve, in many respects, the epithet *unclean*. These
two sects are more especially pointed out in prophecy,
because they, as the representatives of Edom and Ismael,
have alternately held possession of Jerusalem since its
destruction by Titus.

From the time of the coming redemption, the prophet
declares that none of the uncircumcised and the unclean
shall ever again enter the gates of the Holy city. In the
same manner says the prophet (Joel iii. 17), " And Jerusalem shall be holy, and no stranger shall enter therein."
Respecting the same two nations, says the prophet Isaiah,
" They that sanctify themselves and purify themselves in
the gardens behind one in the midst of them, who eat the
flesh of swine and the abominations and the mice, they
shall perish altogether, saith the Lord." Those persons
who sanctify and purify themselves are obviously the
Ishmaelites who defile themselves by the most licentious
indulgences. The reflective form of the Hebrew verb,

as used in this quotation, conveys the idea of pretension and false claim, and in such a position are those of whom the prophet says, they " sanctify and purify themselves." The expression, the eaters of swine's flesh and other abominations, has allusion to the Christians, and their creed will therefore perish during the wars of the latter times. Concerning the people of Israel, however, Isaiah says, chap. xvi. 20, " And they shall bring all your brethren from all the Gentiles as an offering unto the Lord, on horses and chariots, and in litters, and upon mules and upon swift beasts, to my holy mount of Jerusalem, saith the Lord, as the children of Israel bring an offering in a holy vessel into the house of the Lord."   The nations surviving the wars of the latter times shall show honour to the Israelites, and hasten to join the true service of the Lord; hence the prophet says (chap. lxvi. 23), " And it shall come to pass, that from one new moon to the other, and from one Sabbath to the other, all flesh shall come to bow down before me, saith the Lord."   In the prophecy of Zechariah, we likewise find (chap. xiv. 16), " And it shall come to pass, that all who have been spared of all the Gentiles who come up against Jerusalem, shall come up from year to year to bow down before the King, the Lord of Hosts, and to celebrate the feast of Tabernacles."   The prediction of a periodical visit to Jerusalem by all the Gentiles, for the observance of the festivals of the Lord, is an evident proof that they are to be united with the ancient nation of Israel. With this view the prophet Zechariah says (chap. viii. 23), " Thus saith the Lord of Hosts, At that time ten men from all the tongues of the Gentiles shall take hold of the skirts of a man that is a Jew, saying, We will go with you, for we have heard that God is with you." The same prophet declares in another place (chap. ix. 7), " And I shall remove his guilt of blood from his mouth, and his abomination from beneath his teeth, and also he shall be left unto our God." This proves that they will abstain from eating unlawful food, like those who are born Israelites. We have already dwelt on this point, and refer the reader to the Chapters XV. and XXXV. of this work. In order to prove the strength of our doctrine beyond any doubt, we have only to add the clear prediction of the same prophet (Zechariah xiv. 9), " And the Lord shall be king of the whole earth; on that day the Lord shall be one, and his name one." The Lord will no longer be adored under the restricted title of King of Israel, as he actually is described by Isaiah, who says (chap. xliv. 6), " Thus saith the Lord, the *King of Israel* and his Redeemer, the Lord of Hosts, I am the first and I am the last, and besides me there is no other God." And again, chap. xlv. 15, " Surely thou art the God who art hidden, the *God of Israel*, and his Deliverer." In chap. liv. 5, that prophet informs us of the extension of the name of the God of Israel, to that of the God acknowledged by all nations: he says, " For thy Maker is thy Husband, the Lord of Hosts is his name, and thy Redeemer is the Holy One of Israel, he *shall be called the God of the whole earth.*" The one God, and his one and only law of Sinai, will be acknowledged by all the inhabitants of the earth; no principle of Duality or of Trinity will then prevail. " All nations thou hast made will then come, as the Psalmist exclaims (Ps. lxxxvi. 9), " and bow down before Thee and honour Thy name." And as throughout the realms of the universe the Supreme King of heaven will be acknowledged, so throughout all the kingdoms of the earth will his anointed king, Messiah, be the only worldly ruler. We shall have another opportunity of treating on the last mentioned subject when discussing, in the second part of this work, the merits of the contents of the other chapters of the Gospel of John.

We conclude this chapter with the conviction that men of understanding and reading, attentively considering such passages as we have quoted, cannot any longer conscientiously refuse their assent to our belief of the future universal establishment of the Faith of Israel.

CHAPTER XLV.

I HAVE to set forth the following objection to the Christian religion. If our Christian brethren are sincerely anxious to separate truth from falsehood, they ought to examine the passages of the Old Testament quoted in the Gospel, and ascertain whether they are really applicable or not. A brief survey of such topics shows that the quotations in the Gospel can never be considered cogent or satisfactory. Whoever reads the statement made by the prophets must at once grant, that they never had it in contemplation to afford any clue or even a preference for the admission of a change or abjuration of the Faith of Israel. Besides this, the authors of the Gospel have occasionally garbled and perverted the form as well as the sense of the original text, and have thus based their erroneous opinion on an unstable foundation. Even in matters relating to history, where the fact has no relation to prediction and fulfilment, they have resorted to misrepresentation, which does not argue in favour of the veracity of their faith, or of their sound knowledge of the Scriptures. We shall examine these discrepancies in the Second Part of this work, and will now only make a few cursory remarks on one or two points.

Matthew, in the first chapter, (ver. 8) of his Book, says, " And Joram begat Ozias." This is not to be found in the Old Testament. In 1 Chronicles iii. ver. 11, we

read the following genealogy: " Joram his son, Ahaziah
his son, Joash his son, Jotham his son." Azariah,
father of Jotham, here mentioned, was Uzziah, mentioned elsewhere in our Scripture, consequently the
three generations of Ahaziah, Joash, and Amaziah, are
omitted in the Gospel of Matthew. The omission is not
caused by any oversight, but must have been intentional,
in order to reduce the generations to the like number as
those from Abraham to David, and thus to make both
series of genealogy appear to consist of fourteen generations. Nor is the enumeration of the third series of
fourteen generations during the Babylonian captivity,
and coming down to Jesus, anything but a mere invention, in order to lead to the opinion that the three
genealogical divisions ending in Jesus, were ordained
as a special manifestation from the Almighty. Equally
unsound is the tale of Matthew that Jesus was brought
forth by a Virgin, in order to fulfil the words of
Isaiah vii. 14, " Behold, the young woman [accord-
ing to the vulgate *a virgin*] shall conceive and shall
bear a son, and thou shalt call his name Emmanuel."
What connection with the birth of Jesus has the
address made by Isaiah to King Ahaz, in order to
remove his fear of the two hostile kings then threatening
Jerusalem? What comfort could it possibly have
afforded to Ahaz, and how could it have allayed his
terror, if the prophet, in proof of his divine mission, had
given him a sign which could not and was not to be realized
for more than five centuries after the death of the king?
A fair examination of the entire passage in Isaiah will
be found in Chapter XXI. of this work. The same dis-
cordance between the word of Scripture and its application in the New Testament, will be found in referring
to the following passage of Matthew ii. 14, 15, " And
he [Joseph] arose and took the young child and his

mother by night, and departed into Egypt. And he was there until the death of Herod; that it might be fulfilled which was spoken of the Lord by the prophet, saying, "Out of Egypt have I called my son." The prophet alluded to in this portion of the gospel is Hosea, who in reality says (in chap. xi. 1), "When Israel was a youth I loved him, and from Egypt I called my son." The fulfilment had not been delayed to the times of Jesus, but had taken place in the days of Moses when the Lord had told him (Exodus iv. 22, 23), "And thou shalt say unto Pharaoh, Thus saith the Lord, Israel is my first-born son;" and again, "Send away my son that he may serve me." What connection between Prophecy and the New Testament can be discovered in the following passage of St. Matthew? (chap. ii. 16, 17, 18,) "And Herod sent forth and slew all the children that were in Bethlehem from two years old and under. Then was fulfilled that which was spoken by Jeremiah the prophet, (chap. xxxi. 15), saying, Rachel is weeping for her children, and would not be comforted because they are not." Whoever reads the complete passage delivered by Jeremiah, will soon perceive that he speaks of the *captives*, who, he says, ibid. ver. 16, "Shall return from the land of the enemy." And subsequently the prophet continues to say, (ibid. ver. 17), "And the children shall return to their boundary." It is thus quite evident, that Jeremiah is representing the lamentations of an afflicted mother, who alludes to the children who are living in captivity, and not those who have been massacred by a tyrant : the ten tribes being called by the name of Ephraim the descendants of Rachel; who was represented as a becoming emblem of maternal grief for her unhappy children. Moreover, if the prophet had intended to point out the affliction created by the massacre of the children in

Bethlehem Judah, he would have selected Leah as the representative of the wounded spirit of a bereaved mother; for she and not Rachel was the female ancestor of the inhabitants of Bethlehem. Various other remarks on this passage have already been made in the Chapter XXVIII. of this work.

In the same second chapter of Matthew, ver. 23, we read, " And he came and dwelt in the city called Nazareth, that it might be fulfilled which was spoken by the prophets, " He shall be called a ' Nazarene.' " It is quite certain that the writings of our prophets afford not the slightest authority in support of this quotation.

In Matthew v. 43, Jesus is made to say, " Ye have heard that it hath been said, thou shalt love thy neighbour and hate thine enemy." Now we maintain that the additional injunction of *hating the enemy* flowed from the inventive mind of the author of the Gospel, and that it is not to be found in any part of the Jewish law. What we find in our law concerning the treatment of our enemy, is conveyed in totally different terms. See Exodus xxiii. 4, " If thou meet thine enemy's ox or his ass going astray, thou shalt surely bring it back to him again. If thou seest the ass of him that hateth thee, lying under his burden and wouldst forbear to help him, thou shalt surely help with him." Again, see Leviticus xix. 17, 18, " Thou shalt not hate thy brother in thine heart, thou shalt in anywise rebuke thy neighbour, and not suffer sin upon him. Thou shalt not avenge, nor bear any grudge against the children of thy people, but thou shalt love thy neighbour as thyself." The same precept is reproduced in Proverbs xxv. 21, " If thine enemy be hungry, give him bread to eat; and if he be thirsty, give him water to drink."

In Matthew xxiii. 35, Jesus reproaches the Jews for

having slain Zacharias, son of Barachias, " between the
temple and the altar." In this reproach an insufficient
acquaintance with our Holy Books is shown, inasmuch
as it was Zachariah, the son of Jehoiada, the priest, who
was slain (see 2 Chronicles xxiv. 22). Some Christian
commentators endeavour to explain away this discrepancy, asserting that the father of Barachias had two
names. But this is a clumsy subterfuge, for the priest
Zechariah, the son of Jehoiada, lived in the days of
Joash, king of Judah, while Zechariah, the son of
Berachiah, prophesied during the reign of Darius ;
therefore several centuries intervened between the existence of the two men bearing the name Zechariah.

In Mark ii. 13, Jesus is made to say to the Pharisees,
" Have ye never read what David did when he had
need, and was an hungered, he and they that were with
him? How he went into the house of God in the days
of Abiathar, the high-priest, and did eat the shew-bread,
which is not lawful but for the priest, and gave also to
them that were with him?" This author of the Gospel
likewise evinces an inattentive perusal of our Scriptures,
since David did not go to Abiathar, but he went to
Ahimelech, the father of Abiathar. See 1 Samuel xxi.
1, " And David came to Nob to Ahimelech the priest;"
and ibid, chap. xxii. 20, "And one of the sons of
Ahimelech, the son of Ahitub, named Abiathar, escaped
and ran after David." Nor did David come to Ahimelech
with his followers, as the above quotation from Mark
would lead one to suppose. For Ahimelech asked David
(1 Samuel xxi. 1), " Why art thou alone, and no man
with thee?" In St. John iii. 34, Jesus communicates
to his disciples, "A new commandment I give unto you,
That ye love one another." This commandment is
decidedly not new. Moses laid it down in the words
" Thou shalt love thy neighbour as thyself.

In Acts vii. 4, is to be seen, " Then came he (Abraham) out of the land of the Chaldeans and dwelt in
Haran, and from thence, when his father was dead, He
[God] removed him into the land wherein ye now
dwell." This is erroneous, for Abraham quitted Haran
during his father's lifetime. And since Terah, the
father of Abraham, died in Haran at the age of 205
years, he must have resided there for sixty years after
the departure of Abraham. The following statement
will prove this, according to the account given in
Genesis:—Terah was seventy years old when he begat
Abraham, and the latter, when seventy-five years old,
quitted his father; and Terah having died at the age of
205, he must, therefore, have been still living for sixty
years after his son's departure. The order in which the
history of Terah and Abraham is given in Genesis xi.
and xii. has most probably led to the inaccuracies we
have pointed out.

In Paul's Epistle to the Romans ix. 24, the Gentiles
are declared to be on an equality with the Chosen People.
" Even us whom he hath called not of the Jews only,
but also of the Gentiles. As he says also in Hosea,
" I will call them my people which were not my people,
and her beloved which was not beloved." Whoever
peruses the first and second chapter of Hosea will find
that Paul made use of the most tortuous means in order
to shew that the Gentiles are meant by that prophet.
So long as the people of Israel, through sin, forfeited
the favours of God, they were stigmatized by the designation "*Loammi* (no more my people), and *Lo-ruchamah*
(not received in mercy), but on returning to God,
the Judgment was, according to the prophet, to
be reversed, and they would bear the title " *Ammi*" (my
people), and " *Ruchamah*" (received in mercy). The
contents of Hosea's prophecy completely refute Paul's
attempt to assimilate the Gentiles with the Jews.

In the same ninth chapter of Paul (ver. 33) a quotation from Isaiah is inserted, " Behold I lay in Zion a stumbling-stone and rock of offence, and whosoever believeth on him shall not be ashamed." This quotation is a mere fabrication of the author. In Isaiah viii. 14, we find only, " And he shall be for a sanctuary, and for *a stone of stumbling and for a rock of offence* to both houses of Israel; for a gin and for a snare to the inhabitants of Jerusalem." In chapter xxviii. 16 of the same prophet, we read " Therefore, thus saith the Lord God, *Behold I lay in Zion for a foundation* a stone of trial, a precious corner-stone, which shall be well founded, yea securely founded; he that believeth shall not hasten from it." Paul thus combines various distinct passages to make them serve his own views.

In chap. x. 11 of Paul's Epistle to the Romans and 1 Peter ii. 6, an inaccurate version of the above is given, " He that believeth on him shall not be ashamed" (or confounded). Scripture thus mutilated can certainly not uphold the fabric of human faith. Again, Paul says in Rom. x. 6, 7, " Say not in thine heart, Who shall ascend into heaven? (that is, to bring Christ down from above); or who shall descend into the deep? (that is, to bring up Christ again from the dead.) But what saith it? The word is nigh thee; even in thy mouth and in thy heart : that is the word of faith which we preach." The words separated by Paul from their context, allude to the Divine promise contained in Deuteronomy xxx. 3, " God will turn the captivity of Israel and replace all evils with blessings," ver. 2, "if thou wilt turn to the Lord with all thy heart and with all thy soul." " For this commandment or precept which I command thee this day is not hidden from thee, neither is it far off. It is not in heaven that thou shouldst say, Who shall go up for us to heaven and bring it unto us, that we may hear it and do it." Ibid. 11, 12, The grace of the Almighty here points out to us the magnitude of the duty of repentance, and the ease of accomplishing it. Commonly the value of worldly advantages is estimated according to the difficulty of obtaining them. But the preciousness of repentance consists in the means which the Almighty has placed within our reach; and therefore the subject closes with the terms ibid. ver. 14, " but the thing is very nigh unto thee. It is in thy heart and in thy mouth that thou mayst do it."

In the Epistle to the Hebrews x. 5, Paul quotes the following words from our Scriptures:—" Sacrifice and offering thou wouldst not, but a body thou hast prepared me." The true passage occurring in Psalm xl., is, however, thus worded: " Sacrifice and offering thou didst not desire, mine ears hast thou opened," etc. The Psalmist touched here only on the subject of obedience as agreeing with the announcement made by Moses previously to the delivery of the Decalogue. See Exodus xix. 5, where it is said, " And it shall come to pass, if ye diligently hearken unto my commandments and keep my covenant, that ye shall be unto me a distinct people from among all nations, for mine is the earth." The matter is further developed by Jeremiah, who says in his book, chap. vii. 22, 23, " For I spoke not unto your ancestors, and I commanded not unto them concerning the burnt offering and sacrifices; but this I commanded them, saying, Hearken unto my voice." Again, in 1 Samuel xv. 22, obedience is enforced in preference to sacrifice, " Hath the Lord as great delight in burnt offerings and sacrifices as in obeying the voice of the Lord? Behold obedience is better than sacrifice, to attend *unto Him* is better than the fat of rams." We thus see that sacrifices were not ordained for their intrinsic value, but were intended to lead sinners into the temple, where they might contemplate on the mercy of God while performing the prescribed offering. Sacrifices consequently produced the same sanctifying effect on the mind, as healing medicines do on the body. We have here selected only a few Scriptural passages from those incorrectly cited in the New Testament, but will resume the subject more minutely in the Second Part of this work.

Many Christian commentators have lost their way, while attempting to reconcile those inconsistencies which we perceive in the New Testament, and they have found it necessary to assert, that it is not right to argue on those dubious matters. If that principle be true, it certainly would be better if the Jews were left unmolested by the assailants of their ancient religion, and if they were left free from the obtrusion of doctrines which interest neither faith nor reason.

CHAPTER XLVI.

THERE is a striking instance of the fulfilment of prophetic warnings exhibited in the chastisement inflicted on the Gentiles, who relentlessly persecuted the Jews. There has never yet been a ruler exercising tyranny over the Jewish people who escaped with impunity. For although the Almighty deems it proper to visit Israel's transgressions, He does not suffer mortal man to act arbitrarily and fiendishly, where he is employed as the instrument of Divine Providence. Thus Pharaoh, Sennacherib, Nebuchadnezzar, Haman, and other persecutors of the Jews, met with the retribution suited to their excesses, notwithstanding the calamities of exile falling upon the Israelites for their continuance in sin. They had not forfeited the title of God's people and His heritage, and He never disowned them so far as to destroy them totally; for the sole object of His corrections was to bring them back from their iniquitous

conduct. And because He never rent asunder the tie of
the covenant made with their fathers, He is in all parts
of Scripture mentioned as *their God*. This is illustrated
by the following quotation:—Leviticus xxvi. 44, " And
even this I will do, when they shall be in the land of
their enemies, I will neither despise nor loathe them so
as to consume them, and to break my covenant with
them, for I am the Lord their God." In their own
country they committed sins arising from their prosperity and affluence, their punishment was, therefore,
adjusted to their evil ways. The loss of the " goodly
land," and the degradation from an independent to a
dependent state, and from riches to poverty, were the
chastisements proportioned to their withdrawal from
the ways of God. In this respect, they shared the fate
of a king's minister who has fallen into disgrace with
his sovereign; even after his estate has been confiscated,
he still remains a subject of his master, and in lowering
him the king merely exercises his royal prerogative.
Should now a stranger undertake to cast further
humiliation upon the fallen courtier, will not his master
direct his displeasure and vengeance upon him who
tramples on the fallen man? History has, indeed, amply
shewn that in the very same countries in which the Jew
suffered persecution for his faith, the persecutors soon
engaged in sanguinary conflicts among themselves under
various pretexts. After the expulsion of the Jews from
England, France, Spain, and Germany, unheard of
cruelties ensued, the description of which excites the
utmost horror in every breast, while, on the other hand,
the countries in which the Jew was left unmolested,
bore the most undeniable proofs of civilization, and
obtained by providential retribution the enjoyment of
prosperity. This state of quietude will ever remain
uninterrupted wherever toleration prevails, although new
sects may start up in defiance of newly established creeds.

This opinion is founded on our own experience as well as on the following Scriptural testimonies:—See Deuteronomy vii. 15, " And the Lord shall remove from thee every sickness and all the evil diseases of the Egyptians; He shall not put them upon thee, but give them upon thine enemies." Ibid. chap. xxx. 7, " And the Lord thy God shall put all these oaths upon thine enemies and upon thy haters who have persecuted thee." See also Isaiah xli. 11, 12, " Behold all those who were incensed against thee shall be ashamed and confounded; they shall be as nothing, and they that strive with thee shall perish. Thou shalt seek them and not find them. Even them that contended with thee; they that war against thee, shall be as nothing, and as a thing of nought." Ibid. chap. xlvii. 5, 6, " Sit thou silent and get thee into darkness, O daughter of the Chaldeans; for thou shalt no more be called the Lady of Kingdoms. I was wroth with my people, I have polluted mine inheritance, and given them into thine hand. Thou didst shew them no mercy: upon the ancient thou hast very heavily laid the yoke." Ibid. chap. xlix. 26, " And I will feed them that oppress thee with their own flesh, and they shall be drunken with their own blood as with sweet wine, and all flesh shall know that I the Lord am thy Saviour and thy Redeemer, the mighty one of Jacob."

See also Jeremiah ii. 3, " Israel is holiness unto the Lord and the first fruits of his increase; all that devour him shall offend; evil shall come upon them, saith the Lord."

Ibid xxx. 16, " Therefore all they that devour thee shall be devoured; and all thy adversaries every one of them shall go into captivity, and they that spoil thee shall be a spoil, and all that prey upon thee, will I give for a prey." Joel iii. 2, " I will gather all nations, and bring them down into the valley of Jehoshaphat, and will

plead with them there for my people and for my
heritage Israel, whom they have scattered among the
nations, and divided my land." The same prophet says,
at the conclusion of his book, chap. iii. 19, " Egypt
shall be a desolation, and Edom shall be a desolate
wilderness for their violence against the children of
Judah, because they have shed innocent blood in their
land." Obadiah, in his prophecy (ver. 10), says, " For
the violence against thy brother Jacob, shame shall
cover thee, and thou shalt be cut off for ever." See
also the remaining part of this prophecy. Zephaniah
ii. 9, 10, " Therefore as I live, saith the Lord of hosts, the
God of Israel; surely Moab shall be as Sodom, and the
children of Ammon as Gomorrah, even as the breeding
of nettles, and salt pits, and a perpetual desolation; the
residue of my people shall spoil them, and all the
remnant of my people shall possess them. This they
shall have for their pride, because they have reproached
my people and magnified themselves." And at the
conclusion of the book, the prophet says, (ver. 19),
" Behold at that time I will undo all that afflict thee;
and I will save her that halteth and gather her that
was driven out, and I will set them as praise and fame
in every land where they have been put to shame."
Zechariah i. 15, " I am very sore displeased with the
nations that are at ease; for I was but little displeased,
and they helped forward the affliction." Ibid. ii. 8 and
9, " For thus saith the Lord of hosts, after the glory
hath he sent me unto the nations which have spoiled
you; for he that toucheth you toucheth the apple of his
eye. For, behold, I will turn my hand upon them, and
they shall be a spoil unto their own servants, and ye
shall know that the Lord of hosts hath sent me." See
also Psalm lxxxiii. 1, commencing " O God, keep not
thy silence." Chapters xxv., xxvi., xxxv., and that

portion of xxxvi., to verse 16, of the book of Ezekiel, afford further elucidations on the subject.

CHAPTER XLVII.

THE following argument may be raised against the Christians who oppose Judaism. They either believe that the Jews tormented and crucified Jesus *with* his will or *against* his will. If with his will, then the Jews had ample sanction for what they did, and could in that case only have merited the Divine approbation, acting as they then did in conformity with the ejaculation of David in Psalm xl. 8, " I have been desirous to perform Thy will;" and Psalm cxliii. 10, " Teach me to perform Thy will." The Jews must also have followed the admonition of Ezra x. 11, " And now give ye thanks unto the Lord the God of your fathers, and execute his desire." In addition to this we must ask, that if Jesus was really willing to meet such a fate, what cause was there for complaint or affliction? And why did he pray in the manner narrated in Matthew xxvi. 39, " And he [Jesus], went a little further and fell on his face and prayed, saying, O my Father, if it be possible let this cup pass from me, nevertheless not as I will but as thou wilt." After Jesus had been fixed to the cross he gave evident proof of his non-identity with the Deity by exclaiming, " My God! my God! why hast thou forsaken me?" This argues that the will of God was different from that of Jesus, and that he bore no closer relation to the Creator than belongs to every other mortal.

We will now proceed to the other alternative, and suppose that the crucifixion of Jesus was done with his will. In this case the question arises, How could he be designated a God while he was incapable of resisting

the power of those who brought him to the cross, and
how could he be held as the Saviour of all mankind who
could not save his own life?

The adoration paid to Jesus after his death recalls
to our mind the passage in Ezekiel xxviii. 9, " Wilt
thou say before him that slayeth thee, I am God; but
thou art a man and not a God in the hand that slayeth
thee."

CHAPTER XLVIII.

WE would submit to discussion the question whether
the Christians have any foundation for the belief that
Jesus wrought his beneficial works for the salvation of
the souls of his believers, and through his sufferings and
his blood, he saved the followers of his creed from
everlasting perdition in hell? If that were the case,
the Christians would be dispensed from doing good
actions, and be irresponsible for evil deeds. A passage
occurring in St. Paul's First Epistle to the Corinthians
(chap. vi. 9,) will moreover show that the fall of Jesus
was only of advantage to the upright, but not to sinners.
" Know ye not that the unrighteous shall not inherit
the kingdom of God." Of this we find a detailed
explanation in the subsequent verses. Now, if sinners
devoid of merit cannot be saved, why should the
righteous who have merits require any intercession in
order to obtain the Divine favour? It would appear
then that the death of Jesus serves neither for the
salvation of the sinner, nor for the salvation of the
righteous.

Should the Christians argue that the death of Jesus
was intended only to rescue from hell the souls of those
who were involved in the sin of Adam, then we would
refer back to the pages wherein we have fully proved

that the prophets and the pious could not reasonably, and according to Scriptural evidence, incur damnation on account of the fall of Adam.

CHAPTER XLIX.

AN extraordinary degree of inconsistency presents itself in numerous points, when we compare the doctrine of the Christians with the teachings of Jesus and his Apostles.

In the first place, we find that Jesus does not, in any part of the New Testament, call himself " *God*," but continually calls himself " *Man*," or " *the Son of Man.*" The title of Divinity attributed to Jesus is consequently conferred upon him without the sanction of that Book, the authority of which can alone be of value to the Christians.

In the second place, we notice that Jesus expresses himself, in various places, that he did not come to abolish the law of Moses, but to uphold it. Thus we read in Matthew v. 17, 18, " Think not that I am come to destroy the law or the prophets: I am not come to destroy, but to fulfil: for verily I say unto you, till heaven and earth pass, one jot, or one tittle, shall in no wise pass from the law, till all be fulfilled." In a similar manner, we find in Luke xvi. 17, " And it is easier for heaven and earth to pass, than one tittle of the law to fail." Nevertheless, the Christians persist in believing that the Mosaic dispensation is no longer in force, but has been superseded by that of Jesus.

In the third place, we observe, from the words of Jesus, that he thought everlasting bliss depended on the obedience to the holy laws of Moses, for when asked by the rich man, what he was to do in order to earn beatitude in life everlasting, Jesus answered (Matthew

xix. 17, 18, "If thou wilt enter into life, keep the commandments. The rich man said unto him, Which commandment? Jesus answered, Thou shalt do no murder; thou shalt not commit adultery; thou shalt not steal; thou shalt not bear false witness; honour thy father and thy mother; and thou shalt love thy neighbour as thyself." The Christian of our day adds, that the sole condition on which life eternal depends, is the belief in Jesus as the Saviour of the soul. Jesus moreover taught the young man "If thou be perfect, go and sell that thou hast, and give to the poor." This precept we have never yet seen performed by any Christian.

In the fourth place, we do not anywhere find the Christian who submits to the humiliation enjoined by Jesus on his disciples, when he said (Luke vi. 29) "And unto him that smiteth thee on the one cheek, offer also the other; and him that taketh away thy cloak, forbid not to take thy coat also," etc.

In the fifth place, we have to point out that, while the Christians believe that Mary, after having given birth to Jesus, still remained a virgin, Jesus himself was not of that opinion; for, according to John ii. 4, he said, " *Woman*, what have I to do with thee"?

In the sixth place, we find the Christians at variance, not only differing from the Mosaic, or rather Noachic prohibition of eating blood, but even from the injunction we read in Acts xv. 20, " But that we write unto them, that they abstain from pollutions of idols, and from fornication, and from things strangled, and from blood." See also ibid. xv. 29 and xxi. 25.

CHAPTER L.

WE would ask the Christians who take the New Testament as a substitute for the Mosaic law, how they could venture to add, or diminish from the doctrines set forth in that law, seeing that the most severe denunciations are pronounced against him, who would dare either to add to, or omit the doctrines contained therein.

As points of addition, we must consider — First, The dogma of the Trinity. The New Testament itself furnishes us only with proofs *against* the existence of a Trinity, as we have already shown in the tenth chapter of this book.

Secondly, We do not learn from the New Testament that Jesus called himself God, or that he arrogated to himself the unbounded power of the Almighty.

Thirdly, We have to ask those members of Christianity who worship images, how they could introduce a worship which runs counter to the stringent prohibitions of Jesus regarding this matter? For he prohibited his disciples from tasting the very flesh of animals sacrificed in honour of images. The defence attempted by those who bow to images is perfectly untenable. They allege that the images merely recall to mind the memory of holy men and women, and that they do not pay adoration to their inanimate representations. They, however, cannot deny that the form is polytheistic, and that, in their estimation, their bowing and prostration, and praying before those figures of saints, imparts a Divine character to those images.

Fourthly, The Christians, in visiting upon the Jews the death of Jesus, are acting against his expressed opinion; for, according to Luke xxiii. 34, Jesus said, "Father, forgive them, for they know not what they do."

The wide scope to cruelty which has been given by the assumption of the right of avenging the death of Jesus on the Jews, has been sadly demonstrated in the conduct of the worst of men, who have heaped upon the inoffensive false accusations and acts of violence. As to the Christians' omission of acts enjoined by Jesus, we will point out—

First, The non-adoption by Christians of the precept to sell their property and distribute among the poor the money thus realized: Matthew xix. 16, and Luke xviii. 22. No Christian, according to our knowledge, ever acquiesces in this mode of doing charity.

Secondly, The Christians do not practise the following admonition, contained in Luke vi. 35, " Love ye your enemies, and do good, and lend, and hope for nothing again;" and Matthew v. 44, " Love your enemies, bless them that curse you, do good to them that hate you, and pray for them who despitefully use you and per-secute you."

Thirdly, The Christians have, without authority, abolished the law, repeated in the New Testament, that they should abstain from eating blood and the flesh of the strangled, as we have shewn in the preceding chapter, by citing Acts xv. 29, and xxi. 25.

If Christians thus evade well-defined doctrines of the New Testament, they cannot cast any reproach on the Jew, who, from conscientious motives, refuses adherence to the new doctrines of the Christian religion.

Thus we have fairly established our objections to Christianity in the various arguments adduced in the preceding chapters, wherein we have refuted the attacks made by Christians upon the Jewish faith.

Let not the reader blame us for having occasionally made repetitions. Our desire has by no means been to swell the volume, but merely to render our arguments more clear and effective.

END OF THE FIRST PART.

SECOND PART.

BEING A REFUTATION OF STATEMENTS CONTAINED IN THE NEW TESTAMENT. THE VERSION OF THE NEW TESTAMENT USED BY THE AUTHOR WAS THAT MADE BY SIMON BUDNI, PUBLISHED IN 1572, WHOSE VERSION IS CONSIDERED THE MOST AUTHENTIC.

INTRODUCTION.

IT is notorious that, in no part of the New Testament do we find that Jesus intended to pass as the author of a New Law, but, on the contrary, that he admitted the perpetual duration of the Mosaic Law, as we have shewn in the 19th, 20th, 24th, 29th, and 30th chapters of the FIRST PART of this work. Besides, it is ascertained that the New Testament was composed many years after Jesus. It has been averred even by Jerome, in his Latin version of the New Testament, that Mark and Luke wrote merely from hearsay. Jerome seems to have thereby indirectly acknowledged the Apocryphal character of those compositions, and admitted the true origin of the incongruities and contradictions which occur in various parts of those books. We must also direct the attention of the reader to the incorrect manner in which portions of our prophets are quoted and explained therein. Very frequently the words of our Scripture are there actually changed and perverted from their true signification. In fact, after a careful perusal of the Christian Canon of faith, we have been impressed with the conviction that the authors of the New Testament have overlooked, either intentionally or unintentionally, the real meaning and bearing of our original Sacred writings.

CHAPTER I.

MATTHEW i. contains an account of the genealogy of Jesus, and traces back the descent of Joseph, the husband of Mary, to Solomon son of David. The enumeration of his ancestors terminates thus (ver. 15, 16, 17), " And Eliud begat Eleazar, and Eleazar begat Matthan, and Matthan begat Jacob, and Jacob begat Joseph, the husband of Mary, of whom was born Jesus, who is called Christ. So all the generations from Abraham to David are fourteen generations, and from David until the carrying away into Babylon are fourteen generations, and from the carrying away into Babylon unto Christ are fourteen generations."

In Luke iii. 23, 24, however, the genealogy of Jesus differs from that given by Matthew; for he assigns the descent of Joseph, the husband of Mary, to Nathan the son of David. The parentage of Jesus is there described as follows: " And Jesus was the son of Joseph, which was the son of Heli, which was the son of Matthat, which was the son of Levi, which was the son of Melchi, etc., etc. Thus while, according to Matthew, there are forty-two generations, reckoning back to Abraham, there are twenty-six according to the names mentioned in Luke. Besides this, the list of names given in Matthew is not calculated to afford a correct knowledge of the descendants of David, for three generations, Ahaziah, Jaos, and Amaziah, are omitted, and Uzziah is represented to be the son of Joram. See the correct genealogy in 1 Chron. iii., and in the historical part of the Second Book of Chronicles beginning at chapter xxii. etc.

It appears that the omission of three generations of kings was done advisedly, in order to make out Matthew's three series of fourteen generations. However, after all it must be owned, that contradictory accounts of the generations have no reference to Jesus, but only to Joseph. For, as Mary is stated to have remained a virgin, even after her marriage with Joseph, we do not see the use of putting forth a long string of names which had no relation to the founder of the Christian religion.

This perplexing matter has not escaped the enquiry of Christian scholars, and they meet it by asserting that Luke does not contradict the account of Matthew, but mentions the same Kings under different names, in the same manner as Solomon is called Uzziah, Azariah, and Jehoiachin. This defence is not admissible, as Luke mentions Nathan, the brother of Solomon, as the ancestor of Jesus; it cannot, therefore, be supposed that Solomon bore the name of Nathan. We further observe that Matthew reckons eighteen generations, and Luke twenty-three, from David to Zerubabel. Again, from Abraham to Jesus, Matthew makes out forty-two, and Luke forty generations. This cannot be reasoned away but by taking various names as the designation of the same person. Besides, we find in *our* Scriptures only two or three of those contained in the list of the ancestors of Jesus who had several names. And as to those men who lived between Abraham and David, not one is represented in our Sacred Writings as having possessed two names, so that the contradictory enumerations in the New Testament still remain unreconciled. Some scholars have contrived to offer another palliation of the suspicious account. They say Matthew alone gave the ancestral origin of Joseph, but that Luke stated that of Mary, who was also of the seed of David by his son Nathan, and that Mary's origin was mixed up with that of her husband, because man and wife are one flesh. Such apologies are frustrated by the very words of Luke (chap. iii.), who speaks expressly of Joseph to show that through him the royal ancestry of Jesus was established. Those who assert that Jesus took his pedigree from his mother, only ought to find in the genealogy of Jesus the son of Mary, the son of Heli, the son of Matthew, etc.; thus all suspicion of error would have been obviated. Those who make an attempt to defend their position by quoting " Man and wife are of one flesh," should recollect that this expression has reference only to their conjugal fidelity and affection, but not to their descent.

CHAPTER II.

MATTHEW i. 22 and 23, sets forth that Jesus was born of a virgin, in order that it might be fulfilled which was spoken by the prophet, " Behold, a virgin shall be with child and shall bring forth a son, and they shall call his name Emmanuel."

The reader will remember from the First Part of this work that we have had frequent occasion to speak of the method employed in the New Testament and other Christian works, of citing from our Scriptures certain passages, which, on careful examination, have no reference whatever to the immediate subject. Thus they quote also the passage from Isaiah vii. 14, " Behold הָעַלְמָה " (meaning the young woman and not virgin) "is with child, and about to bring forth a son." The prophecy was given to Ahaz, King of Judah, in order to allay his apprehensions regarding the two kings who were to come to carry on war against Jerusalem.

What connection could there subsist between a sign necessary to convince the King of Jerusalem, and the event of the birth of Jesus which happened so many centuries after? How could Ahaz receive consolation from prophecy, the fulfilment of which he was not to live to see?

CHAPTER III.

MATTHEW i. concludes with these words concerning Joseph, the husband of Mary; "And [he] knew her not until she had brought forth her first-born son, and he called his name Jesus." The wording of this passage shows, in the first place, that after she had brought forth "her first-born son" Joseph did "know her;" and secondly, the appellation of Jesus the "first-born son," proves that the same mother bore more children than one, otherwise the term *first*-born could not be applicable. This harmonizes well with Matthew xiii. 55, where Jesus, "the carpenter's son," is mentioned together with his brothers "James, and Joses, and Simon, and Judas." This passage is an incontrovertible contradiction of the opinion of those who consider Mary to have been a virgin before and after she had given birth to Jesus.

The English version of Matthew i. 23, has, "And *they* shall call his name Emmanuel;" but in the Hebrew original, we have וקראת "*and she shall call.*"

It is also a striking fact that the name *Emmanuel* was not given to Jesus by the virgin. Nor do we find that the Emmanuel mentioned in Isaiah was ever to be considered the Messiah.

CHAPTER IV.

MATTHEW ii. 14 and 15, " When he [Joseph] arose, he took the young child and his mother by night and departed into Egypt.   And was there until the death of Herod, that it might be fulfilled which was spoken by the prophet, saying, " Out of Egypt have I called my son."

The misapplication of the evidence taken from Hosea xi. 1, is perfectly obvious.   He speaks of the chosen people delivered from bondage.   He says, "When Israel was young I did love it, and out of Egypt I called my son."   This allusion to the pristine state of Israel fully agrees with the message Moses gave to Pharaoh.   Exod. iv. 22 and 23, " Thus saith the Lord, Israel is my first-born son, and I have said unto thee, send away my son that he may serve me."

CHAPTER V.

MATTHEW ii. 16, 17, " And Herod sent forth and slew all the children that were born in Bethlehem, and in all the coasts thereof, from two years old and under.   Then was fulfilled that which was spoken by Jeremiah the prophet, chap. xxxi. 15, saying, "Rachel [was] weeping for her children, and would not be comforted because they are not."

The construction of these words of the prophet is incompatible with what follows.   For we read in the same chapter of Jeremiah, ver. 17, " And the children shall return to their boundaries."   This cannot mean *slain*, but only *captive*, children.   The ten tribes are here alluded to as the captives who are mentioned under the collected name *Ephraim*, because their first king Jeroboam was of the tribe of Ephraim, the descendant of Rachel. Had Jeremiah's prophecy had any connection with the extermination of the infants of *Bethlehem Judah*, it would not have been for Rachel to weep, but for Leah, the ancestress of the children of Judah. See chapter xxviii of Matthew.

CHAPTER VI.

MATTHEW ii. 23, " And he came and dwelt in a city called Nazareth, that it might be fulfilled which was spoken by the prophets, He shall be called a Nazarene." This quotation has been falsely made, and is not to be found in any part of our prophetic writings; which subject has been more fully treated of in the former part of this work. See chapter 23 of FIRST PART.

CHAPTER VII.

MATTHEW iv. 1—11, " Then was Jesus led up of the Spirit into the wilderness to be tempted of the Devil. And when he had fasted forty days and forty nights, he was afterwards an hungered. And when the tempter came to him he said, If thou be the Son of God, command that these stones be made bread. But he answered and said, It is written, Man shall not live by bread alone, but by every word that proceedeth out of the mouth of God. Then the Devil taketh him into the Holy City, and setteth him on a pinnacle of the Temple, and saith to him, If thou be the Son of God, cast thyself down: for it is written, He shall give His angels charge concerning Thee; and in their hands they shall bear thee up, lest at any time thou dash thy foot against a stone. Jesus saith unto him, It is written again, Thou shalt not tempt the Lord thy God. Again, the Devil taketh him up into an exceeding high mountain, and sheweth him all the kingdoms of the world, and the glory of them, and saith unto him, All these things will I give thee, if thou wilt fall down and worship me. Then saith Jesus unto him, Get thee hence, Satan; for it is written, Thou shalt worship the Lord thy God, and him only shalt thou serve."

The same subject occurs in Luke iv. The reader must certainly perceive by this narrative that the Jesus tempted by Satan, is not intended to pass for a God incarnate. For can any man, in his sound senses, suppose that Satan would have presumed to tempt one whom he knew to be a God; or can it be imagined that he would have dared, as a creature, to lead him away by force against his will? Reason recoils from such a belief.

CHAPTER VIII.

MATTHEW iv. 13—15, "And leaving Nazareth, he [Jesus] came and dwelt in Capernaum, which is upon the sea coast, in the borders of Zebulon and Naphthali. That it might be fulfilled which was spoken by Esaias the prophet, saying, The land of Zebulon and the land of Naphthali, by the way of the sea beyond Jordan, Galilee of the Gentiles." Let the reader refer to Isaiah ix. 1, and see whether the detached passage, as given in the New Testament, proves anything relating to Jesus. There we read that the anguish is not abating which is poured down upon "her" [Israel]. "The first time it came lightly upon the land of Zebulon, and

the land of Naphthali; and the latter time, it fell heavily
upon her by the way of the sea, on the side of Jordan,
and the boundary of the Gentiles." The prophet had
spoken of the preponderance of the empire of Ashur
over that of Israel, and he stated that Tiglath Pilessar,
king of Assyria, had at first extended his conquest over
the lands of Zebulon and Naphthali; and therefore the
calamity was deemed to be confined to a narrow compass in the sight of Israel. But afterwards the misery
became oppressive, when Sennacherib marched against
Judah, and took all its fortified cities; so that Jerusalem was the only country that escaped. The whole
country of Palestine being thus ravaged, the prophet
pointed out the utmost limits of the country as the
marks of the extent of the devastation; hence the
allusion to Jordan and the sea, which were the boundaries of the nation. The borders of the neighbouring
Philistines were therefore called " the boundaries of
the Philistines." When Sennacherib came up to attack
Jerusalem, the angel of the Lord destroyed 185,000
warriors. Then it was that, according to Isaiah viii. 2,
" The people who had walked in the darkness of trouble
saw "—namely, the light of deliverance, after the total
fall of Sennacherib. That salvation is termed " light,"
is shown by the expression in Esther viii. 16, " Unto
the Jews was light." Isaiah continues, chap. ix. 3,
" Thou hast made great the nation (namely, in their
position among other nations); Thou hast increased
their joy before Thee, according to the joy in harvest";
thus expressing their gratitude and devout sentiments
at the miraculous escape from the overwhelming number
of the enemy, and their exultation during the distribution
of the spoil found in the Assyrian camp. " For Thou
hast broken the yoke of his burden"; that is, Thou hast
frustrated the designs of the cruelty of the Assyrian

king; " And the staff of his shoulder, and the rod of his oppression, as in the day of Midian." [When Gideon, with a handful of men, routed in the night the army of the invading Midianites; so that also then a supernatural help saved Israel from utter ruin.] For the attack of the assailants was as the shock of an earthquake — that is to say, this warfare differed from all others in which garments were rolled in blood; whereas in this war there was no bloodshed by human weapons, but the weapons of destruction were " burning and of full fire." The prophet then continues to say, " For unto us a child has been born, unto us a son has been given, and the government has [fallen] on his shoulders." By this prediction was meant Hezekiah, king of Judah, in whose days the signal deliverance happened. This prophecy was given to Ahaz after the birth of Hezekiah, and in consideration of the future piety of this child, this Divine consolation was given. The son who was given us, and who was proved to have been Hezekiah, was nine years old when Ahaz ascended the throne.

CHAPTER IX.

MATTHEW iv. 18, 19, " And Jesus, walking by the shores of Galilee, saw two brethren, Simon, called Peter, and Andrew his brother, casting a net into the sea, for they were fishermen, and he said unto them, Follow me, and I will make you fishers of men." The same is related in Luke v. 10, " And Jesus said unto Simon, Fear not, from henceforth thou shalt catch men." This metaphorical language employed by Jesus, appears most inapt and undignified. The net catches the unwary by stealth, and those who are caught are destined to death by those who spread the net.

CHAPTER X.

MATTHEW v. 17, 18, 19, " Think not that I am come to destroy the law, or the prophets. I am not come to destroy but to fulfil. For verily I say unto you, till heaven and earth pass away, one jot or one tittle shall in no wise pass from the law till all be fulfilled. Whosoever, therefore, shall break one of these least commandments, and shall teach men so, he shall be called the least in the kingdom of heaven: but whosoever shall do and teach them, he shall be called great in the kingdom of heaven." So in Luke xvi. 17, " And it is easier for heaven and earth to pass away than one tittle of the law to fail." These words are in direct opposition to the belief and the assertion of the Christians, that the law of Moses has been superseded by the coming of Jesus. Thus, circumcision is replaced by baptism, and the sanctity of the seventh day is deferred to the keeping of the first day of the week. With the same inexcusable freedom, many other Divine laws have been rejected by the Christians, only few having been retained, such as those regarding incest and moral enactments, respect to parents, love to our neighbour, charity to the poor, avoidance of theft, rapine, adultery, murder, shedding of blood, and some other crimes which reason enforces, and which other nations, who were without revelation, had acknowledged before the coming of Jesus. On this subject we have enlarged in Chap. XIX. of the First Part of this work.

CHAPTER XI.

MATTHEW v. 43, " Ye have heard that it hath been said, " Thou shalt love thy neighbour, and hate thy enemy."

This passage, which is pretended by Matthew to be taken from some part of our Scriptures, originated partly in his own imagination. Scripture no where bids us to hate our enemy, but teaches us a totally different doctrine; for we find in Exodus xxiii. 4, 5, " If thou meet thine enemy's ox or his ass going astray, thou shalt surely bring it back to him again. If thou seest the ass of him that hateth thee, lying under his burden, and wouldst forbear to help him, thou shalt surely help with him." See also Levit. xix. 17, 18, " Thou shalt not hate thy brother in thine heart: thou shalt rebuke thy neighbour and not suffer sin upon him. Thou shalt not avenge nor bear any grudge against the children of thy people, but thou shalt love thy neighbour as thyself. I am the Lord." Again, in the Book of Prov. xxiv. 17, " When thine enemy falleth do not rejoice, and when he stumbleth let not thine heart rejoice." And ibid xxv. 21, " If thine enemy be hungry, give him bread to eat, and if he be thirsty, give him water to drink."

CHAPTER XII.

MATTHEW viii. 19, 20, " And a certain scribe came and said unto him, Master, I will follow thee whithersoever thou goest. And Jesus said unto him, The foxes have holes, and the birds of the air have nests, but the Son of Man hath not where to lay his head." The same saying is recorded in Luke ix. 57. This passage we deem a strong proof of the consciousness of Jesus that he was not God. For, if he had really been filled with such a conceit, why should he have called himself *the Son of Man?* And moreover, why should he have dissuaded others from relying on him? Perhaps he bore in mind the admonition given in Psalm cxlvi. 3, "Do not rely in princes nor trust in the son of man, for salvation belongeth not unto him." Or perhaps the words of Jeremiah in chap. xvii. 5, "Cursed is the man who relieth on man." Had he imagined he was God, why should he have said he had nowhere to lay his head? Would he not have considered the whole earth to be his own resting-place; for does not the Psalmist remind us in Psalm xxiv. 1, "That the earth is the Lord's, and the fulness thereof, the world, and the inhabitants therein?"

CHAPTER XIII.

MATTHEW x. 34, "Think not that I am come to send peace on earth: I came not to send peace, but a sword. For I came to set a man at variance against his father, and the daughter against her mother, and the daughter-in-law against her mother-in-law." The same matter is treated on in Luke xii. 51, and is a strong indication that Jesus was not filled with that spirit of peace so indissolubly attached to the office of Messiah. For, regarding the expected Messiah, Zechariah, in chap. ix. 10, says, "And he will speak peace unto the nations." Concerning that period it was prophecied by Isaiah in chap. ii. 4; and in Mic. iv. 3, "Nation shall not lift up the sword against nation." How much less will it then be allowable that a man should "be set at variance against his father?" On the contrary, the Divine promise runs thus (in conclusion of Malachi), "And he shall restore the heart of the fathers unto the children, and the heart of the children unto their fathers."

CHAPTER XIV.

Matthew x. 40, Jesus is made to say to his apostles, "He that receiveth you receiveth me, and he that receiveth me receiveth him that sent me." By this expression the Christians are reduced to the necessity of believing that Jesus and his apostles are identical; and as they are taught that three make one, they ought, by parity of reasoning, to deduce the inference from the present passage, that the trinity, with the twelve apostles, make altogether one unity.

CHAPTER XV.

Matthew xi. 13, 14, Jesus is made to say, "All the prophets and the law prophesied until John, and if ye will receive it, this is Elias which was for to come." See the same passage in Luke xvi. 16. From this it would seem that it was intended to inculcate a belief, that the law and the prophecies had only a certain temporary object in view, which was to find its point of completion in John, a contemporary of Jesus. On the other hand, Jesus declared in Matthew v. 17, "Think not that I am come to destroy the law or the prophets; I am not come to destroy, but to fulfil." (see our opinion on this subject in Chap. XIX. of the First Part of this work). We would ask the question, how did he fulfil the predicted ingathering of the Ten Tribes, and the carrying on of the war against Gog and Magog? We would also notice a discrepancy between the opinion held out in this chapter of Matthew, that John was the Elias (Elijah) of the Bible, and the following statement made by the author of the Gospel of John: "And they asked him, What then? Art thou Elias? And he saith, I am not. Art thou the Prophet? And he answered, No." (See Chap. XXXIX. of the First Part of this work).

CHAPTER XVI.

Matthew xii. 32, "And whosoever speaketh a word against the Son of Man it shall be forgiven him, but whosoever speaketh against the Holy Ghost it shall not be forgiven him, neither in this world, neither in the world to come." See also Luke xii. 10. Both Matthew and Luke acknowledge, by this warning, that Jesus is the Son of Man; and that he and the Holy Ghost are not identical, consequently they were fully convinced that there is no doctrine in the Testament enforcing the belief in a triune deity, and that such a notion rests merely on imagination.

CHAPTER XVII.

Matthew xiii. 55; it is related there that the Jews said of Jesus, "Is not this the carpenter's son? And is not his mother called Mary, and his brethren James, and Joses, and Simon, and Judas? And his sisters, are they not all with us?" See also Mark vi. 3. How then can the Christians constantly worship Mary as a virgin, she having given birth to the several brothers and sisters of Jesus?

CHAPTER XVIII.

Matthew xv. 1 to 25, When the Pharisees blamed his

disciples for eating without previously washing their hands, Jesus argued that whatever enters the mouth does not defile man, but *that* defiles him which goes out of the mouth. The same is said in Mark vii. from the beginning to verse 24. If that were true, why should the Law of Moses prohibit us from eating certain unclean things? See also Levit. xi. 8, " And ye shall not defile yourselves with them [viz. the unclean animals] lest ye grow unclean through them." This shows, that a certain class of food is considered by Divine authority as impure and unlawful. By what right then did Jesus dare to contradict the law, and to absolve his Jewish followers from prohibited meats? If unclean food did not defile the mouth of the eater, why did the Apostles forbid the eating of blood and of the flesh of strangled animals? And did not Adam commit a sin, even according to the belief of the Christians, by the act of eating of that of which he was enjoined not to eat? How much strong drink is able to defile the soul of man is early demonstrated in Scripture, as we learn from the history of Noah and Lot. While on the other hand the expression of Jesus that words coming out of the mouth of man alone defile him, is subject to great limitation. For all praises and thanksgiving offered up to the Almighty, as well as all wise, moral and social converse do not defile the soul.

CHAPTER XIX.

Matthew xix. 16 and subsequent verses, " And behold one came and said unto him, Good master, what good thing shall I do, that I may have eternal life? And he said unto him, Why callest thou me good? There is none good but one, that is God;" an expression which proves that Jesus is not God. Then Jesus continued, " If thou desirest spiritual salvation keep the commandments." An injunction indicating that there is no salvation without the observance of the law of Moses. He [the querist] saith unto him, " Which? " Jesus said, " Thou shalt do no murder. Thou shalt not commit adultery. Thou shalt not steal. Thou shalt not bear false witness. Honor thy father and thy mother, and thou shalt love thy neighbour as thyself." Further he said, " If thou wilt be perfect, go and sell that which thou hast and give to the poor." The same is to be found in Mark x. 21. In Luke xviii. 22, Jesus thereby advises, " Sell all that thou hast and distribute unto the poor," etc. Jesus, in saying there is none good but one, that is God, taught his followers a monotheistic principle. He taught them at the same time that salvation depends on the observance of the Divine commandments. All these injunctions, given by Jesus, are renounced by Christians; and thus, having thrown off those inconvenient and onerous observances taught in the New Testament, they might well allege that the severe precepts of the Mosaic Law were abrogated, and must give place before a Lawgiver whose laws they think proper to disregard. We would ask, which precept is the most severe, that of Jesus, which demands that a man should divest himself of his property for the benefit of the poor, or the Mosaic Law, which ordains that a tithe only should be devoted to holy purposes, leaving the remainder at the free disposal of the owner of the property?

CHAPTER XX.

MATTHEW xx. 23, Jesus, addressing his disciples, namely

the two children of Zebedee, says, "To sit at my right hand and at my left is not mine to give, but it shall be given to them, for whom it is prepared of my Father." The reader will find the same idea expressed in Mark x. Now if the Son is less powerful than the Father, how can it be asserted that the Father and Son are all one?

CHAPTER XXI.

MATTHEW xx. 28, Jesus thus communicates to his disciples, "Even as the Son of Man came not to be ministered unto, but to minister," etc. The same is stated in Mark x. 45. By this passage, Jesus makes the declaration destructive of the dogma of his divinity, that he, being the son of man, is a servant and not a master; or in other words, that he is not the King Messiah of whom it was said of Zechariah, in his book, chap. ix. 10, "And his kingdom shall extend from sea to sea, and from the river to the ends of the earth." Also, in Psalm lxxii. 11, "And all kings shall bow down unto him, all nations shall serve him." And in Daniel vii. 14, "And all rulers shall serve and obey him."

CHAPTER XXII.

MATTHEW xxiii. 35, "That upon you may come all the righteous blood shed upon the earth from the blood of the righteous Abel unto the blood of Zacharias, son of Barachias, whom ye slew between the temple and the altar." This reproach rests on an error regarding the names, for it was Zechariah, the son of Jehoiada the priest, whom they slew (See 2 Chro. xxiv). It is impossible to admit the attempted reconciliation according to which Zechariah, the son of Jehoiada the priest, and Zechariah, the son of Berachiah, are identical. For the priest of that name was slain in the days of Joash, king of Judah, about two hundred and fifty-four years prior to the destruction of the temple; while the prophet Zechariah did not prophesy until the second year of Darius, the son of Artachsasta, during the Babylonian captivity. Such errors in the mouth of Jesus are decidedly unfavourable to the divine inspiration attributed to him, as well as to the authors of the New Testament.

CHAPTER XXIII.

MATTHEW xxvi. 6, 7, " Now when Jesus was in Bethany, in the house of Simon the leper, there came unto him a woman having an alabaster box of very precious ointment, and poured it on his head." In Mark xiv. 3, the narrative is given in the following words, " And being in Bethany, in the house of Simon the leper, there came a woman having an alabaster box of ointment of spikenard, very precious, and she brake the box and poured it on his head." In Luke vii. 37, however, the version is far different; " And behold a woman brought an alabaster box of ointment, and stood at his feet behind him, and anointed them with ointment." Then Jesus said to Simon, the master of the house (ver. 46), " my head with oil thou didst not anoint, but this woman hath anointed my feet with ointment.'

In John xii. 3. the story is narrated thus: " Then took Mary a pound of ointment of spikenard, very costly, and anointed the feet of Jesus." These extracts, from the several books of the New Testament, are curious specimens of the want of agreement between the several authors, who of necessity would have been in perfect unanimity, had they been under the influence of Divine inspiration.

CHAPTER XXIV.

MATTHEW xxvi. 39, "And he (Jesus) went a little further and fell on his face, and prayed, saying, O, my Father, if it be possible, let this cup pass from me; nevertheless, not as I will, but as thou wilt." See likewise Mark xiv. 35, and Luke xxii. 41. This passage refutes the Christian belief, that Jesus offered himself spontaneously as the sacrifice for the salvation of mankind. If that had been the case, why should he have hesitated and prayed for the removal of the bitter cup of his portion; and why should he have exclaimed, " My God, my God, why hast Thou forsaken me"! (see Matthew xxvii. 46). This is another proof that the Father and the Son are not identical, and that the design of the one does not accord with that of the other.

CHAPTER XXV.

MATTHEW xxvii. 9, 10, " Then was fulfilled that which was spoken by Jeremy the prophet, saying, "And they took the thirty pieces of silver, the price of him that was valued, and whom they of the children of Israel did value, and gave them for the potter's field, as the Lord appointed me." Here, again, we meet with the usual misapplication of Scriptural passages. The quotation, taken from Zechariah xi. 12, 13, runs as follows: " So they weighed for my price thirty pieces of silver. And the Lord said unto me, Cast it unto the potter," etc.

The unbiassed reader need merely refer to the context from which this passage is extracted, in order to obtain the conviction that the prophet wished to convey a far different idea than Matthew found in it. Zechariah, in the chapter before us, represents the fate of the children of Judah during the captivity, who had become the prey of their enemy for having transgressed the commandments of the Almighty, and hence he designates the Jews of the second temple as the flock of the slaughter.

The prophet Zechariah's account (in chap. xi. 7) of his taking two staves, the name of the one being "Beauty," and the name of the other "Bands," must not be viewed in its literal, but in its metaphorical sense. The staves signify the leaders of Israel, for the shepherd conducts his flock by means of the staff or crook in his hand. Now the prophet hereby intimates that Israel would be treated according to the merit of their doings. *The Staff* "*Beauty*" (*i. e.* lenient treatment) was used in the early days of the second temple, when such leaders as Nehemiah and Zerubbabel stood at the helm of Government; while the misgovernment of the succeeding rulers, which crippled and ultimately destroyed the energies and well-being of Israel, was designated "Bands" (*i. e.*, harsh treatment). The simultaneous death of three righteous leaders, alluded to by the prophet, may have been in reference to Haggai, Zechariah, and Malachi, after whose decease severe calamities came upon the Jewish nation.

The shepherd in the prophecy claims his wages—that is to say, he demands that the pious observance of the Divine statutes should be offered as a compensation for the special favours of the Almighty. The thirty pieces of silver are a figurative representation of the righteous men of the time, who were cast to their potter (*i. e.*

literally thrown upon the mercy of their Former or Creator). The Staff (termed *Bands*) was broken; for we learn from our history that the misrule prevailing in Jerusalem was productive of Israel's overthrow. Indeed, it seemed as if every successive bad Government had been destined to be the avenger of the misdeeds of its predecessor. Whether it be correct or not, to refer the details of the prophecy to certain known historical characters, this much is evident, that the political government of the Jews, and their destiny, are the circumstances alluded to by the prophet. No thinking man can, however, admit that the prophecy had reference to Jesus, in whose fate his Jewish contemporaries were so little concerned.

CHAPTER XXVI.

MATTHEW xxvii. 46, " And about the ninth hour, Jesus cried with a loud voice, saying, ' Eli, Eli, lama sabachthani,'—that is to say, ' My God, my God, why hast thou forsaken me' "? See the same passage in Mark xv. 34.

By this exclamation, Jesus clearly announced that he was not a God, but was like other mortals, who invoke God in the day of trouble.

CHAPTER XXVII.

MATTHEW xxviii. 18, " And Jesus came and spake unto them (*i. e.* his disciples), All power is given unto me in heaven and in earth." This passage does not show that he was a Divine Being; for, had he been so, he would not have asserted that the power was *given* to him. To God, nothing can be given; for "Unto him belongeth the dominion and the power." He is the Giver, and not the Receiver. It could not be maintained that Jesus received the dominion from his Father, for in that case the Bestower and the Acceptor must incontestably be considered as two separate and distinct Beings. This concludes our views concerning the book of Matthew.

CHAPTER XXVIII.

MARK ii. 25, "And he [Jesus] said unto them, Have ye never read what David did when he had need and was an hungered, he and they that were with him? How when he went into the house of God, in the days of Abiathar, the high priest, and did eat the shewbread, which is not lawful to eat, but for the priests, and gave thereof to him that were with him." This passage is also to be found in Matthew xii. 3, and in Luke vi. 3; but all these authors have fallen into the same error, and labour under the same misconception. For this happened in the time of Ahimelech, the priest, and not in the time of Abiathar, as may be seen in 1 Samuel ii. 1, " David came to Nob, to Ahimelech, the priest," etc. But Abiathar was one of the sons of Ahimelech, the son of Ahitub, who escaped and fled after David. Now, from the express question put to him, we see that David came alone to Ahimelech, and that no one was with him: " Why art thou alone, and no man with thee?"

CHAPTER XXIX.

MARK iii. 31—35, " There came then his brethren and his mother, and standing without, sent unto him, calling

him; and the multitude sat about him, and they said
unto him, Behold thy mother and thy brethren without
seek thee.   And he answered them, saying, Who is my
mother, or my brethren?   And he looked round about
on them which sat about him, and said, Behold my
mother and my brethren.   For whoever shall do the
will of God, the same is my brother, and my sister, and
mother."   The same subject occurs in Matthew, at the
close of chap. xii.; and in Luke viii. 19.   It appears from
these statements, that his own mother, and brothers, and
sister, would not believe in him, and be his disciples, and
that he would not go to meet them who were of his own
flesh.   The allusion to mutual discord between them is
confirmed by the statement in John vii. 5, " For neither
did his brethren believe in him."

CHAPTER XXX.

MARK xi. 11, 12, 13, " And on the morrow, when they
were come from Bethany, he (Jesus) was hungry; and,
seeing a fig-tree afar off having leaves, he came, if haply
he might find anything thereon; and when he came to
it, he found nothing but leaves, as the season of figs was
not yet come.   And Jesus answered, and said unto it,
No man eat fruit of thee for evermore."   See also
Matthew xxi. 18.   Jesus acted here neither as a Divine
person, nor as a man in whom the Divine Spirit dwelt.
For he surely might have known that the fig-tree bears
its fruit only at the appointed season; nor would any
discreet person cast a malediction on a tree merely for
being thus disappointed.   Moreover, if Jesus, by his
mere word, was able to render a tree barren, might he
not as well, by the power of his word, have made the
tree bring forth its fruit at the bidding of the moment,

in order to appease his hunger? I, having once made use of this argument with a Christian, he explained it away by asserting that the passage has only a spiritual signification, and that the fig-tree named was but a symbol used by Jesus to represent the Jewish nation, in like manner as the prophets designate them the "vine-tree," and that Jesus had cursed Israel for having rejected him as their spiritual teacher. I rejoined that, in our prophecies regarding the time of the expected and true Messiah, we are promised that in the days of the Messiah, knowledge and prophecy shall increase and prevail throughout the world; as it is said in Joel ii. 27, 28, "You shall know that I am in the midst of Israel, and that I am the Lord your God, and none else, and my people shall then never again be put to shame. And then I shall pour out my spirit upon all flesh, and your sons and your daughters shall prophecy." From this prophecy, it is clear that many of the indispensable conditions, requisite for the advent of the Messiah, had not yet been fulfilled, but were still to come.

CHAPTER XXXI.

MARK xiii. 32, Jesus is made to say to his disciples, "But of that day and that hour knoweth no man, no, not the angels which are in heaven, neither the Son but the Father." Here we have a clear proof that Jesus, who is called "the son of Mary," is not a God, seeing that he could not foretell events.

CHAPTER XXXII.

LUKE i. 26, There it is related that the angel Gabriel

came as a messenger sent by God to Mary in her virgin
state, when she was espoused to Joseph of the house of
David, and that He announced to her she would conceive and bear a son, who would be holy, and be called
a son of the highest; that the throne of David would be
assigned to him by the Lord God for occupation, and
that he would reign over the house of Jacob for ever,
and of his kingdom there should be no end."

The statement disagrees with those made in other
parts of the New Testament, and cast strong suspicion
on the veracity of a book asserted to be written under
the influence of inspiration. If Mary had received
such a divine message, why did she and her children
refuse faith in, and obedience to that Son of God, and
why did she and her offspring keep away from the
circle of the disciples of him whom she had borne through
the intervention of a miracle? See Mark iii. 31. A
marked contrast also appears between the words of
Luke i. 26, and those in John vii. 5, which we had
occasion to quote in a former chapter, viz., " His
brethren did not believe in him." Would it not have
been the duty of the virgin-mother to inform her
children what a strong claim her first-born had on their
pious attachment to him? Again, why did Mary name
her son " Jesus?" If he were to be named *Emmanuel*,
according to the interpretation given to the famous
passage in Isaiah, which is especially cited in Matthew i. 22,
why did the angel hold out the never-fulfilled promise
that Jesus would sit on the throne of David? Moreover,
why was Jesus called the descendant of David, since it
is alleged that he was not the offspring of Joseph, of
the house of David, but was begotten of the Holy
Ghost? The number of contradictions also is increased
by the words of Paul in his First Epistle to the Corinthians, chap. xv., ver. 28, for there it is said, " Then

shall the son also himself be subject unto him, that put all things under him." This is an additional proof that the kingdom of Jesus is not intended to continue throughout eternity, but is to be only of a temporary nature; hence, we arrive at the conclusion, from the very authorities of the Christian faith, that the Father and the Son are totally distinct personages.

CHAPTER XXXIII.

This chapter is omitted by the translator as unimportant in itself, and inapplicable to the general argument.

CHAPTER XXXIV.

LUKE ii. 33, " And Joseph and his mother marvelled at those things which were spoken of him."

" The child tarried behind in Jerusalem, and *his parents* knew not of it." " And when they saw him they were amazed, and his mother said unto him, Son, why hast thou thus dealt with us? Behold *thy father* and I have sought thee sorrowing?" ver. 43, 48. Ibid. iv. 22, " And they said, Is not this *Joseph's son?*" See also John i. 45, " Jesus of Nazareth, the *son of Joseph;*" and ibid. vi. 42, " Is not this Jesus the *son of Joseph, whose father* and mother we know?"

These passages afford a complete refutation of the doctrine of the miraculous conception of Jesus, and thereby undermine the groundwork of the Christian faith.

CHAPTER XXXV.

LUKE iii, 23, The genealogy of Jesus, as treated in this and the subsequent verses, is contradictory to that in Matthew i. For Luke commences thus: " The list of the descent of Jesus"—" And Jesus [as was supposed],* was the son of Joseph, the son of Heli, the son of Matthat, the son of Levi, the son of Malachi," etc. etc. In Matthew, where the origin of Joseph is traced back to Solomon, the Son of David, the enumeration of the ancestors of Joseph closes in the following manner:— " And Eliud begat Eleazar, and Eleazar begat Matthan, and Matthan begat Jacob, and Jacob begat Joseph, the husband of Mary, of whom was born Jesus." We have already shown above that Matthew enumerates forty-two generations, from Abraham our father; but Luke counts only twenty-six. From these contrary statements one might fairly ask, which Joseph was the husband of Mary? Was it Joseph, the son of Heli, the son of Matthat, the son of Levi, as Luke supposes; or was it Joseph, the son of Jacob, the son of Matthan, the son of Eleazar, as Matthew supposes? If we are to believe the words of Luke then the statement of Matthew must be incorrect, and *vice versâ.* Luke, in tracing back the descent of Jesus to the first ancestor, says that Jesus was the son of *Adam, the Son of God.* Hence it would seem that Jesus has no better title to the designation of *the Son of God,* than every other descendant of Adam.

---

* The words " *as was supposed,*" inserted here in the copies of the translators of Luke, are a gratuitous interpolation, intended to make us Jews believe that the author himself used the words, from the apprehension that he was affording an argument militating against the Divinity of Jesus.—NOTE BY THE TRANSLATOR.

CHAPTER XXXVI.

LUKE iv. 17—21, " And there was delivered unto him (to Jesus) the book of the prophet Esaias, and when he had opened the book, he found the place where it was written, 'The Spirit of God is upon me, because he hath anointed me to preach the Gospel to the poor. He hath sent me to heal the broken-hearted, to preach deliverance to the captives, and recovery of sight to the blind, to set at liberty them that are bruised, to proclaim the acceptable year of the Lord.' And he closed the book, and he gave it again to the minister, and sat down. And he said unto them, ' This day is this Scripture fulfilled in your ears." Isaiah lxi. is here quoted in a garbled manner. In order to lay more stress on the healing powers attributed to Jesus, the gift of restoring sight to the blind is added to the mission of the pretended Messiah. On the other hand, it is omitted to be quoted that this would be—" A day of vengeance to our God, to comfort all mourners, to give to the mourners of Zion glory instead of ashes, the oil of gladness instead of mourning, the cloak of praise instead of a gloomy spirit". Jesus had no right to attribute to himself the glory of deeds he had not performed. Isaiah spoke here of *himself*. And by the words, " The Lord hath anointed me," he meant nothing more than that he had received the Divine unction as a prophet. It was he who was sent forth to offer consolation, in order that the Israelites, during their long sufferings, should not despair of the Divine aid, and of their future restoration. They, the exiled children of Israel, were addressed by the prophets " as the afflicted, the broken-hearted, the captives, the prisoners, the mourners of Zion." They alone stood in need of the prophetic consolatory promises, and to whom alone they had reference.

CHAPTER XXXVII.

LUKE vi. 27—29, " Love your enemies, do good
to them that hate you. Bless them that curse you,
and pray for them which despitefully use you. And
unto him that smiteth thee on the one cheek offer also
the other, and him that taketh away thy cloak, forbid
not to take thy coat also." This injunction is a repetition of what is to be found in Matthew v. 39. These
injunctions were and are, however, not only disregarded
by the members of the Christian religion, but were not
even practised by Jesus himself in the spirit in which the
words imply. For in John xviii. 22, we find that
Jesus, when beaten by a bye-stander, instead of offering
quietly his other cheek, very naturally argued with
him on the unfairness of such summary proceeding.
Nor did Paul silently submit to the order given by the
priest, that he should be smitten on the mouth, (Acts
xxiii. 2, 3), or offer his cheek in meek contentment,
but indignantly swore " God shall smite thee, thou
whited wall." If the precept were broken, obviously
from its extreme rigour, by the very disciple who
promulgated it, it is strange to ascribe to the doctrines
of Jesus, as is done in certain parts of the Gospel, a
greater degree of practicability than to the original laws
of Moses, a fact that must convince every thoughtful
man that Christian doctrines are not always infallible.

CHAPTER XXXVIII.

LUKE xi. 37, 38, and 41, " And he [Jesus] went in
and sat down to meat, and when the Pharisees saw it,
they marvelled that he [Jesus] had not first washed

before dinner." To this expression of purpose Jesus responded, "Now do ye Pharisees make clean the outside of the cup and the platter; but your inward part is full of ravening and wickedness. Ye fools, did not he that made that which is without make that which is within also? But rather give alms of such things as ye have, and behold all things are clean unto you."

These arguments are merely quoted here, to show how illogical some of the replies are, which are put into the mouth of the assumed Son of God.

The negligent, and those who are indifferent to cleanliness, might screen themselves under such dicta; plain sense, however, would have suggested an answer of a different character. Other sayings of similar inconsistency in the replies of Jesus are recorded in the book of Matthew.

CHAPTER XXXIX.

LUKE xvi. 22, 23, Lazarus is stated to enjoy after his death the bliss of immortality in the bosom of Abraham, whilst the rich man, who indulged in the pleasures of this world, is to suffer the torments of hell. It is further said, that there subsists an infinite distinction between the abode of glory and that of perdition.

According to this account, it does not appear that either Abraham or Lazarus were after their death doomed to the punishment of hell, although the alleged work of the redemption of mankind had not yet been achieved by Jesus. We are therefore at a loss to know what the Christians mean by salvation wrought by Jesus, and what can be the danger of the original sin, when we see that it did not affect those who died unredeemed.

CHAPTER XL.

LUKE xxiii. 34, " Then Jesus said, Father pardon them, they know not what they do."

This appeal refutes the opinion of the Christians, who maintain that the Jews suffer the punishments of the Almighty for having put Jesus to death.

Can the Christians believe that God would not accept the supplication of Jesus?

Whether the supplication was accepted or not accepted, it is clear that the Jews do not lie under the punishment of the Almighty, in consequence of that deed.

CHAPTER XLI.

JOHN i. 21, " And they asked him, What then? Art thou Elias? and he said, I am not. Art thou that prophet? and he answered, No."

This verse completely contradicts the statement made in Matthew xi. 13, 14, according to which John is included in the list of prophets, and is held to be the last of them. The words used in that book, which we have had occasion to adduce, run as follows: " All the prophets and the law prophesied until John; and if ye will receive it, this is Elias [Elijah], which was for to come." In Matthew xvii. 12, 13, Jesus, in alluding to John, affirms that the forerunner of himself as a Messiah had come, although he had not been acknowledged as such. He says there, " Elias [Elijah], is come already, and they knew him not, but have done unto him whatever they listed. Likewise shall also the Son of Man suffer of them. Then the disciples understood that he spake of John the Baptist."

Once, on representing this contradiction to a Christian, he evaded a direct answer by the retort, that Samuel likewise denied his true mission, for he told Saul that he was on his way to offer up sacrifices, while his real object was to anoint David as king of Israel.

The cogency of this reply is not apparent, for Samuel made no secret of his mission to David to whom he had to communicate the Divine will, but observed the necessary caution with Saul, to whom he had *not* been sent. Different, however, was the case with the pretended Elias.

If he [John], had to bring the Jews the tidings of the advent of the Messiah, he very strangely performed his duty, by denying his character and concealing his message.

CHAPTER XLII.

JOHN ii. 4, " Jesus saith unto her (viz., to his mother Mary), Woman, what have I to do with thee?" and ibid. chap. xix. 26, " When Jesus, therefore, saw his mother and the disciple standing by, whom he loved, he saith unto his mother, Woman, behold thy son." If he had believed that his mother had miraculously given birth to him, and still continued in her virgin state, would he not have addressed her by the more endearing and exalting appellation than the simple term *woman*? The mode in which he addressed his mother here, and on various other occasions narrated in the New Testament, shows that he was not at all impressed with the sanctity of the commandment, " Honour thy father and thy mother."

CHAPTER XLIII.

JOHN ii. 18—20, " Then answered the Jews, and said unto him [viz., to Jesus], What sign showest thou unto us, seeing that thou doest these things? Jesus answered and said unto them, Destroy this temple, and in three days I will raise it up. Then said the Jews, Forty and six years was this temple in building, and wilt thou rear it up in three days?"

Could Jesus prove his divine character by thus advising the Jews to lay a sacrilegious hand on the sacred edifice? And, moreover, it was most unreasonable to ask that the Jews, who did not believe in his divine power, should commit an action that should consign the temple to everlasting destruction, merely for the sake of testing the reality of his character.

CHAPTER XLIV.

JOHN vi. 38, " For I [viz., Jesus], came down from heaven not to do mine own will, but the will of Him that sent me."

If Jesus alludes here to the descent of his soul to the earth. in order to inhabit the body, then he has pronounced a common-place doctrine, for every human body is possessed of a soul; but if he meant that he descended from heaven in flesh, then the assertion is at variance with the other accounts, according to which he was born of a woman in Bethlehem, in a manger. See Luke ii. 7. Moreover, we see here an acknowledgment of the all-important fact of his non-identity with the Godhead, as he professed to be only the agent of Him who sent him.

CHAPTER XLV.

JOHN vii. 5, "For neither did his brethren believe in him." If his own brothers, men of the same flesh and blood, and the nearest judges of the powers attributed to him, felt no inducement to admit his pretensions; surely we Jews may be excused for discrediting what his own contemporaries and brothers rejected as incredible.

CHAPTER XLVI.

JOHN vii. 15, "And the Jews marvelled, saying, How knoweth this man letters, having never learned?"

Talmudical tradition informs us that he had a teacher, who was named R. Joshua Ben Perachiah, and that master and scholar had fled into Egypt to escape the persecution of King Janai.

CHAPTER XLVII.

JOHN viii. 3, " And the scribes and Pharisees brought unto him a woman taken in adultery; and when they had set her in the midst, they said unto him, Master, this woman was taken in adultery, in the very act. Now Moses, in the law, commanded us that such should be stoned. But what sayest thou? And he said unto them, 'He that is without sin among you, let him first cast a stone at her." And he said to the woman (verse 11), " Neither do I condemn thee; go, and sin no more."

The laxity of this sentence is not only opposed to the Mosaic injunction, " Thou shalt remove the evil from the midst of thee": but it is also practically disavowed by the Christian legislation, according to which, the adulteress is subjected to the severest rigour of the law, on account of the injury it would necessarily occasion to the happiness of society.

CHAPTER XLVIII.

JOHN viii. 4, " But now ye seek to kill me, a man that hath told you the truth which I have heard of God."

If he had been identical with God, he would not have told the Jews that he had received his revelation *from* God. The truth proceeds from his own mouth, that he was not a Deity incarnate. What the opinion of his disciples was regarding this Divinity subsequently attributed to him, is sufficiently manifest, in spite of the many obscure expressions that occur in the New Testament; for instance, Paul says plainly, in his epistle to the Romans, chap. v. 15, " The gift of grace which is *by One Man*, Jesus Christ, hath abounded unto many." In every part of the New Testament where Jesus speaks of himself, he represents himself as the Son of Man, and not as God.

CHAPTER XLIX.

JOHN x. 16, " And other sheep I [Jesus] have, which are not of this fold; them also I must bring, and they shall hear my voice, and there shall be one fold and one shepherd."

The truth which is contained in this passage has no reference to himself, for the union of faith was not accomplished by him, and will only take place at a future period, when the proper time shall arrive. This is testified by the following passages of Scripture. Isaiah, in chap. xlv. 23, says, " Thus I have sworn by myself, the word is gone out of my mouth in righteousness, and shall not return, For unto me every knee shall bow, and every tongue shall swear." Zephaniah iii. 9, " For then will I turn to the people a pure language, that they may all call upon the name of the Lord, to serve Him with one consent." The predominance of Judaism over all the religions of the Gentiles is dwelt on in the following extracts from the prophets: Isaiah lii. 1, " Awake, awake, put on thy strength, O Zion; put on thy beautiful garments, O Jerusalem, the Holy City; for henceforth there shall no more come unto thee, the uncircumcised and the unclean." Ibid. chap. lii. 1, " And it shall come to pass, that from one new moon to another, and from one Sabbath to another, shall all flesh come to worship before me, saith the Lord." Zechariah xiv. 16, " And it shall come to pass, that every one that is left of all the nations which came against Jerusalem shall even go up from year to year to worship the King, the Lord of Hosts, and to keep the feast of tabernacles." As to the attribution of the sovereignty of empires to the future King Messiah, we find in Daniel ii. 44, " And in the days of these kings shall the God of Heaven set up a kingdom which shall never be destroyed, and the kingdom shall not be left to other people; but it shall break in pieces and consume all those kingdoms, and *it* shall stand for ever."

Ibid. vii. 27, " And the kingdom and the dominion, and the greatness of dominion under the whole heaven, shall be given to the people of the saints of the Most

High, whose kingdom is an everlasting kingdom, and all the dominions shall serve and obey Him." Numbers xxiv. 17, "I see it [it will not happen] now, I behold it, but not nigh; there shall come a star out of Jacob, and a sceptre shall rise out of Judah, and he shall smite the corners of Moab, and overthrow the children of Sheth."

CHAPTER L.

JOHN x. 30, "I [Jesus] and my Father are one." According to the opinion prevailing among the Christians, Jesus declared in these words his perfect identity with the Godhead; but we have already noticed a passage which completely refutes this view. For we find in Mark xiii. 32, "But of that day and that hour knoweth no man, no, not the angels which are in heaven, neither the son, but the Father."

Every attempt to reconcile the two contradictory verses, only leads to new perplexities. The more we examine into the purport of the New Testament, the more clearly we perceive its general tenor is not to deify Jesus; and that the doctrines which assign to him the title of God, have arisen from want of due investigation, and are not upheld by the force of sound argument.

CHAPTER LI.

JOHN x. 33—36, "The Jews answered him [Jesus], For a good work we stone thee not; but for blasphemy, and because that thou, being a man, makest thyself God.

"Jesus answered them, Is it not written in your law,

I said ye are gods? If he called them gods unto whom the Word of God came, and the Scripture cannot be broken: say ye of him, whom the Father hath sanctified and sent into the world, Thou blasphemest, because I said, I am the Son of God"?

The equivocal reply of Jesus for styling himself God, argues more against than in favour of his claim. In quoting in his above defence the words of Psalm lxxxii. 6, "I have said, Ye are gods, and sons of the Most High altogether," he has not borne in mind that the psalmist spoke with the very purpose of showing that those who call themselves sons of God, betray by their own nature that they delude themselves and others; for he goes on to say, "But surely ye die like other men, and fall like any one of the princes." The occurrence of the word Elohim (gods), does not even show that the Divine Being is really alluded to. We have instances that both *angels and judges* are designated by that term, and that it is equal to the expression of higher powers or authorities. See Judges xiii. 22, "We must die, for we have seen an "Elohim" (a superior being). In Exodus xxii. 9, we read, "The cause of both men shall come before the Elohim" (the judicial authorities), and whom those Elohim find guilty, "he shall pay a double portion to his neighbour." Similar use is made of the word Elohim in various places of our Scriptures. In Psalm lxxxii. 1, the word gods [Elohim] has the same signification as angels and messengers of the Almighty.

When God said to Moses, "Behold I have made thee a god unto Pharaoh," He spoke merely of him as of a messenger who came in the name of the Most High. The misquoted passages abounding in the New Testament betray the scanty and superficial knowledge its authors possessed of the language and purport of our Holy Scripture.

CHAPTER LII.

John x. 38, " That ye may know and believe that the Father is in me, and I in Him." The same is repeated in chap. xiv. 11. In chap. xvii. 21, it is said, " That they all may be one, as thou, Father, art in me, and I in Thee, that they also may be one in us; that the world may believe that Thou hast sent me. And the glory which Thou gavest me, I have given them, that they may be one even as we are one. I in them, and Thou in me, that they may be made perfect in one," etc.

The junction of Father and Son is conferred also upon the twelve apostles. If, therefore, the Christians thought it necessary to change their belief in the Divine unity, they were not justified in adopting the term " Trinity," inasmuch as the twelve apostles are placed on an equality with Jesus, and they might, with the same latitude of argument, be well included in the coalition of Divine personages.

CHAPTER LIII.

John xiii. 3, " Jesus, knowing that the Father had given all things into his hands," etc. See also ibid. xvi. 15, " All things that the Father hath are mine;" and Matthew xxviii. 18, "All power is given unto me in heaven and in earth." This assumption of Supreme dominion is in total opposition to the often-quoted passage of Mark xiii. 32, " But of that day and that hour knoweth no man, no, not the angels which are in heaven, neither the son, but the Father only." A like inconsistency in ascribing to Jesus at one time the possession, and at another a deficiency, of Supreme dominion, is perceptible in Matthew xx. **23**, where Jesus owns that it is not within his power to allot to the meritorious certain distinctions in future life. We have before quoted from Matthew viii. **19**, that Jesus confessed he had no place on which to rest his head, and was poorer than the fox in the field and the bird of the heavens. In John xiv. **28**, he states, "The Father is greater than I." Such repeated discrepancies must deprive the New Testament of all title of a genuine and an inspired work.

CHAPTER LIV.

JOHN xiii. **34**, Jesus asserts, "A new commandment I give unto you, that ye love one another," etc. This commandment was by no means a new one. Moses had inculcated it in the words, "Thou shalt love thy neighbour as thy self." Matthew xix. 19, and xxii. 39, admit that Moses was the first who promulgated this precept.

CHAPTER LV.

JOHN xvii. 3, Jesus says, " And this is life eternal, that they might know Thee, the only true God, and Jesus Christ, whom thou hast sent."

In this verse, Jesus acknowledged himself to be merely a messenger, and not an integral part of the Deity. The awe and worship due to the Almighty is also, in Timothy i. 17, declared to belong to God alone; for we find there, "Now unto the king eternal, immortal, invisible, the only wise God, be honour and glory for ever and ever, amen."

If Jesus does not share the glory of God, he must be

dependant on the will of his Creator, like every other
creature.

CHAPTER LVI.

JOHN xviii. 3, etc., "Judas Iscariot having received a
band of men from the chief priests and pharisees, cometh
with lanthorns," etc., and was asked by Jesus, "Whom
seek ye? and they answered and said, Jesus of Nazareth.
Jesus saith unto them, I am he.   And Judas also, who
betrayed him, stood with them."

This account of the betrayal differs from that given
in Matthew xxvi. 47; Mark xiv. 43; and Luke xxii.
47; for according to those authors of the respective
parts of the Gospel, Judas gave a secret sign to his
companions, saying, "Him whom I shall kiss, that same
is he, hold him fast."

CHAPTER LVII.

JOHN xix. 15, "The chief priests answered, We have no
king but Cæsar."

Those who are of opinion that the Jews lost their
independence on account of their putting Jesus to death,
find here a complete refutation.   The Cæsar alluded to
was the Emperor Tiberius, who had, according to
Luke iii., placed Pilate over Jerusalem.

CHAPTER LVIII.

JOHN xx. 17, "Jesus saith unto her [Mary Magdalene],
Touch me not; for I am not yet ascended to my Father;

but go to my brethren, and say unto them, I ascend unto my Father and your Father, and to my God and your God."

Jesus showed here clearly that he was no God, but was in the same subjection to God as his brethren.

It cannot, therefore, be asserted on the authority of this passage, that Jesus meant anything more by styling himself "the Son of God," than the Holy Scriptures indicate by such passages as Deut. xiv. 1, "Ye are children of the Lord your God." The expression "*Son of God*," has not the slightest reference to a Superhuman Being.

CHAPTER LIX.

ACTS i. 6 and 7, "When they [the Apostles], therefore, were come together, they asked of Jesus, saying, Lord wilt thou at this time restore again the kingdom to Israel? and he said unto them, It is not for you to know the times or the seasons which the Father has put in *his own* power."

The enquirers were evidently awaiting the restoration, and learnt from his own avowal, that he did not con- sider himself the restorer of the kingdom of the Jews. At the same time he owned, that the termination of Israel's exile is only known to the Almighty. If Jesus had considered himself divinely inspired, he would have given an answer in unison with his supernatural knowledge.

CHAPTER LX.

ACTS v. 34, " Then stood there up one in the council, a

pharisee, named Gamaliel, a doctor of the law, and said
unto the Jews, Ye men of Israel, take heed to yourselves
what ye intend to do as touching these men; for if this
council, or this work, be of men, it will come to nought:"
(verse 39) "but if it be of God, ye cannot overthrow
it; lest, haply (perhaps) ye be found even to fight
against God."

The subject is cited here for the purpose of following
the order of the passages which claim a refutation.
We have already noticed that the duration of a sect
does not constitute a proof of the veracity of their
tenets, otherwise, the Mahommedan faith would be
entitled to nearly the same belief as that of the Christians.

CHAPTER LXI.

ACTS vii. 4, "Then came he out of the land of the
Chaldeans and dwelt in Charran, and from thence, when
his father was dead, they brought him into this land
wherein ye now dwell." We have already pointed
out that this statement of Abraham's departure from
Charran, after the death of his father, is erroneous.
Instead of recapitulating our proof, we refer the reader
to chap. xlv., of the first part of this work.

It is true that the death of Therah, though happening
after the departure of Abraham, is mentioned before it;
but that is the frequent mode of Scripture narrative.
In the same way we find the death of Isaac recorded
before the selling of Joseph, although a brief calculation
would show that he survived thirteen years after the
selling of his grandson.

CHAPTER LXII.

Acts vii. 7, "And the nation to whom they shall be in bondage will I judge, said God, and afterwards shall they come forth and serve me in this place."

From this quotation it appears, that the disciples of Jesus were but superficially versed in biblical knowledge. For in Genesis (chap. xv.) no such words as "in this place," are to be found; and in Exodus iii. 12, the expression is, "When thou shalt bring out this people from Egypt, ye *shall serve God on this mountain*."

CHAPTER LXIII.

Acts vii. 14, " Then sent Joseph, and called his father Jacob to him, and all his kindred, threescore and fifteen souls. So Jacob went down into Egypt and died, he and our fathers, and were carried over into Sychem, and laid in the sepulchre that Abraham bought for a sum of money of the sons of Emmor, the father of Sychem."

The many errors put together in so a small compass are sufficiently obvious. In the first place, we know that Jacob's family that came down to Egypt, inclusive of Joseph and his sons, amounted to seventy persons, and not to seventy-five. See Genesis xlvi. 27, and Deut. x. 22.

Secondly, Jacob was not buried in Sychem (Schachem), but in the cave of Machpelah, in Hebron.

Thirdly, The " fathers" of the several tribes were not buried in Egypt, Joseph only being buried there, but his remains Moses carried away with him at the time of the departure of the Israelites from Egypt.

Fourthly, Abraham did not buy the cave of Mach-pelah of the children of Emmor (Hamor), the son of Schachem," but of Ephron, the Hittite.

Fifthly, the plot of field, situated near Schachem, was purchased by Jacob, and not by Abraham. The author of the Acts had but a confused idea of the several purchases made by the patriarchs Abraham and Jacob, and his statements respecting them must have been from hearsay.

Sixthly, Schachem (Schechem, Sychem), was the son, and not the father of Emmor (Hamor).

CHAPTER LXIV.

Acts vii. 43, " Yea, ye took the tabernacle of Moloch, and the star of your god Remphan, figures which ye made to worship them, and I will carry you away beyond Babylon." This quotation from the prophecy of Amos is incorrect. In chap. v. 26, 27, it is thus expressed: " But ye have borne the tabernacle of your Moloch, and Chiun your images, the star of your God, which ye made to yourselves. Therefore I will cause you to go into captivity beyond Damascus," etc. Quotations misapplied, or garbled, destroy the authenticity of a work instead of supporting it.

CHAPTER LXV.

Acts viii. 9, 10, 11, " There was a certain man called Simon, which before time in the same city, used sorcery, and bewitched the people of Samaria, giving out that himself was some great one, to whom they all gave heed from the least to the greatest, saying, This man is the great power of God, and to him they had regard, because that of long time he had bewitched them with sorceries."

In days when credulity and superstition were rife, and sorceresses were deemed to be inspired messengers of the Almighty, it was easy to impress a belief that the son of a woman was an incarnate deity, but in an age, when sorcery is discredited, and superstition discouraged, it is strange that such a belief should be inculcated, and that men should attempt to convert the Jews to the inconsistent doctrines that still prevail, that Jesus was a God on earth.

CHAPTER LXVI.

ACTS x. 11—15, " And Peter saw heaven opened; and a certain vessel descending unto him, wherein were all manner of four-footed beasts of the earth, and wild beasts, and creeping things, and fowls of the air. And there came a voice to him, saying, arise, Peter, kill and eat. But Peter said, Not so, Lord, for I have never eaten anything that is common or unclean. And the voice spake unto him again the second time, What God hath cleansed, that call not thou common." The same is stated ibid. chap. xi. 6. In Paul's first epistle to the Corinthians, chap. x. 25, the following doctrine is taught: " Whatsoever is sold in the shambles, that eat, asking no questions for conscience sake." Mark, (chap. vii. 16,) declares only such things unclean which come out of the mouth, but not those which go into the mouth. We have already animadverted on the inconsistency of such declarations when compared with the stringent injunction enforced in the very same book, to abstain most rigidly from blood and flesh of torn or strangled beasts. See what we have noticed before, when treating on Matthew xv. in the Second Part of this Work.

CHAPTER LXVII.

ACTS xiii. 21, Paul says of the Israelites, "And afterwards they desired a king, and God gave unto them Saul, the son of Kish, a man of the tribe of Benjamin, by the space of forty years."

Paul erred in assigning to Saul such a protracted reign. Saul had governed only two years when his dereliction of the will of God, in his war against the Amalekites, threw him into disfavour, so that he forfeited his crown. Samuel was then immediately sent to anoint David, who was about twenty years old; when he [David] ascended the throne, he was but thirty years of age (see 2 Samuel v. 4); consequently Saul could not have governed Israel more than ten years. If we follow an hypothesis of Albo, the author of the book, entitled Sepher Ikkarim, Saul did not occupy the throne even so long a time; but certainly could not have remained king for forty years.

CHAPTER LXVIII.

ACTS xiii. 33, Paul proves that Jesus is the Son of God, by quoting from the second Psalm : "Thou art my Son, this day have I begotten thee "

The reference to that psalm is objectionable, since the royal psalmist spoke here of his own person. It was against himself that the Gentiles raged, and carried on their warfare, when he had commenced his government.

See 2 Samuel v. 17, "And the Philistines had heard that they had anointed David king over Israel, and all the Philistines came to seek David," etc.

He called himself justly the Messiah, Anointed of the Lord, for that title was lawfully given to him as the ruler of his people. Having been established as the chief of Israel, by the express command of the Lord, he was justified to mark those rebelling against him as rising "against the Lord, and against His Anointed." The words in Psalm ii., "And I have anointed my king," occur in the actual history of David, in 1 Samuel xvi. 1, "I shall send thee to Jesse, of Bethlehem, for among his sons I have seen for myself a king." "Zion, my holy mountain," (Psalm ii.), which was the metropolis, and was called "the city of David." It was that king to whom it was said, "Thou art my son, I have this day begotten thee." The title *Son*, was given to all those who, by faithful obedience, attached themselves to the service of God. In Exodus iv. 22, Israel was called "my first-born son"; and in Hosea i. 10, "It will be said unto them, Ye are the sons of the living God." On the day when Samuel anointed David as king of Israel, "he was changed into another man"; and we read in 1 Samuel xvi. 13, "And Samuel took the horn of oil, and anointed him in the midst of his brethren, and the Spirit of the Lord descended upon him." The adoption of man by God is called, in biblical language, "to beget." See Deuteronomy xxxii. 18, "Thou hast forgotten the rock that begat thee." The words, "Ask of me, and I shall give nations for an inheritance," were fulfilled to David, who humbled the Philistines (2 Samuel viii.), and made Amon, and Moab, and Edom, tributary to himself. With reference to Jesus, he had no dominion whatever to merit the title of a *Messiah* (Anointed King). He said of himself that he was "not come to be ministered (served) unto, but to minister " (serve others). Moreover, why should Jesus have been invited to " Ask of me, and I will give nations for an inheritance," since as the incarnate Son of God, the whole earth ought to have belonged to him, and not some selected portion of it?

CHAPTER LXIX.

ACTS xiii. 35 — 37, Paul says, "Wherefore, he says also in another *psalm*, Thou shalt not suffer thine Holy One to see corruption.   For David, after he had served his own generation by the will of God, fell on sleep, and was laid unto his fathers, and saw corruption; but he whom God raised again, saw no corruption."

The addition, that " David saw corruption," shows that Paul misunderstood the sense of the passage he quoted.   The word *schachet* (rendered " corruption ") means *a pit*, and is synonymous with *grave ;* for David relied on the salvation of the soul of the righteous, and expressed his conviction, that the body alone goes down to the pit, and not the soul with it, into perdition.

Passages, in which the word *schachet* (*pit*) occurs, in Psalm xciv., " Until a *pit* is dug for the iniquitous man."   Proverbs xxvi. 27, " He who diggeth a *pit*, shall fall into it."   Psalm vii. 15, " He who makes a hole and diggeth it, will fall into the *pit* he hath made." We cannot perceive, therefore, the authority Paul had to apply the words of that psalm otherwise than in a sense in which its author had evidently designed it.

CHAPTER LXX.

Acts xv. from ver. 1 to 12. It is there related that certain men of the sect of the Pharisees rose up, and said that the Gentiles could not be saved unless they abided by the law of Moses, and that, upon the delivery of this opinion, the apostles and elders came together to deliberate; and they argued much upon this matter. Peter then settled the dispute by saying, "Why tempt ye God to put a yoke upon the neck of the disciples, which neither our fathers nor we were able to bear. But we believe that, through the grace of the Lord Jesus Christ, we shall be saved even as they."

Peter, by this remonstrance, contradicts the opinion held by Jesus, as is shown by the advice given to the rich man, who had consulted him respecting which of the laws he should observe, etc. (See Matthew xix.) We have, moreover, in a former chapter, shown that the law of Jesus, when carried out to the letter, is more rigorous than the Mosaic code, and utterly impracticable in the affairs of social life. We have already pointed out that the suggestion made by Jesus to the rich man, to the effect that he should sell all he had and distribute the money among the poor, was wisely disregarded by all his disciples and followers. Paul also deemed it proper to designate the law of Moses "a yoke of bondage" (Galatians v. 1), and that he would not submit to the passive endurance of the humiliation recommended by Jesus. See Chap. XXVII. of the Second Part of this work.

CHAPTER LXXI.

Acts xv. 17, the Apostle James cites a verse from Amos ix., changed into the following terms:—"That the residue of men might seek after the Lord, and all the Gentiles upon whom my name is called, saith the Lord, who doeth all these things."

The true passage runs thus:—"In order that those may inherit the remainder of Edom, and of all the Gentiles upon whom my name is called, saith the Lord who doeth this." The prophecy does not predict the acquisition of the inheritance in favour of other men, but in favour of Israel, " upon whom the name of the Lord is called. See Deut. xxviii. 10, " And all the people of the earth shall see that the name of the Lord is called upon thee"

CHAPTER LXXII.

Acts xv. 20, 29. The apostles enjoin on their followers the frequently-repeated commands to abstain from sacrifices to idols, and from fornication, and from things strangled, and from blood." How the Christians respect these prohibitions we have already adverted to in Chap. XLIX. and L. in the First Part of this work.

CHAPTER LXXIII.

Acts xvi· 1, " Paul, going to Derbe and Lystra, met Timothy, the son of a certain woman who was a Jewess, and he took and circumcised him because of the Jews who were in those quarters." From this quotation and the records of history, it is evident that original Christianity did not dispense with the circumcision of Jews received within its pale. Is it not then sinful to attempt to persuade Jews to abandon those rites which the founders and first propagators of the Christian religion actually confirmed by their own acts?

CHAPTER LXXIV.

ACTS xvi. 2.   Paul, by circumcising Timothy, proved that the Mosaic dispensation of circumcision had not been abrogated. On the other hand, he wrote to the Galatians (chap. v. 2), " Behold, I, Paul, say unto you, that, if ye be circumcised, Christ shall profit you nothing; for I testify again to every man that is circumcised, that he is a debtor to do the whole law." If circumcision were of no avail for Timothy, why did his master circumcise him? If, however, that sacred act was indispensable, and bound the man fully through the covenant of Abraham to adhere to the commandments and the laws of Moses, how is it that Paul deemed it perfectly consistent to break by precept those very teachings of Moses?

CHAPTER LXXV.

ACTS xvi. 30.   The keeper of the prison asked Paul and Silas, " Sirs, what must I do to be saved? and they said, Believe on the Lord Jesus Christ, and thou shalt be saved and thy house."

The answer of the apostles does not coincide with the answer given by Jesus in Matthew xix. 16; Mark x. 17; and Luke xviii. 19; wherein he exacted of the inquirer full obedience to the laws of Moses, in order to obtain salvation.

CHAPTER LXXVI.

Acts xxviii. 3.   Paul being bitten by a viper, felt no harm from the effects of the poisonous bite, and was, therefore, held by the *barbarians* surrounding him, to be a God.

The ease with which a human being was deified in those days, accounts for the astonishing superstitious belief that Jesus was at the same time mortal and a God.

CHAPTER LXXVII.

PAUL'S EPISTLE TO THE ROMANS.

Romans v. 14, " Nevertheless death reigned from Adam to Moses, even over them that *had not sinned* after the similitude of Adam's transgression."

Other copies have the contrary. " Who *had sinned after* the similitude," etc.

If death reigned to the days of Moses only, how is the question to be explained: How could Jesus be considered the Saviour of mankind, if the dominion of death had been made to cease through the laws of Moses, " which, if a man performeth, he *liveth in them?*" See the question fully discussed in chapter one of the First Part of this work.

CHAPTER LXXVIII.

ROMANS ix. 24,—26, " Even us, whom he has called, not of the Jews only, but also of the Gentiles. As he says also in Hosea, I will call *them* my people, which were not my people, and *her* beloved which was not beloved. And it shall come to pass, that in the place where it was said unto them, Ye are not my people, there shall they be called the children of the living God."

It is immaterial for us to know whether it was ignorance or intentional perversion which prompted Paul to refer to Hosea for a purpose which that prophet had not in view. It suffices to refer to Hosea i., in order to ascertain that the prophet alludes not to the Gentiles, but exclusively to Israel, who, when obedient to the law of God, were to be called Ammi, (" my people)," and " Ruhamah," " (she who is pitied) ;" but when disobedient they were to be called Lo-Ammi, " (not my people)," and Lo Ruhamah " (not to be pitied)." And again in ver. 10, we read, "And it shall come to pass that in the place where it was said unto them, Ye are the sons of the living God."

CHAPTER LXXIX.

ROMANS ix. 33, " As it is written, Behold, I lay in Zion, a stumbling stone and a rock of offence, and whosoever believeth on him shall not be ashamed."

This passage is a collection of short sentences, ignorantly or ingeniously packed together, to show that Jesus is the only Saviour of those who found " their stumbling block in Zion." In chap. xviii. 14 of

Isaiah, we find, "And he shall be for a sanctuary and a stumbling stone, as a rock of offence to the two houses of Israel, and as a snare and a gin to the inhabitants of Jerusalem." And the prophet continues, (chap. xxviii. 16), "Therefore thus saith the Lord God, Behold I have laid a foundation in Zion, a tried stone, a precious corner stone, well established, well founded. He who believes shall not hasten (away from it)."

Another incorrect quotation from our Scriptures is also to he found in Romans x. 11, "For the Scripture saith, Whosoever believeth on him shall not be ashamed." Peter in his first Epistle, (chap. ii. 6), quotes from treacherous memory, "Wherefore also it is contained in the Scripture, Behold I lay in Zion a chief cornerstone, elect, precious, and he that believeth on him shall not be confounded."

By arbitrarily detaching or connecting various words of Scripture to verify doctrines, not taught in our Sacred Books, is, according to our opinion, its own refutation, and highly blameable.

CHAPTER LXXX.

ROMANS x. 6—9, "Say not in thine heart, Who shall ascend into heaven? (that is, to bring Christ down from above); or, Who shall descend into the deep? (that is, to bring up Christ again from the dead). But what saith it (viz. Scripture)? The word is nigh thee, even in thy mouth, and in thy heart, that is, the word of faith which we preach: That if thou shalt confess with thy mouth the Lord Jesus, and shalt believe in thine heart that God has raised him from the dead, thou shalt be saved."

If those to whom Paul was preaching had referred to

the thirtieth chapter of Deuteronomy, they might have perceived that the words of Moses were misconstrued by the Apostle. That part of our law tells us merely that it is within the reach of every man to be penitent, and obtain mercy and pardon.

Our lawgiver having spoken in general terms, "If thou wilt turn to the Lord thy God, with all thy heart and all thy soul," etc., goes on to say, "For the commandment which I give thee this day is not hidden from thee, nor is it too far off. It is not in heaven that thou mightest say, Who shall go up into heaven for us, and bring it down for us that we may practice it?" etc.

It having been shown that the nature of the gift of mercy is put in juxtaposition with the ease of acquiring it, we are enabled to comprehend the expression, " This matter is very near unto thee, it is in thy heart and thy mouth that thou mayest do it."

CHAPTER LXXXI.

ROMANS xi. 26, " And so all Israel shall be saved, as it is written, There shall come out of Zion the deliverer, and shall turn away ungodliness from Jacob."

The true words of the prophet (Isaiah lix. 20), do not indicate that the Messiah will turn away ungodliness from Jacob, but that "a redeemer will come to Zion, and *to those* who return from transgression in Jacob, saith the Lord."

CHAPTER LXXXII.

ROMANS xvi. 20, " And the God of peace shall bruise

Satan under your feet shortly," etc. In 1 Thessalonians ii. 18, Paul says, " We would have come unto you. again, even I, Paul, but Satan hindered us."

The Christians, in consequence of the above quotations, maintain the belief that the power of Satan was broken by the death of Jesus, who " bruised the head of the serpent." If so, how then did it happen that Satan, after the death of Jesus, had such sway as to obstruct the very apostles of Jesus in the pursuit of their ministrations?

CHAPTER LXXXIII.

PAUL'S FIRST EPISTLE TO THE CORINTHIANS.

1 CORINTHIANS v. 1, Paul reproaches his followers that " there be fornication among them, and that one of them had committed incest by marrying his father's wife "

If Paul, as all his writings indicate, considered the Christians dispensed from observing the Mosaic Law, where was their boundary of religious duties or transgressions, seeing that Jesus had not promulgated a new code of laws? Surely, no permission had been granted by the founder of Christianity, so that his followers should observe part of the Mosaic laws, and reject the remainder.

CHAPTER LXXXIV.

1 CORINTHIANS vi. 3, Paul says, " Know ye that we shall judge angels?" Great must have been the Apostle's presumption if he believed that corporeal man should be the judge of incorporeal beings! The greatest

prophets of Israel admitted that the angels were beyond the comprehension of our finite sense. How could the invisible be summoned before the tribunal of the visible?

CHAPTER LXXXV.

1 CORINTHIANS vii. 18—20, " Is any man called being circumcised, let him not become uncircumcised. Is any called in uncircumcision, let him not be circumcised. Circumcision is nothing, and uncircumcision is nothing, but the keeping of the commandments of God. Let every man abide in the same calling wherein he was called." In the Epistle to the Galatians, chap. v. 3, he also says, " For I testify again to every man that is circumcised that he is a debtor to do the *whole law.*" These words ought to be kept in constant remembrance by those Christians who urge us to abandon our holy faith and adopt their religious observances.

CHAPTER LXXXVI.

1 CORINTHIANS x. 8, " Neither let us commit fornication, as some of them committed, and fell in one day three and twenty thousand."

In this brief passage there is an error, which in every other work might pass unnoticed. A book, which assumes to be dictated by inspiration, ought to be accurate in every particular. In Numbers xxv., we read that *four and twenty thousand*, and not *three and twenty thousand*, fell by the visitation of pestilence

CHAPTER LXXXVII.

1 CORINTHIANS xv. 54, " So, when this corruptible shall
have put on incorruption, and this mortal shall have
put on immortality, then shall be brought to pass the
saying that is written, Death is swallowed up in victory;
O Death, where is thy sting! O grave, where is thy
victory"! This passage is not a true quotation from
our Scripture, being a mixture of two unconnected
verses.   Isaiah, chap. xxv. 8, says only, " He has
swallowed up Death to perpetuity "; and Hosea,
chap. xiii., says, " Where are thy pestilences, O Death?
Where are thy destructions, O grave?

CHAPTER LXXXVIII.

PAUL'S EPISTLE TO THE GALATIANS.

GALATIANS i. 18, " Then, after three years, I went up
to Jerusalem to see Peter, and abode with him fifteen
days.   But other of the Apostles saw I none, save
James, the Lord's brother."   Paul represents here,
James, the brother of Jesus, as an apostle of Jesus, and
he contradicts thereby the statement made by John,
chap. vii. 5, " For neither did his [viz., Jesus'] brethren believe in Him."   We have enlarged on these
contradictions in our discussions on Luke ii. and
Mark iii.

CHAPTER LXXXIX.

GALATIANS iii. 13, Paul says, " Christ has redeemed us
from the curse of the law, being made a curse for us:

for it is written, Cursed is every man that hangeth on a tree." It is a most extraordinary conclusion, that an ignominious death, suffered by Jesus, should have become the means of releasing his followers from their adherence to the ancient law of God, in order not to be subjected to the curse of the law. Surely submission to, and not abandonment of the law, should have been recommended.

CHAPTER XC.

GALATIANS iii. 16, " Now to Abraham and his seed were the promises made: He saith not, and to *seeds* as of many; but as of one, and to thy SEED, which is Christ."

Want of acquaintance with the genius of the Hebrew language, has led the author of the epistle to a wrong conclusion. When seed signifies *posterity*, it is never put in the plural number. See Genesis xiii. 15, " For all the land which thou seest, I will give to thee, and to thy seed for evermore." Immediately after this promise, we read, " And thy seed shall be like the dust of the earth." This relates to the numbers of individuals, and not to a single individual. Again, we find in Genesis xv. 5, " And He caused him to go out (of the house) and He spake, Look now up to heaven, and count the stars, if thou canst count them; and He said unto him Thus shall be thy seed."

Ibid. ver. 13, " And He spake unto Abraham, Thou shalt surely know that thy seed shall be strangers in a land which is not their's." These examples may suffice, but similar ones may be found in various parts of Scripture. These annotations afford abundant proof that the term *seed*, in the promise given to Abraham, refers to an entire nation.

CHAPTER XCI.

Paul's Epistle to the Ephesians.

Ephesians iv. 8, " Wherefore, he saith, when he ascended up on high, he led captivity captive, and gave gifts unto men."

The quotation seems to be made from memory. The psalmist (lxviii. 18) who addresses the Almighty, says, " Thou hast *taken gifts* from men," and not *thou hast given gifts*.

CHAPTER XCII.

Paul's First Epistle to the Thessalonians.

1 Thessalonians ii. 10, Paul says, "Ye are witnesses, and God also, how holily, and justly, and unblameably, we behaved ourselves among you that believe."

In a teacher of men, whose object it was to establish a new faith, it appears unbecoming to mention *first*, men, *as witnesses*, and *secondly*, *God*. A candid perusal of the writings of Paul accounts for this peculiarity of arranging his ideas. He impresses on the reader the suspicion that he was guided by expediency, more than by true religious feeling, and that his mind was not influenced by the elevated sentiments of piety.

CHAPTER XCIII.

Epistle of James.

James ii. 14, to the end of the chapter. The author of

this Epistle recommends good works as superior to mere faith, and then he continues, "Was not Abraham, our father, *justified by works*, when he had offered Isaac, his son, upon the altar? Likewise also, was not Rahab, the harlot, *justified by works*, when she had received the messengers, and had sent them out another way? For as the body without the spirit is dead, so faith without works is dead also."

The opinion here cited meets with the contradiction of Paul, who writes in his Epistle to the Romans, chap. iii. 19, "Therefore, *by deeds of the law* shall no flesh be *justified.*" Again, he says, in the same chapter, ver. 28, "Therefore, we conclude that a man *is justified by faith without the deeds of the law.*" In his Epistle to the Galatians, chap. ii. 16, Paul repeats the assertion, that faith in Jesus is of greater avail than the observance of the law, by saying, "Knowing that *a man is not justified by the works* of the law, but by *faith* in Jesus Christ." At the end of that chapter, he maintains, "If righteousness come by the law, then Christ is dead in vain." The like doctrine is enforced in chap. iii. from the beginning to the end. Also throughout the Epistle to the Hebrews, chap. xi., it is maintained that *faith* is preferable to *works*. See again ibid. ver. 17, where it is said, "Abraham, tried by *faith*, offered up Isaac." Again, ibid. v. 31, "By *faith* the harlot Rahab perished not with them that believed not, when she had received the spies in peace." We, Jews, are not anxious to reconcile the discrepancies occurring in the New Testament, and to decide whether more truth is to be found in one than in the other of those opinions. All our aspirations lead us to adopt a mode of life in exact conformity with the Holy Law, which tells us, "*And it shall be accounted to us as righteousness if we keep and fulfil all these commands.*

CHAPTER XCIV.

Epistle to the Hebrews.

This Epistle is the production of an anonymous writer. Some have ascribed it to Luke, others to Paul. In the early days of Christianity it was rejected as Apocryphal.

CHAPTER XCV.

Hebrews i. 5—9, "For unto which of the angels said he, in former times, Thou art my son, this day have I begotten thee? And, again, I will be to him a father, and he shall be to me a son. And again, when he bringeth in the first begotten into the world, he says, Let all the angels of God worship him. And of the angels, he saith, Who maketh his angels spirits, and his ministers a flame of fire? But to the Son he saith, Thy throne, O God, is for ever and ever. A sceptre of righteousness is the sceptre of thy kingdom. Thou hast loved righteousness and hated iniquity; therefore God, even thy God, hath anointed thee with the oil of gladness above thy fellows."

The errors of the author of this epistle are as many as the quotations with which he strives to confirm his views   The connexion established between Jesus and the seventh verse of Psalm ii., "Thou art my son, this day have I begotten thee," we have already presented in a proper light in our remarks on Acts viii. 33. We have there fully proved that David applied those elevated words to *himself.* Hence Christians are not justified in deducing from it doctrinal points. The promise made in 2 Samuel viii., " I shall be unto him as a father, and he shall be to me as a son," was made regarding Solomon, the son of David. The Christians themselves would not like to refer these words to Jesus, since the prophecy contains the prediction, "Whom, if he commit iniquity, I shall chastise him with the rod of men, and with the stripes of the children of men." As to Jesus, it is well known that his worshippers are impressed with the conviction that he never committed any sin.

The author of the Epistle pretends to discover in our Scripture, that the angels of God were bound to worship Jesus. We find, in Psalm xcvii., "All ye gods worship *him,*" viz., *that God* who is spoken of as the Lord of the whole earth. The words, " Thy throne, O God, is for ever and ever," are wrongly quoted from Psalm xlv. 6. We read there *Kis-au-hau Elohim*, which means, " Thy throne (is) *of* God, " and not " Thy throne, *O God.*" Thus we find, in 1 Chron xxix. 23, " And Solomon sat on the *throne of the Lord.*" The Lord being the acknowledged king of Israel, the throne occupied by David and his posterity was described as the throne of the Lord. This throne is to be occupied by the descendants of David for time everlasting. Thus Daniel prophesies, in chap. ii.,"The God of heaven will establish a throne which shall not be destroyed throughout eternity."

To be convinced that our interpretation is correct, let the reader merely refer to the continuation of the words of Psalm xlv. 7, " Thou lovest righteousness and hatest iniquity ; therefore hath God, *even thy God,* anointed thee. " If Jesus is God, could the Psalmist address him with such words as *thy God?*

CHAPTER XCVI.

HEBREWS ii. 7, " Thou madest him a little lower than
the angels, thou crownedst him with glory and honour."
In verse 9, it is said, " Jesus who was made a little
lower than the angels. "   It is remarkable that Jesus,
as the inferior being, should have been destined to be
worshipped by the angels, who were his superiors.   On
referring to the eighth Psalm, ver. 3, 4, 5, 6, we find
that the author of the Epistle, in quoting some words,
has perverted their real purport.   The Psalmist in
using the ejaculation, " When I behold the heavens, the
works of thy fingers, and the moon and the stars which
thou hast fixed, " must be understood as if he had expressed himself in the following words:—I am so struck
with awe and wonder, that I feel the utter nothingness
of human creatures ; and I say to myself, " What is
mortal man, that thou rememberest him, and the son
of man, that thou takest note of him. "   The frailty and
mortality of man, suggested to the Psalmist the sense
of a deep humility ; on the other hand, man is rendered
conscious of his noble state, as the possessor of an
immortal spirit, which makes him almost an equal to
the ministering angels on high.   It is with respect to
this supreme endowment that the Psalmist exclaims,
" Thou hast made him but little less than the angels and
hast crowned him with glory and honour."   Blessed
with intelligence, he rules the inferior creatures of the
field and the forest, of the air and the sea.

This Psalm has, consequently, no allusion to any non-
Jewish doctrine, but is a sublime amplification of the
divine resolve, as contained in Genesis, " We will make
man in our image, according to our likeness, and they
shall rule over the fish of the sea, and the birds of the

heaven, and the beasts, and over the whole earth."
Taking this plain view of the several portions of Scripture, the candid reader will agree with us, that the
inflexible truth of our revealed writings does not allow
the shade of a proof in favour of the rank given to
Jesus in the mystical theology of the Christians.

CHAPTER XCVII.

HEBREWS viii. 8. The following quotation is made
from Jeremiah xxxi. 31, "Behold the days come, saith
the Lord, when I will make a new covenant with the
house of Israel".

A refutation of the interpretation given by the
Christians to this verse, has been offered in the First
Part of this work, Chap. XXIX. The author of the
Epistle to the Hebrews, in ver. 13 of the same chapter,
says, "In that he saith a new covnant, he hath made
the first *old*. Now that which decayeth and waxeth
old is ready to vanish away." The writer was not
aware that spiritual matters are worn out like old
garments. He might have found a correct opinion in
Psalms cxi. 7,8,. "The works of His hands are truth and
judgment; faithful are all His ordinances; *well sup-
ported for ever* and made with truth and integrity."

Equally decided are the words of Isaiah on this
subject. He says, chap. xl. 8, "Grass drieth up, the
flower withereth, but *the word of our God shall stand
for ever.*"

CHAPTER XCVIII.

HEBREWS x. 5. Referring to Psalm xl., Paul states,

"Wherefore when he cometh into the world, he saith, Sacrifice and offering thou wouldst not, but a body thou hast prepared me." The quotation is erroneous. The Psalmist says, "Sacrifice and offering thou wouldst not, mine ears thou hast opened; burnt offering and sin offering thou didst not desire." The Psalmist expressed by this, that obedience to God is the chief duty of man, and that listening to Him is better than an offering, and hearkening to Him "is more acceptable than the fat of rams."

That pious feelings, and not mere ceremonials, were the essential requisites, we have already demonstrated in the First Part of this work.

CHAPTER XCIX.

Revelation.

Revelation vii. 5. In enumerating the Twelve Tribes of Israel, the tribe of Dan is omitted, and that of Manasseh mentioned in its stead, although the *tribe of Joseph* might have naturally included that of Manasseh. This shows that the author of the Revelation was imperfectly acquainted with the very rudiments of Biblical history. If the instructor himself be un-instructed, what can his disciple profit by the knowledge emanating from such a source?

CHAPTER C.

Revelation xxii. 18, 19, "For I testify unto every man that heareth the words of the prophecy of this book, If any man shall add to these things, God shall add unto him the plagues that are written in this book. And if any man shall take away from the words of the book of this prophecy, God shall take away his part out of the book of life, and out of the Holy City, and from the things that are written in this book."

The Christians have nevertheless ventured to make changes of a most glaring nature. The removal of the sabbath to the first day of the week is not authorised by Jesus or any of his apostles. The eating of blood, and the flesh of strangled beasts, etc., is a palpable infringement of the dictates of the apostles, as has been amply proved in Chap. III. of the First Part of this work.

Thus, having accomplished all my intention, I offer thanks to God, who is One and Indivisible; He is the first and the last; besides Him there is no God.

THE END.

INDEX OF QUOTATIONS.

GENESIS.

Chap. XXIX. - Verse 20 - Page 46 | Chap. II. - Verse 17 - Page 81
" I. - " 26 - " — | " XXV. - " 18 - " 83
" XI. - " 7 - " — | " XXIV. - " 14 - " 96
" XVII. - " 17 - " 47 | " XII. - " 1 - " 101
" XI. - " 7 - " — | " XXIII. - " - " 104
" II. - " 17 - " 51 | " XVII. - " 7 - " 108
" XXVII. - " 31 - " — | " XII. - " 8 - ,, 115
" XXV. - " 17 - " 53 | " XXVIII ·- " 14 - " ——
" XV. - " 13 - ,, 58 | " XXIV. - ,, 20 - " 126
" XXXVII.- " 35 - ,, 59 | ,. XXI - " 32 - ., 155
" III. - " 15 - " — | ,, X. - " 10 - " 167
" XXII. - " 18 - ,, 60 | ,. XXX. - ,, 1 - " 168
" XXVI. - " 4 - " 61 | " XV. - ,, 7, 18 " 172
" XXVIII - " 14 - " — | " X. - ,, 1, 2 " 180
" XVIII. - " 18, 19 " — | " XIV. - ,, 18 - ,. 193
" XLIX. - " 10 - " 63 | " XXIV. - ,, 10 - " 198
" XXVIII. ., " 15 - " 66 | " XLVI. - " 27 - ,, 271
" XVII. - " 7,8 - " 80 | ;, XIII. - ,, 15 - ,, 287
" XXVIII. - " 21 - " — | " XV. - ,, 5, 13 ,, ——

EXODUS.

Chap. XII. - Verse 9 - Page 3, 45 | Chap. XXXV. - Verse 22 - Page 166
" VII. - " 1 - " 45 | " II. - ,, 25 - " 177
" XXI. - " 20 - " 58 | " XV. - " 16 - " 195
" XIX. - " 13 - ,, — | ,, XXII. - " 37 - " 198
" XX. - ,, 8 - " 89 | " IV. - ,, 22, 23 " 211
" XVI. - ,, 29 - " — | " XXIII. - ,, 4 - ,, 212
,, XXI. - " 16 - " 90 | " XIX. - ,, 5 - ,, 216
" II. - ,, 8 - " 96 | " IV. - ,, 22, 23 " 232
" XVII. - " 15 - " 104 | " XXIII. - ,, 4, 5 - ,, 238
,, XIX. - " 5 - " 114 | " III. - ,. 12 - ,, 271
" XIX. - ,, 6 - ,, 115 | " IV. - ,, 22 - ,, 275
" XV. - ,, 26 - ,, 121 | " XX. - ,, - ,, 285
., XXIII. - " 8 - ,, 159 |

₂ It may not be superfluous to remind the biblical student, that this elaborate abstract has been supplied, in order to afford facility of reference, a desideratum without which this work could not be considered complete.

LEVITICUS.

Chap. XXVI. - Verse 38 - Page 38   Chap. XXVI. - Verse 11, 12 Page 79
"   XXVI. - " 34, 35 " 39   "   XVIII. - " 5 -   " 81
"   XXVI. - " 38 -   41, 42   "   XXII. - " 3 -   " 83
"   XXVI. - " 44 -   " 42   "   XXII. - " -   " 136
"   VII. - " 27 -   " 53   "   XXVI. - " 44 -   146, 151
"   XXII. - " 3 -   " —   "   XXVI. - " 42 -   " 155
"   XVIII. - " 5 -   " 55   "   XIX.   - " 17, 18 " 212
"   XXVI. - " 9 -   " 57   "   XXVI. - " 44 -   " 218
"   XI.   - " 1, 43, 44 " 67   "   XIX.   - " 17, 18 " 238
"   XX.   - " 25, 26 " 68   "   XI.   - " 8 -   " 242
"   XXVI. - " 42, 31 " 74

NUMBERS.

Chap. XXIV. - Verse 3 - Page 29   Chap. XXV. - Verse 13 - Page 108
"   X.   - " 32 -   " 62   "   X.   -   " 32 -   " 116
"   X.   - " 13 -   " 64   "   XV.   -   " 12 -   " 155
"   VII. - " 12 -   " 64   "   II.   -   " 20 -   " 167
"   XXIII. - " 10 -   " 84   "   XXIV. -   " 17 -   " 264

DEUTERONOMY.

Chap. XXX.   - Verse 6 - Page 10   Chap. XIV.   - Verse 1, 2 Page 81
"   XXVIII. - " 64 -   " 23   "   XXII.   -   " 46, 47 " 82
"   XXX.   - " 3 -   " 24   "   XXXIII. -   " 29 - } ,,82, 83
"   IV.   - " 30, 31 " 26   } 85
"   XXX.   - " 3, 4, 5, 6 } " 27   "   XXXII. -   " 50 -   " 83
"   XXX.   - " 6 -   " 35   "   IV.   -   " 2, 8   " 91
"   XXX.   - " 6 -   " 36   "   XXXIII. -   " 4 -   " —
"   VII.   - " 6 -   " 37   "   XXVII. -   " 1 -   " 92
"   XXX.   - " 6 -   " 40   "   I.   -   " 5, 6   " 112
"   XXX.   - " 146 - " 41   "   XXX.   -   " 26 -   " —
"   XXXII. - " 15 -   " 45   "   XXXII. -   " 9 -   " 115
"   VI.   - " 4 -   " 47   "   XXX.   -   " 5 -   " 124
"   IV.   - " 35, 39 " —   "   XV.   -   " 10 -   " 129
"   XXIV.   - " 16 -   " 52   "   XXVIII. -   " 47 -   " 129
"   XXXII. - " 50 -   " 53   "   III.   -   " 24 -   " 137
"   I.   - " 10 -   " 61   "   IV.   -   " 30 -   " 140
"   XXXIII. - " 21 -   " 66   "   XXX.   -   " 1–7 - " —
"   XXXVIII.   " 57 -   " —   "   XXXII. -   " 40 -   " 144
"   VII.   - " 24 -   " —   "   XI.   -   " 12 -   " 174
"   XIV.   - " 13 -   " 67   "   VII.   -   " 6 -   " 198
"   XIV.   - " 1, 2, 3, 21 } " 68   "   XXVI.   -   " 19 -   " 199
"   XXVI.   - " 26 -   " 70   "   XXVII. -   " 1 -   " —
"   XXVIII. - " 15 -   " 71   "   XXX.   -   " 2, 3, 11, 12 } " 215
"   XXVII. - " — -   " 72, 73   "   XXX.   -   " 14 -   " 216
"   XXIX.   - " 29 -   " —   "   VII.   -   " 15 -   " 219
"   XXVIII. - " 29 -   " 75   "   XXX.   -   " 7 -   " —
"   XXIX.   - " 12 -   " 77   "   X.   -   " 22 -   " 271
"   XXX.   - " 1--10 " 77, 78   "   XXXII. -   " 18 -   " 275
                                        "   XXVIII. -   , 10 -   " 278

JOSHUA.

Chap. VII. - Verse 7, 8 - Page 183.

THE BOOK OF JUDGES.

Chap. I. - - Verse 1 - Page 64 | Chap. XII. - Verse 22 - Page 265

RUTH.

Chap. II. - - - - Page 96.

THE FIRST BOOK OF SAMUEL.

Chap. XIV.	- Verse 49 - Page 58	Chap. XII.	- Verse 22 - Page 150
„ XXII.	- „ 16 - „ —	„ XX.	- „ 5 - „ 159
„ VIII.	- „ 7 - „ 65	„ XVII.	- „ 12 - „ 164
„ XXV.	- „ 29 - „ 86	„ II.	- „ 7 - „ 175
„ XVII.	- „ 56, 58 „ 96	„ XXI.	- „ 1 - „ 213
„ XIII.	- „ 14 - „ 101	„ XXII.	- „ 20 - „ —
„ XV.	- „ 28 - „ —	„ XV.	- „ 22 - „ 216
„ VII.	- „ 1 - „ 102	„ II.	- „ 1 - „ 249
„ XVIiI.	- „ 14 - „ 118	„ XVI.	„ 13 - „ 275
„ I.	- „ 22 - „ 137		

THE SECOND BOOK OF SAMUEL.

Chap. VII.	- Verse 26 Page 137	Chap. V. -	- Verse 4 - Page 274
„ XII.	- „ 10 - „ 138	„ IV. -	- „ 17 - „ 275
„ XXI.	- „ 17 - „ 193	„ VIII. -	- „ 271

THE FIRST BOOK OF KINGS.

Chap. IX. -	- Verse 13 - Page 25	Chap. II. -	- Verse 26 - Page 108
„ XII.	- „ 16 - „ 26	„ VIII. -	- „ 9 - „ 130
„ II. -	- „ 37 - „ 51	„ XVIII. -	- „ 2I - „ 190

THE SECOND BOOK OF KINGS.

Chap. VIII.	- Verse 5 - Page 58	Chap. XVII.	Verse 20 Page 140, 146
„ XVI.	- „ 9 - „ 98	„ II.	- „ 4 - „ 159
„ XV.	- „ 29, 30 „ —		

THE FIRST BOOK OF CHRONICLES.

Chap. XVII.	- Verse 20 - Page 48	Chap. III.	- Verse 11 - Page 209
„ V. -	- „ 2 - „ 64	„ III., XXII.	- „ 228
„ XXVIII. -	- „ 4 - „ —	„ XXIX. -	- „ 23 - „ 291
„ XXIX. -	- „ 22 - „ 108		

THE SECOND BOOK OF CHRONICLES.

Chap. XXXVI. -	Verse 20 - Page 28	Chap. XXI.	- Verse 12 - Page 190
„ XXXVI. -	„ 21 - „ 39	„ XXIV. -	- „ 244
„ XXXI. -	104		

EZRA.

Chap. II. -	- Verse 1 -	Page 23	Chap. II., III., X.				- Page 104
„ I. -	- „ 2 -	„ 24	„ X. -	- - Verse 11 -	„ 221
„ IX. -	- „ 9 -	„ 28			

THE BOOK OF NEHEMIAH.

Chap. IV. -	- Verse 2 -	Page 28	Chap. IX. -	- Verse 6 -	Page 48
„ IX. -	- „ 36, 37	„ 29	„ IX -	- „ 30 -	„ 75
„ VII.	- „ 3 -	„ —			

THE BOOK OF ESTHER.

Chap. VIII. - Verse 16 - Page 235.

THE BOOK OF JOB.

Chap. XVII.	- Verse 2 -	Page 46	Chap. XXXIII. -	Verse 30 -	Page 87
„ XIV.	- „ 13 -	„ 59	„ V. -	„ 16 -	„ 119
„ XI.	- „ 8 -	„ —	„ XXXIII.	„ 16 -	„ 203

THE BOOK OF PSALMS.

Psalm XXII.	- Verse 11 -	Page 7	Psalm LXV.	- Verse 4 -	Page 128
„ XIX. -	„ 12 -	„ 19	„ LXIX. -	„ 9 -	„ —
„ XIV. -	„ 70 -	„ 22	„ XXV. -	„ 2 -	„ —
„ XCVII. -	„ 7 -	„ 33	„ CXV. -	„ 1 -	„ —
„ XL. -	„ 38 -	„ 42	„ CXLIII. -	„ 11 -	„ —
" XC. -	„ -	„ 43	„ XLIV. -	„ 26 -	„ —
„ L, -	„ 22 -	„ 45	„ LXXX -	„ 3 -	„ —
„ LXXXVI.	„ 10 -	„ 48	„ LXXXV. -	„ 9 -	„ 169
„ XLIX. -	„ 15 -	„ 58	„ XCV. -	„ 11 -	„ 174
„ CXXXIX.	„ 8 -	„ 59	„ XLIV. -	„ 10 -	„ 123
„ LXVII. -	„ 1 -	„ 62	„ CXXX. -	„ 8 -	„ 160
„ CL. -	„ -	„ 72	„ CXIII. -	„ 2 -	„ 189
„ XIX. -	„ -	„ 84	„ CXV. -	„ 4 - 9	„ 189
„ XXVII. -	„ 13 -	„ —	„ CXXV- -	„ 19 -	„ —
„ CXVI. -	„ 8, 9 -	„ —	„ CX. -	„ 1 -	„ 191
„ XXVI. -	„ -	„ —	„ II. -	„ 7 -	„ 192
„ XVI. -	„ 10, 11	„ —	„ LXXIX. -	„ 1 -	„ —
„ XLIX. -	„ 15 -	„ —	„ XCVI. -	„ 1 -	„ —
„ XXV. -	„ 12, 13	„ —	„ XX. -	„ 1 -	„ —
„ XXXI. -	„ 19 -	„ —	„ XCVI. -	„ 6 -	„ 194
„ XXXVI. -	„ 7, 8, 9	„ —	„ XCVIII. -	„ 16 -	„ —
„ LXXIII. -	„ 35 -	„ 85	„ XCIV. -	„ 7 -	„ 195
„ XLI, -	„ 4 -	„ —	„ LXXII. -	„ 7 -	„ 203
„ XIX. -	„ 7-9	„ 91	„ LXXXVI.	„ 9 -	„ 218
„ CXIX. -	„ -	„ —	„ LXXXIII.	„ 1 -	„ 220
„ CXXXVI.	„ 22 -	„ 111	„ XL. -	„ 8 -	„ 221
„ XCVI. -	„ 3 -	„ 115	„ CXLIII. -	„ 10 -	„ —
„ CXXXV.	„ 4 -	„ —	„ CXLVI. -	„ 3	„ 239
„ XLIV. -	„ 11 -	„ 122	„ XXIV. -	„ 1 -	„ —
„ XLIV. -	„ 22 -	„ 123	„ LXXXII.	„ 11 -	„ 244

Psalm II. - Verse — } Page 274, 275
„ VII. - „ 15 - „ 276
„ LXVIII. - „ 18 - „ 288
„ II. - „ — - „ 290
„ XCVII. - „ — - „ 291

Psalm XLV. - Verse 6, 7 Page 29
„ VIII. - „ 3, 4, 5, 6 } „ 292
„ CXI. - „ 7, 8 „ 293
„ XL. - „ — - „ 294

THE PROVERBS.

Chap. XXX. - Verse 7 - Page 66
„ XI. .. „ 7 - „ 85
„ XIV. - „ 32 - „ —
„ XXIII. - „ 17, 18 „ —
„ XXIV. - „ 14 - „ —
„ I. - „ 8 - „ 95

Chap. III. - Verse 11 - Page 169
„ XXV. - „ 21 - „ 212
„ XXIV. - „ 17 - „ 288
„ XXV. - „ 21 - „ —
„ XXVI. - „ 27 - „ 276

ECCLESIASTES; OR THE PREACHER.

Chap. XII. - Verse 7 - Page 53
„ IX. - „ 10 - „ 59
„ II. - „ 8 - „ 80

Chap. III. - Verse 21 - Page 85
„ IV. - „ 8 - „ 107
„ VII. - „ 20 - „ 142

THE BOOK OF THE PROPHET ISAIAH.

Chap. II. - Verse 4 - Page 6
„ LII. - „ 1 - „ 8
„ LXVI. - „ 17 - „ -
„ LXVI. - „ 23 - „ 9
„ XIV. - „ 16 .. „ -
„ VIII. - „ 23 - „ -
„ II. - „ 18 - „ -
„ II. - „ 4 - „ 11
„ XI. - „ 6, 7, 8 „ —
„ LXV. - „ 16, 19 20, 21, 22 } „ 12
„ XI. - „ 9 - „ 14
„ II. - „ 18 - „ 20
„ XLIII. - „ 5 - „ 27
„ XI. - „ 12 - „ 28
„ LX. - „ 10 - „ —
„ LX. - „ 11 - „ 29
„ XXXIV. - „ 3 - „ 30
„ IV. - „ 22 - „ —
„ LXVI. - „ 20 - „ —
„ XI. - „ 15, 16 „ 32
„ LXVI. - „ 23 - „ 33
„ II. - „ 13 - „ —
„ XLVII. - „ 16 - „ —
„ LX. - „ 10 - „ —
„ II. - „ 4 - „ 34
„ XI. - „ 6, 7, 8, 9 } „ —
„ LXV. - „ 6 - „ —

Chap. LX. - Verse 21 - Page 35
„ LXV. - „ 16 - „ —
„ LXV. - „ 19 - „ 36
„ XXVI. - „ 19 - „ 37
„ LXII. - „ — - „ 38
„ XXVII. - „ 13 - „ 42
„ LXVI. - „ 22 - „ —
„ XLIV. - „ 6, 8 „ 45
„ XIX. - „ 4 - „ —
„ XLIII. - „ 2 - „ 47
„ XLIV. - „ 6 - „ —
„ XLV. - „ 5 - „ —
„ XLV. - „ 6 - „ 48
„ XL. - „ 18 - „ —
„ XLV. - „ 7 - „ —
„ XL. - „ 18 - „ 49
„ XXXVIII. - „ 10 „ 50
„ XIV. - „ 1 - „ 62
„ LVI. - „ 6, 7 „ —
„ LX. - „ 3 - „ —
„ XXXVII. - „ 35 - „ 71
„ XXII. - „ 3 - „ 75
„ LVIII. - „ — - „ 83
„ XLV. - „ 17 - „ 85
„ VI. - „ 10 - „ 86
„ LVII. - „ 8 - „ —
„ XIV. - „ 1 - „ 92
„ LI. - „ 4 - „ 93
„ II. - „ 4 - „ 94

ISAIAH (continued).

Chap. VII.	-	Verse 14	-	Page 95	Chap. LXII.	-	Verse 1	-	Page 151
„ LIV.	-	„ 4	-	„ 96	„ I. -	-	„ 14	-	„ 156
„ VII.	-	„ 2	-	„ 97	„ LVI.	-	-		„ 157
„ VIII.	-	„ 3	-	„ 99	„ LV.	-	„ 6, 7	„	163
„ VII.	-	„ 16	-	„ 100	„ XLIII.	-	„ 19	-	„ 164
„ VIII.	-	„ 8	-	„ 101	„ XXI.	-	„ 13	-	„ 174
„ VII.	-	„ 15	-	„ 103	„ LIV.	-	„ 1, 2	-	„ 176
„ IX.	-	„ 6	-	104, 105	„ XXXI.	-	„ 38	-	„ —
„ II. -	-	„ 7	-	„ 107	„ XLII.	-	„ 2	-	„ 178
„ IX. -	-	„ 7	-	„ —	„ XI. -	-	„ 12	-	„ 186
„ LII.	-	„ 1	-	„ 108	„ XXXIV. -	-	„ 1, 2	„	—
„ XLIV.	-	„ 9	-	„ —	„ LX.	-	„ 8	-	„ 197
„ LII.	-	„ 13	-	„ 109	„ LX.	-	„ 12	-	„ 198
„ XLIV.	-	„ 21	-	„ 111	„ LXII.	-	„ 12	-	„ —
„ XLV.	-	„ 4	-	„ —	„ XII.	-	„ 2	-	„ 199
„ LIII.	-	„ 4, 5		„ —	„ XXXVII.		„ 13	-	„ —
„ XIV.	-	„ 1	-	„ 114	„ XLI.	-	„ 14	-	„ —
„ LXI.	-	„ 6	-	„ 115	„ IV. -	-	„ 3	-	„ 200
„ LXVI.	-	„ 22	-	„ 116	„ LX.	-	„ 21	-	„ —
„ LIII.	-	„ 5	-	„ —	„ LI. -	-	„ 6	-	„ 202
„ LIII.	-	„ 12	-	„ 117	„ XI. -	-	„ 4, 5	„	—
„ LII.	-	„ 1	-	„ —	„ LX.	-	„ 21	-	„ 203
„ LIV.	-	„ 1, 9, 10	„	—	„ LXI.	-	„ 3	-	„ —
„ LI.	-	„ 22	-	„ —	„ XLV.	-	„ 6	-	„ 204
„ LII.	-	„ 13	-	„ 118	„ XLV.	-	„ 23	-	„ 205
„ LIII.	-	„ 3	-	„ 120	„ LII.	-	„ 1	-	„ 206
„ LIII.	-	„ 6	-	„ 121	„ XVI.	-	„ 20	-	„ 207
„ LXI.	-	„ 5	-	„ 122	„ LXVI.	-	„ 23	-	„ —
„ XLIX.	-	„ 23	-	„ —	„ XLIV.	-	„ 6	-	„ 208
„ LIII.	-	„ 7, 8	„	—	„ XLV.	-	„ 15	-	„ —
„ LIII.	-	„ 9	-	„ 123	„ VII.	-	„ 14	-	210, 215
„ LXV.	-	„ 22	-	„ 124	„ XXVIII.-		„ 16	-	„ 215
„ LIII.	-	„ 11	-	„ 125	„ XLI.	-	„ 11, 12	„	219
„ LXIV.	-	„ 5	-	„ 127	„ XLVII.	-	„ 9, 6	„	—
„ XLVIII. -		„ 11	-	„ 129	„ XLIX.	-	„ 26	-	„ —
„ XLIII.	-	„ 25	-	„ —	„ VII.	-	„ 4	-	„ 230
„ II. -	-	„ 2	-	„ 131	„ IX.	-	„ 1	-	„ 234
„ LVI.	-	„ 6, 7		„ 132	„ VIII.	-	„ 2	-	„ 235
„ XIV.	-		-	„ 137	„ IX.	-	„ 3	-	„ —
„ XXXII. -		„ 14	-	„ 138	„ II. -	-	„ 4	-	„ 239
„ LXVI.	-	„ 20	-	„ —	„ XLV.	-	„ 23	-	„ 263
„ XLIV.	-	„ 22	-	„ 141	„ LII.	-	„ 1	-	„ —
„ XXXVII.		„ 35	-	„ 142	„ XVIII. -		„ 14	-	„ 282
„ LIV.	-	„ 9, 10	„	144	„ XXVIII.-		„ 16	-	„ —
„ LXII.	-	„ 8, 9	„	145	„ LIX.	-	„ 20	-	„ 283
„ I. -	-	„ 25	-	„ 146	„ XXV.	-	„ 8	-	„ 286
„ I. -	-	„ 15, 16	„	149	„ XL.	-	„ 8	-	„ 293
„ XLVIII. -		„ 9, 10, 11	„	150					

THE BOOK OF THE PROPHET JEREMIAH.

Chap. III.	-	Verse 13	-	Page 10	Chap. XI. -	-	Verse 11	-	Page 147
„ XXXI.	-	„ 34	-	„ 14	„ V. -	-	„ 13, 14	„	—
„ XLIII.	-	„ 7	-	„ 52	„ V. -	-	„ 14	-	„ 148
„ III. -	-	„ 17	-	„ 35	„ XIV.	-	„ 7, 11, 12	„	—
„ L. -	-	„ 20	-	„ —	„ XIV.	-	„ 21	-	„ 149
„ II. -	-	„ 3	-	„ 37	„ V. -	-	„ 18	-	„ 150
„ X. -	-	„ 6	-	„ 48	„ XXXII. -	-	„ 41	-	„ 151
„ XXXIII. -	-	„ 20	-	„ 60	„ XXXI. -	-	„ 15, 17	„	152
„ XXX.	-		-	„ 96	„ VII. -	-	„ 15	-	„ 153
„ XII.	-	„ 15	-	„ 101	„ XXXI. -	-	„ 15, 16, 17	„	—
„ XXXIII. -	-	„ 16	-	„ 104					
„ XXX.	-	„ 10	-	„ 111	„ XXXI. -	-	„ 20, 21	„	154
„ X. -	-	„ 19, 20		„ 112	„ XXX.	-	„ 18	-	„ —
„ XXX.	-	„ 12, 17	„	—	„ XXIII. -	-	„ 6	-	„ —
„ XXXIII. -	-	„ 6, 8	„	—	„ XXXI. -	-	„ 31	-	„ 155
„ XXX.	-	„ 11	-	„ 114	„ XXXI. -	-	„ 30	-	„ 156
„ XXXV. -	-	„ 19	-	„ 116	„ XXXIII. -	-	„ 8	-	„ 160
„ XVI.	-	„ 19, 20	„	121	„ L. -	-	„ 20	-	„ —
„ L.	-	„ 17	-	„ 122	„ XXX.	-	„ 7	-	„ 165
„ XXXI.	-	„ 34	-	„ 125	„ II. -	-	„ 16	-	„ 167
„ XXIX.	-	„ 7	-	„ 127	„ XI. -	-	„ 16	-	„ —
„ XXX.	-	„ 21	-	„ —	„ XXIII. -	-	„ 17	-	„ 174
„ XIV.	-	„ 7	-	„ 128	„ XVII.	-	„ 18	-	„ 179
„ XXXI.	-	„ 37	-	„ 129	„ IX. -	-	„ 13	-	„ —
„ III.	-	„ 16	-	„ 130	„ XIV.	-	„ 2	-	„ 196
„ XIX.	-		-	„ —	„ IV. -	-	„ 13	-	„ 197
„ XIV.	-	„ 8	-	„ 132	„ L. -	-	„ 29	-	„ 199
„ XVII.	-	„ 13	-	„ 133	„ XXIX.	-	„ 10	-	„ 200
„ XIII.	-		-	„ —	„ XXX	-	„ 7	-	„ 202
„ XIV.	-		-	„ —	„ XXIII.	-	„ 5	-	„ —
„ III.	-		-	„ 137	„ XXIII.	-	„ 6	-	„ 203
„ XVII.	-	„ 4	-	„ —	„ XXXI.	-	„ 15, 16, 17	„	211
„ XXX.	-	„ 8	-	„ 138	„ VII. -	-	„ 22, 23	„	216
„ XVII.	-	„ 7	-	„ 139	„ II.	-	„ 3	-	„ 219
„ XV.	-	„ 1	-	„ 140	„ XXX.	-	„ 16	-	„ —
„ III. -	-	„ 14	-	„ 141	„ XXXI.	-	„ 15, 17	„	232
„ XXXI.	-	„ 35, 36, 37	„	145					
„ VII.	-	„ 15, 16, 17, 18	„	147					

THE LAMENTATIONS OF JEREMIAH.

Chap. IV. -	-	Verse 22	-	Page 24	Chap. V. -	-	Verse 21	-	Page 128
„ IV.	-	„ 22	-	40, 146	„ II. -	-	„ 6	-	„ 157
„ XXX.	-	„ 11	-	„ 42	„ I. -	-	„ 1	-	„ 194
„ II. -	-	„ 13	-	„ 112	„ IV. -	-	„ 22	-	201, 202

THE BOOK OF THE PROPHET EZEKIEL.

Chap. XXVIII. -	Verse 8	-	Page 7	Chap. XXXVII. -	Verse 23	-	Page 10
„ XXXVI. -	„ 25	-	„ 10	„ XXXIX. -	„ 9, 10	„	11

THE BOOK OF THE PROPHET EZEKIEL (*continued*).

Chap.	XXXIV.	-	Verse	25, 28	Page	12	Chap.	XLIV.	-	Verse 15 -	Page 108
„	XXXVII. -		„	26, 27, } 28, 29 }	„	13	„	XXVII. -		„ 19 -	„ 118
							„	XXXVI -		„ 7 „	„ 124
„	XLIII. -		„	7 -	„	—	„	XXXVIII.		„ 22 -	„ 126
„	XLVIII. -		„	35 -	„	—	„	XXXVI. -		„ 22 -	„ 129
„	XXII. -		„	15 -	„	24	„	XX. -		„ 44 -	„ —
„	XXXIX. -		„	28 -	„	28	„	XXXIX -		„ 6, 29	„ 138
„	XXXVII. -		„	16 -	„	32	„	XXXIII. -		„ 11 -	„ 141
„	XXXVII., } XXXIX. }			-	„	—	„	XVIII. -		„ 21 -	„ 143
							„	XXXVIII.		„ 7, 12	„ —
„	XLVII.		„	1, 12	„	33	„	XXXVI. -		„ 22, 28	„ 144
„	XXXIV. -		„	25 -	„	34	„	XXII. -		„ 15 -	„ 146
„	XXXVI. -		„	25, 26	„	35	„	XVI. -		„ 60, 62	„ 151
„	XXXVII.-		„	28, 24	„	—	„	XXXVII.-		„ 19 -	„ 154
„	XXXVII.-		„	26, 27, 28	„	36	„	XXXVII., XXXIX.		-	„ 164
„	XL., XLV.			-	„	—	„	XXXIX. -		„ 25 -	„ 165
„	XL. -		„	18 -	„	—	„	XLIII. -		„ 9 -	„ —
„	XXII. -		„	15 -	„	39	„	XXXVIII.		„ 19, 20	„ 170
„	XXXVI. -		„	26, 27	„	40	„	XLIII. -		„ 4-7	„ 172
„	XVIII. -		„	19, 20	„	56	„	XXXVII.-		-	„ 179
„	XVIII. -		„	20 -	„	58	„	XXXVI. -		„ 27 -	„ 184
„	XXXVIII.		„	10 -	„	—	„	V. -		„ 7 -	„ 187
„	XVIII. -		„	8, 9 -	„	86	„	XI. -		„ 12 -	„ —
„	XX. -		„	13 -	„	—	„	XXII. -		„ 15 -	„ 202
„	XLV. -		„	35 -	„	104	„	XXVI. -		„ 16 -	„ 221
„	XXXVII.-		„	36 -	„	107	„	XXVIII. -		„ 9 -	„ 222

THE BOOK OF THE PROPHET DANIEL.

Chap.	VII.	-	Verse	27 -	Page	7	Chap.	VII.	-	Verse 27 -	Page 197
„	II.	-	„	28, 44	„	8	„	II.	·	„ 44 -	„ 198
„	IX.	-	„	25 -	„	26	„	VII.	-	„ 21, 22, 25	„ —
„	VII.	-	„	27 -	„	34	„	VII.	-	„ 24 -	„ 199
„	XII.	-	„	2 -	„	37	„	XII.	-	„ 17 -	„ —
„	II.	-	„	44 -	„	—	„	IX.	-	„ 26, 24	„ 200
„	VII.	-	„	18 -	„	—	„	VIII.	-	„ 13, 26	„ 201
„	XII.	-	„	2 -	„	87	„	VIII.	-	„ 13, 14	„ 202
„	IX.	-	„	18, 19	„	128	„	IX.	-	„ 24 -	202, 203
„	XII.	-	„	1 -	„	166	„	IX.	-	„ 25 -	„ 204
„	VII.	-	„	27 -	„	178	„	VII.	-	„ 14 -	„ 244
„	VII.	-	„	18 -	„	195	„	II.	-	„ 44 -	„ 263
„	VII.	-	„	26, 27	„	196	„	VII.	-	„ 27 -	„ —
„	II.	-	„	34 -	„	197					

HOSEA.

Chap.	III. -	-	Verse	5 -	Page	7	Chap.	VI. -	-	Verse 1 -	Page 112
„	II. -	-	„	20 -		11, 12	„	IV. -	-	„ 17 -	„ 121
„	III. -	-	„	4 -	„	26	„	XIV.	-	„ 1, 2 -	„ 141
„	IV. -	-		-	„	34	„	II. -	-	„ 11 -	„ 156
„	II. -	-		28 -	„	—	„	II. -	-	„ 18 -	„ 178
„	XIII.	-	„	4 -	„	48	„	XI. -	-	„ 1 -	211, 232
„	XIII.	-	„	11 -	„	65	„	I. -	-	„ 10 -	„ 275

JOEL.

Chap. II. -	-	Verse 27	-	Page 13	Chap. II. -	-	Verse 28	-	Page 203
„ III. -	-	„ 1, 17	-	„ —	„ III. ᴛ	-	„ 17	-	„ 206
„ III. -	-	„ 18	-	„ 33	„ III. -·	-	„ 2	-	„ 219
„ II. -	-	„ 27	-	„ 36	„ III. -	-	„ 19	-	„ 220
„ II. -	-		-	„ 93	„ II. -	-	27, 28	-	„ 251
„ III. -	-	„ 17	-	„ 132					

AMOS.

Chap. I. -	-	Verse 6, 9	Page 24	Chap. V. -	-	Verse 2	- Page 160
„ I. -	-	„ 9	„ 25	„ IX. -	-	„ 14, 15 }	„ 161
„ I. -	-	„ 5	„ 9ᵈ			12 }	
„ VII. -	-	„ 11	98, 114	„ IV. -	-	„ 18	- „ —
„ II. -	-		„ 154	„ IV., V. -	-	„ 3	- „ 162
„ II. -	-	„ 6	„ 158	„ V. -	-	„ 4	- „ 163
„ V. -	-	„ 12	„ —	„ VIII. -	,	9	- „ 202
„ VIII. -	-	„ 4	„ 159	„ V. -	-	„ 26, 27	„ 272

OBADIAH.

Verse 10 - Page 220.

MICAH.

Chap. VII. -	-	Verse 10	- Page 119	Chap. V. -	-	Verse 5	- Page 166
„ IV. -	-	„ 2	- „ 125	„ V. -	-	„ 5, 6	„ 167
„ V. -	-	„ —	- „ 163	„ V. -	-	„ 7	- „ —
„ V. -	-	„ 4	- „ 165	„ V. -	-	„ 9, 10	„ 168
„ V. -	-	„ 3	- 165, 166	„ IV. -	-	„ 3	- „ 239
„ V. ·	-	„ 4	- „ 166				

ZEPHANIAH.

Chap. II. -	-	Verse 11	- Page 9, 20	Chap. III. -	-	Verse 9	- Page 205
„ III. -	-	„ 13	- „ 10	„ II. -	-	„ 9, 10	„ 220
„ X. -	-	„ 8	- „ 124			„ 19	- „ —
„ XIV. -	-	„ 2	- „ 165				

HAGGAI.

Chap. II. -	-	Verse 9	- Page 169	Chap. II.	-	Verse 21, 22, 25 Page 170

ZECHARIAH.

Chap. IX. -	-	Verse 10	-	Page 6	Chap. XIV.	-	Verse 17	Page 33, 62
„ IX. -	-	„ 10	-	„ 7	„ XIV. -	-	„ 9	„ 33
„ XIII. -	-	„ 2	-	„ 9, 20	„ II. -	-	„ 15	„ 62
„ IX. -	-	„ 10	-	„ 11	„ IX. -	-	„ 7	„ 69
„ II. -	-	„ 14	-	„ 14	„ III. -	-	„ 7	„ 87
„ XIV. -	-	„ 9	-	„ 20	„ VIII. -	-	„ 23	„ 116
„ XIV. -	-	„ 4	-	„ 32	„ VIII. -	-	„ 4	„ 124
„ XIV. -	-	„ 8	-	„ 33	„ XIV. -	-	„ 14	„ 126
„ VIII. -	-	„ 23	-	„ —	„ I. -	-	„ 3	„ 142

ZECHARIAH (*continued.*)

Chap. XIV.	-	-	Verse 16	-	Page 157	Chap. XII.	-	-	Verse 9, 10	Page 183
„ XIV.	-	-	„ 2	-	„ 165	„ XII.	-	-	„ 7	-	„ 185
„ XIII.	-	-	„ 9	-	„ —	„ IV.	-	-	„ 7	-	„ 201
„ II. -	-	-	„ 4	-	„ 168	„ XIV.	-	-	„ 16	-	„ 207
„ II. -	-	-	„ 5, 9	-	„ 169	„ VIII.	-	-	„ 23	-	„ —
„ II. -	-	-	„ 6	-	„ 170	„ IX. -	-	-	„ 7	-	„ —
„ IX. -	-	-	„ 9	-	„ 173	„ XIV.	-	-	„ 9	-	„ 208
„ IX. -	-	-	„ 1, 2	-	„ 174	„ I. -	-	-	„ 15	-	„ 220
„ IX. -	-	-	„ 4, 5	-	„ 175	„ II. -	-	-	„ 8, 9	-	„ —
„ IX. -	-	-	„ 8	-	„ 176	„ IX. -	-	-	„ 10	-	„ 239
„ II. -	-	-	„ 5	-	„ 177	„ IX. -	-	-	„ 10	-	„ 244
„ IX. -	-	-	„ 10, 11, 12	„ 178	„ XI. -	-	-	„ 13	-	„ 246
„ LX.	-	-	„ 12	-	„ 179	„ XI. -	-	-	„ 7	-	„ 247
„ LXI.	-	-	„ 7	-	„ —	„ XIV.	-	-	„ 16	-	„ 253
„ XII.	-	-	„ 10	-	„ 181						

MALACHI.

Chap. IV. -	-	-	Verse 5	Page 7, 93	Chap. I. -	-	-	Verse 2, 12	Page 186
„ IV. -	-	-	„ 4	-	„ 131	„ III. -	-	-	„ 4, 3	„ 188
„ III. -	-	-	„ 7	-	„ 142	„ IV. -	-	-	„ 5	-	„ 190

THE GOSPEL ACCORDING TO MATTHEW.

Chap. X. -	-	-	Verse 3	-	Page 6	Chap. I. -	-	-	Verse 15, 16, 17	Page 228
„ XX.	-	-	„ 28	-	„ 7	„ I. -	-	-	„ 22, 23	„ 230
„ XI. -	-	-	„ 13	-	„ 22	„ I. -	-	-	„ 23	-	„ 231
„ XII.	-	-	„ 32	-	„ 49	„ XIII.	-	-	„ 55	-	„ —
„ X.	-	-	„ 40	-	„ 50	„ II. -	-	-	„ 14, 15 / 16, 17	„ 232
„ XX.	-	-	„ 18, 28	„ —	„ II. -	-	-	„ 23	-	„ 233
„ XV.	-	-	„ 11	-	„ 67	„ IV. -	-	-	„ 1, 11	„ —
„ V. -	-	-	„ 17-20	„ 88	„ IV. -	-	-	„ 13, 15	„ 234
„ XIX.	-	-	„ 21	-	89, 90	„ IV. -	-	-	„ 18, 19	„ 236
„ I. -	-	-	„ 20	-	„ 104	„ V. -	-	-	„ 17, 18 / 19, 43	„ 237
„ XIX.	-	-	-	„ 131	„ VIII.	-	-	„ 19, 20	„ 238
„ X. -	-	-	„ 24	-	„ 173	„ X. -	-	-	„ 34	-	„ 239
„ X. -	-	-	„ 34	-	„ 180	„ X. -	-	-	„ 40	-	„ 240
„ XX. -	-	-	„ 38	-	„ —	„ XI. -	-	-	„ 13, 14	„ —
„ II. -	-	-	„ 10, 11, 12	„ 190	„ V. -	-	-	„ 17	-	„ —
„ XVII.	-	-	„ 10, 13	„ —	„ XII.	-	-	„ 32	-	„ 241
„ I. -	-	-	„ 8	-	„ 209	„ XIII.	-	-	„ 55	-	„ —
„ II. -	-	-	„ 14	-	„ 210	„ XIX.	-	-	„ 16	-	„ 242
„ II. -	-	-	„ 16, 17, 18	„ 211	„ XX.	-	-	„ 23	-	„ 243
„ II. -	-	-	„ 23	-	„ 212	„ XX.	-	-	„ 28	-	„ 244
„ V. -	-	-	„ 43	-	„ —	„ XXIII.	-	-	„ 35	-	„ —
„ XXIII.	-	-	„ 35	-	„ —	„ XXVI.	-	-	„ 6, 7	„ 245
„ XXVI.	-	-	„ 39	-	„ 221	„ XXVI.	-	-	„ 39	-	„ 246
„ V. -	-	-	„ 17, 18	„ 223	„ XXVII.	-	-	„ 46, 9, 10	„ —
„ XIX.	-	-	„ 17, 18	„ 224	„ XXVII.	-	-	„ 46	-	„ 248
„ XIX.	-	-	„ 16	-	„ 226						
„ V. -	-	-	„ 44	-	„ —						

THE GOSPEL ACCORDING TO MATTHEW (*continued*).

Chap.	Verse	Page		Chap.	Verse	Page
XXVIII.	18	248		XXII.	23	267
XXI.	—	250		VIII.	19	—
V.	9	256		XIX.	19	—
XI.	13, 14	258		XXII.	39	—
XVII.	12, 13	—		XXVI.	47	268
XXVIII.	18	266		XIX.	16	279

MARK.

Chap.	Verse	Page		Chap.	Verse	Page
III.	28, 29	50		XV.	34	248
XII.	32	—		II.	25	249
XIV.	27	185		III.	31, 35	—
II.	13	212		XI.	11, 12, 13	250
VI.	3	241		XIII.	32	251
VII.	24	242		III.	31	252
X.	21	243		XIII.	32	264
X.	5	244		XIV.	43	268
XIV.	3	245		VII.	16	273
XIV.	35	246		X.	17	279

LUKE.

Chap.	Verse	Page		Chap.	Verse	Page
III.	1	17		XVIII.	22	243
XII.	10	50		VII.	37, 46	245
XVI.	19	57		XXII.	41	246
XVIII.	22	90		VI.	1	249
II.	11	104		VIII.	19	250
XVI.	17	223		I.	26	251, 252
VI.	29	224		II.	33, 43, 48	253
XXIII.	34	225		IV.	22	—
VI.	35	226		III.	23	254
III.	23, 24	228		IV.	17, 18	255
III.		230		VI.	27-29	256
V.	10	236		XI.	37, 38, 41	—
XVI.	17	237		XVI.	22	256
IX.	57	238		XXIII.	34	258
XII.	51	239		XXII.	47	268
XVI.	16	240		XVIII.	19	279
XII.	10	241				

JOHN.

Chap.	Verse	Page		Chap.	Verse	Page
XIX.	15	17		I.	21	258
I.	21	190		II.	4	259
X.	16	206		II.	18, 20	260
III.	4	213		VI.	38	—
II.	4	224		VII.	5, 15	261
VII.	5	250, 252		VIII.	8, 11	—
I.	45	253		VIII.	4	262
VI.	42	—		X.	16	264
XVIII.	32	256		X.	30, 33, 36	—
				X.	38	266

JOHN (continued).

Chap. XIV.   -   Verse 11 - Page 266 | Chap. XIII.   -   Verse 34 - Page 267
„   XVII.   -   „   21 -   „   — | „   XVII.   -   „   34 -   „   —
„   XIII.   -   „   8 -   „   — | „   XVIII.   -   „   3 -   „   268
„   XVI.   -   „   15 -   „   — | „   XIX.   -   „   15 -   „   —
„   XIV.   -   „   28 -   „   267 | „   XX.   -   „   17 -   „   —

THE ACTS OF THE APOSTLES.

Chap. V. -   - Verse 84,88,89 Page 18 | Chap. VII.   -   Verse 7, 14 Page 271
„   I. -   -   „   6, 7   „   40 | „   VII.   -   „   43 -   „   272
„   XV.   -   „   20 - 69, 73 | „   VIII.   -   „   9 10,11„   —
„   XVI.   -   „   8 -   „   88 | „   X. -   -   „   11-15, 6 „   278
„   XV.   -   „   20 -   „   89 | „   XII.   -   „   21 -   „   274
„   VII.   -   „   4 -   „   214 | „   XII.   -   „   88 -   „   —
„   XV.   -   „   20, 19 -   224 | „   XIII.   -   „   85, 87 „   276
„   XXI.   -   „   25 -   „   — | „   XV.   -   „   1 -   „   277
„   XV.   -   „   29 -   „   226 | „   XV.   -   „   17,20,29„   278
„   XXI.   -   „   25 -   „   — | „   XVI.   -   „   1 -   „   —
„   XXIII.   -   „   2, 3   „   256 | „   XVI.   -   „   2, 80   „   279
„   I. -   -   „   6, 7   „   269 | „   XXVIII.-   „   3 -   „   280
„   V. -   -   „   34 -   „   — | „   XIII.   -   „   33 -   „   290
„   VII.   -   „   4 -   „   270

THE EPISTLE OF PAUL TO THE ROMANS.

Chap. V. -   - Verse 15 · Page 50 | Chap. V. -   - Verse 16 - Page 262
„   V. -   -   „   14 -   „   53 | „   V. -   -   „   14 -   „   280
„   XVI.   -   „   20 -   „   60 | „   IX. -   -   „   24-26,13„   281
„   V. -   -   -   „   82 | „   X. -   -   „   11,6-9 -   282
„   IX. -   -   „   24 -   „   214 | „   XI. -   -   „   26 -   „   283
„   IX. -   -   „   23 -   „   215 | „   XVI.   -   „   20 -   „   —
„   X. -   -   „   11, 6, 7 „   — | „   III. -   -   „   19, 28 „   289

THE EPISTLE OF PAUL TO THE CORINTHIANS.

Chap. V. -   - Verse 1 - Page 89 | Chap. VI. -   - Verse 8 - Page 284
„   VI. -   -   „   9 -   „   222 | „   VII.   -   „   18, 20   „   285
„   XV.   -   „   28 -   „   252 | „   X. -   -   „   8 -   „   —
„   X. -   -   „   25   „   278 | „   XV.-   -   „   54 -   „   286
„   V. -   -   „   1 -   „   284

EPISTLE OF PAUL TO THE GALATIANS.

Chap. V. -   - Verse 1 - Page 277 | Chap. III.   -   Verse 15 - Page 286
„   V. -   -   „   2 -   „   279 | „   III.   -   „   16 -   „   287
„   V. -   -   „   8 -   „   285 | „   II. -   -   „   — ·   „   289
„   I. -   -   „   18 -   „   286

EPISTLE OF PAUL TO THE EPHESIANS.

Chap. IV.   -   Verse 8   -   Page 288.

FIRST EPISTLE OF PAUL TO THE THESSALONIANS.

Chap. II.   -   Verse 18   -   Page 60, 284 | Chap. II.   -   Verse 10   -   Page 288

TIMOTHY.

Chap. I. - Verse 17 - Page 267.

EPISTLE OF PAUL TO THE HEBREWS.

Chap. X. - - Verse 5 - Page 216 | Chap. II. - - Verse 7 - Page 292
„ XI. - - „ 17,ʻ31 „ 289 | „ VIII. - „ 8, 13 „ 293
„ I. - - „ 5, 9 „ 290 | „ X. - - „ 5 - „ —

EPISTLE OF JAMES.

Chap. II. - Verse 14 - Page 288.

FIRST EPISTLE OF PETER.

Chap. II. - Verse 6 - Page 282

REVELATIONS.

Chap. VII.   -   Verse 5   -   Page 294 | Chap. XXII. - Verses 18, 19 - Page 294

ERRATA.

PAGE	LINE	
19	29	*for* proceeds from *read* proceeds not from.
20	7	*for* action *read* actions.
22	24	*for* Psalms xiv. 70 *read* Psalms cxlvii. 19, 20.
24	2	*for* Ezra i. 2 *read* Ezra i. 11.
36	23	*for* Isaiah *read* Elijah.
45	2	*for* Exodus xii. 9 *read* Exodus xxii. 9.
47	8	*for* alterations *read* alternations.
57	6	*for* Levit. xxvi. 9 *read* Levit. xxvi. 39
58	1	*for* viii. 5 *read* viii. 10.
—	3	*for* die *read* to die.
59	15	*for* shall *read* shalt.
61	14	*for* shall *read* shalt.
63	29	*for* belonged to *read* belonged not to.
65	33	*for* exiled *read* exiles.
75	5	*for* Deut. xxviii. 29 *read* Deut. xxviii. 25.
76	24	*for* And *read* at.
84	22	*for* us *read* me.
85	27	*for* chap. lvii. *read* xlv. 17.
—	29	*for* chap. v. *read* lvii. 18.
88	22	*for* Asostles *read* Apostles.
—	29	*for* translater *read* translator.
91	2	*for* principle *read* principles.
93	29	*for* Joel ii. *read* Isaiah ii. 3.
116	13	*for* Nunbers *read* Numbers.
122	2	*for* (shall the Gentiles continue in their accusation *read* (thus the Gentiles will continue their self-accusations, saying).
128	7	*for* xxv. 2 *read* xxv. 11.

PAGE	LINE	
137	7	*for* xiv. *read* xlv. 15.
145	6	*for* ibid chap. lxii. 8, 9 *read* Isaiah lxii. 8, 9.
154	29	*for* chap. xxx. 18 *read* Jer. xxx. 18.
155	13	*for* Numb. xv. 12 *read* Numb. xxv. 12.
159	31	*for* Kings ii. 4. *read* II Kings iv. 23.
161	21	*for* chap. 12 *read* iv. 12.
164	31	*for* עתָה *read* עַתָּה
175	7	*for* יוּרְשֻׁנֶּה *read* יוֹרִשֻׁנֶּה
177	32	*for* יַעֲלוֹ *read* וְעָלוֹ
190	4	*for* Matthew ii. 10 *read* Matthew xi. 10.
204	33	*for* (the shields of salvation *read* the fountains of salvation).
207	8	*for* chap. xvi. 20 *read* chap. lxvi. 20.
213	14	*for* Mark ii. 13 *read* Mark ii. 25.
—	31	*for* St. John iii. 34 *read* St. John xiii. 34.
220	20	*for* (ver. 19) *read* iii. 19.
221	29	*for* with his will *read* against his will.
239	2	*for* in *read* on.
—	22	*for* prophecied *read* prophesied.
244	26	*for* 2 Chron. xxiv. *read* 2 Chron. xxiv. 21.
251	17	*for* prophecy *read* prophesy.
252	10	*for* cast *read* casts.
262	10	*for* viii. 4 *read* viii. 40.
263	18	*for* chap. lii. 1 *read* lxvi. 23.
281	28	*for* chap. xviii. 14 *read* chap. viii 14.
293	18	*for* are worn out *read* do not wear out.

Made in the USA
Charleston, SC
07 September 2010